Distant Water
Stories from Grimsby's fishing fleet

Nick Triplow ~ Tina Bramhill ~ Sophie James

North Wall Publishing

LOTTERY FUNDED

Distant Water: researched, written and edited by Nick Triplow, Tina Bramhill and Sophie James. Book design and layout by Tina Bramhill. Content © The authors 2011. Distant Water is a North Wall publication in association with CPO Media. All Rights Reserved. No part of this publication may be reproduced or transmitted in any form or by any means, electronic or mechanical, including photocopying, recording or any information storage or retrieval systems without prior permission.

Cover painting: *'Distant Water'* by Dale Mackie. Commissioned for the project through Abbey Walk Gallery, Grimsby *www.abbeywalkgallery.com*

ISBN: 978-0-9568175-0-1

CPO Media *www.mycpomedia.com*

Dedicated to the fishermen of Grimsby

CONTENTS

Authors' Note – Oral History and the Distant Water Project

A shortcoming of traditional history is that it tends to focus attention on the recording of momentous historical events. In many ways this approach risks overlooking the most important aspect of history: the everyday life experiences of ordinary people, those who rarely have the opportunity for their voices to be heard.

Distant Water takes traditional historical research and brings it together with oral history – the words, memories and distinctive language of those who lived through the best and, arguably, the worst years of Grimsby's fishing industry. We shed light on the unique lifestyle, work, culture and beliefs of men who lived their lives at sea, one trip at a time.

We hope that *Distant Water* can help to promote a realistic appreciation of a way of life and a level of hardship few of us can imagine. We also hope to address some of the myths and stereotypes which have informed our understanding of this period in Grimsby's history.

The oral history approach recognises that all memories are a mixture of fact and opinion. It is also true that memories are by their nature selective or can become hazy over time. People may be influenced by stories heard later, perhaps remembering only the most extreme aspects or emphasising the importance of their role in a particular event. Where possible, we have verified and cross referenced names, dates, ships and incidents.

The *Distant Water* interviews provided people with the opportunity to make sense of their own experiences as individuals. We are indebted to those who came forward and freely re-visited memories and told their stories. In bringing them together here, we hope to create a greater understanding of Grimsby and its history, and tell the story of the industry which, for 150 years, was the measure of the town's success.

Nick Triplow, Tina Bramhill, Sophie James
April 2011

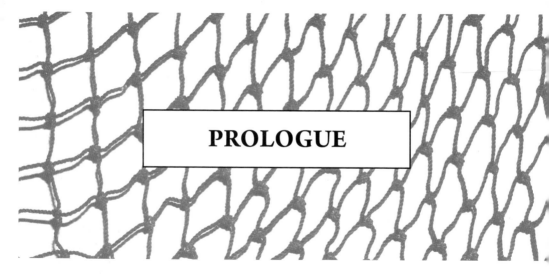

PROLOGUE

'Mac of the Pic' and the Isernia

February 1959

AS THE FIRST COD WAR was beginning to impact on Britain's fishing industry, the *Sunday Pictorial*, forerunner of the *Sunday Mirror*, sent a photo-journalist to Grimsby in order to take a trip on a trawler and witness the conflict at first hand. The London-based journalist, named McKenzie, whose previous assignment had been Beirut covering the 1958 Lebanon crisis, travelled to Grimsby and boarded Northern Trawlers' ship the *Isernia* skippered by Alf Kissack. Derek Grant was the ship's third hand.

'We were due out on the three a.m. tide. It was the third hand's role to take her out the lock pits so I was on the bridge with the skipper and I saw this guy stood there. He was like a lamp-post, about six foot seven and he had this long dark coat on. He definitely didn't look like a fisherman. You could see he wasn't one of ours. I thought he probably belonged to Marconi – we used to get compass adjusters aboard.

'The weather was that bad that we didn't get out on that tide; they didn't even unlock the gates, which was unusual, so we sailed on the afternoon tide. I still thought he was a compass tester, but as we kept going down the river I realised he couldn't be.

'He stayed on the bridge until we got clear of the river. When the ship started moving around he went down below. He was too tall to get in a bunk. They were going to sleep him in the chart room, but he couldn't fit in there either, so he had to go into the skipper's berth. They put a bed on the deck and Alf went into the chart room; there was a good berth in there as well.

'Once we got clear, we didn't see this guy anymore until we got to the north of Scotland. He was that seasick. He disappeared for about thirty hours then come onto the bridge for a breath of fresh air. I came on watch and we were running in front of the wind. The weather was atrocious, as it was all that trip, and Mac was looking out the front window of the bridge. You could feel what was gonna happen with the ship, it just went quiet. She went down and shuddered a bit and she took a load of water on and there was steam and spray and you name it. He gave one big yell and we never saw him n'more until we got to Faroe.

'He was really shaken up. I went down below. I knew he hadn't eaten and that's when I started to get concerned. The rest of the crew knew he was there, it was a joke, y'know, "Is he dead yet?" I managed to get some crusts down him and look after him a bit. If he'd been a kid, a decky learner, he would have been dragged out. I've seen a load like that, just told to get out on deck. Including me.

'We got down to Iceland and he started to rally round; it takes about four or five days to shake it off. Once we started fishing and slowed down to about five knots it was a steadier movement and you get used to it and Mac perked up.

'We had about six or seven days fishing, but we didn't have the makings of a good trip so Alf decided to come back from Iceland to Faroe to this place where you could get these big coley and make a bit of weight up that way. So we never saw any action, never came across any gunboats; we knew they wouldn't come out in that weather. But Mac was all over the place taking those photographs.

'One time he said, "D'you get jellied eels?"
I says, "What d'you mean, do we get eels you can jelly?"

'If we were gonna get any, we'd get 'em there, used to get congers. Anyway we caught one, about three or four feet. I told one of the lads to

Derek Grant on the deck of the *Isernia*

put it aft in the ice locker. When we got the anchor down in the river, I said to the lad, "Go get that eel, but don't let him see it." I went down and he'd packed his case, I opened it and put this eel in.

'He was staying at the Humber Royal Hotel and he said, "In the morning, when your market's finished, I'd like to buy you a drink, will you come and have a drink?" So I went down, got settled up and my wife Shirley came with me. He was on one of these high stools in the hotel bar and he looked at me and said, "You bastard."

'Mac had arrived at his hotel room, put the case down, noticed a smell, but thought nothing of it. He went to eat and when he came back up the smell was worse. He called the maid who agreed, yes, there definitely was a strange smell. She brought the manager in and they all looked around the room for the source of the smell. Eventually, the manager asked, where had he been? He said, "I've been on a trawler for three weeks." So the manager asked, did he have any fishy clothes and would he mind opening up his case? So he opened up and found, "…that bloody thing!" He said, "I wouldn't have minded, but I put my case right near the radiator." I said, "Well you did ask for jellied eels."'

The *Isernia* was away for three weeks in what was acknowledged to be the worst time of year for weather conditions. By his own admission, for Mac it had been 'one hell of an experience' seeing the conditions in which men worked, how tough it was keeping going through an 18 hour shift on deck in all weathers with six hours off.

Some weeks later when Derek returned from sea, a brown envelope had arrived with a short note and the prints Mac had taken on the trip, a 'thank you' from Mac of the Pic.

For the first time since their original publication in the Sunday Pictorial, *Distant Water* is reproducing Mac's photographs. The authors are grateful to Derek Grant for lending us these extraordinary images of a trawler at work, and to Mirrorpix/Sunday Pictorial for allowing us to publish them.

1. McKenzie/Grant photo collection

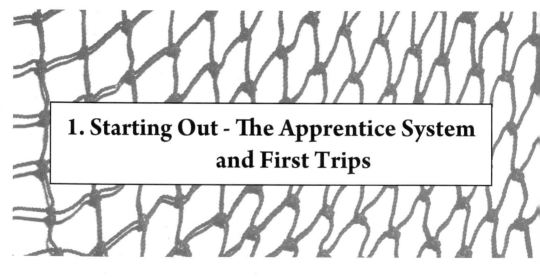

1. Starting Out - The Apprentice System and First Trips

"You go below son, you've had enough."

Fishing in Grimsby was a family trade. With few other employment options and a barely adequate education system, lads coming of age in Grimsby were destined for the sea. Many were willing to follow in the footsteps of their grandfathers, fathers, brothers and uncles in becoming part of an industry whose hierarchies, hardships, ritual dangers and larger than life characters would define their adult lives.

By the late 19th century, the small local community could no longer provide sufficient manpower to feed the industry's rapid expansion. The number of smacks had increased from 219 in 1869 to at least 625 in 1881 and the Grimsby fleet was catching one third of the fish landed in England and Wales. Smack owners began to take advantage of a plentiful source of labour, apprenticing young, poor and underprivileged boys from workhouses, reformatories and charitable institutions across the country, focusing particularly on poverty stricken urban areas. This activity was legal under the archaic Elizabethan Poor Law Act of 1601 which stated that all destitute children should be apprenticed to a trade, minimising their cost to local authorities. Boards of guardians from overcrowded workhouses were eager to supply the needs of Grimsby's smack owners, even paying them a small fee to accommodate the boys.

By the 1860s the system had begun to attract criticism. Complaints of malnourishment and physical abuse of young fisher-lads was becoming widespread. In 1865 the problems were brought to public attention when the skipper and first mate of the *Comet*, a Hull fishing smack, were prosecuted for the manslaughter of their 13 year-old apprentice Jacob Keslier. The trial found that the first mate Thomas Anderson had beaten the apprentice, kicking and rope ending him, and when the boy was so weakened that he was unable to do his work, Anderson tied a rope to him and hauled him from the cabin to the deck. The Leeds Mercury reported that the day before Keslier died he was 'used by Anderson is a most disgusting manner'. On the return voyage, the ship's skipper 'laid strict instructions on the rest of the crew not to reveal anything in reference to the violence in which they had indulged towards the deceased'. The charge of manslaughter was lowered to one of common assault and both men were sentenced to imprisonment with hard labour.

With apprentices bound to their masters, they were forced to serve time at sea regardless of their fear or dislike of seafaring life. One of the most controversial aspects of the apprentice system was the number of young boys imprisoned in Lincoln Gaol for refusing to go to sea, or 'stopping-ship' by jumping off the vessel and back onto the dock. Some boys claimed to 'prefer the treadmill of Lincoln to the deck of their vessel' and saw no disgrace in taking a trip to 'Lincoln College'.

In 1873, the Lincolnshire Chronicle reported that 500 apprentices were sent annually to prison by Grimsby magistrates. In the same year the issue was debated in the House of Commons where it was declared that 'reports which had appeared in the local newspapers were grossly exaggerated', and that only 253 apprentices had been charged with absenting themselves from work in the previous year, with 100 of these discharged with a reprimand. Of the 153 sentenced to imprisonment, 60 were charged with other offences including assault and wilful damage. Nonetheless, it was noted that on arrival the apprentices were 'being driven chained six or seven together like dogs through the streets of Lincoln'. Consequently, arrangements were made to transport the lads in proper prison vans.

Despite the House of Commons apparent acceptance of the apprentice system, it was admitted that 'there was quite sufficient foundation for making complaints' and that a full inquiry would follow.

Appointed by the Local Government Board, Baldwyn Fleming wrote his report *The Treatment of Pauper Apprentices to the Grimsby Fishing Trade* in 1873. He estimated that 2,000 apprentices were engaged in the industry with the youngest just 12 years old. Although Fleming generally found favour with the system, he believed that its regulation did not appear to have 'kept pace with its extraordinary development' and made several recommendations for improvement. As well as demanding full reports on masters, vessels and lodgings, and that closer attention should be paid by each lad's Board of Guardians, Fleming spoke of the moral corruption of the apprentices. He believed there was a need for 'continued education and moral training after joining the sea service', and that strict controls on public houses and brothels were urgently required. With only three days on shore between trips, many youngsters followed the example of the older fishermen, spending their allowances on an immediate orgy of excess and becoming frequent drinkers from the age of 14. The record of apprentice Frederick Turner tells of the lad's roaming in Freeman Street, saying, 'he keeps bad habits and frequents public houses. Takes other boys with him ... gets drunk and makes filthy mess in the house and brings in filthy literature'. Turner was cautioned and 'promised amendment'.

Regardless of Fleming's recommendations, clashes between masters and apprentices continued. Apprentice Charles Tierney accused his skipper of forcing

him to eat meat with soot and turpentine on it, kicking him and striking him with a poker, and having the mate throw buckets of water thrown over him. A deck hand testified in court that he had seen the skipper hit the lad with a shovel because he did not move about the deck fast enough. The skipper's defence claimed Tierney was an 'idle, dirty and indolent boy' and that the skipper and mate 'were placed in a very difficult position' when they had to deal with boys of that character. The skipper was let off with a fine of five pounds, despite the judge's declaration to 'protect the 2,000 boys sailing out of Grimsby'.

19th century images of Grimsby fishing smacks

Some apprentices chose to defend themselves against ill treatment. William Harris was charged with murderous assault when he struck his skipper over the head with an iron pump stanchion. The skipper was 'knocked insensible' and later claimed the lad was trying to jump ashore with two fellow apprentices who had already escaped the ship. Some lads were so desperate to avoid going to sea they would take any measures to get home, like Lawrence Sullivan, who walked from Grimsby to his home in Nottingham. The lad was brought back by his father and forced to resume his indenture.

In 1873 The Times printed two letters written by apprentices in defence of their masters. Thomas Winter wrote, 'I am well satisfied with my master and mrs. Like wise my grub and clothing and spending money…it is our own faults if we go to gaol…' James Brooks claimed that if apprentices were 'good boys' and 'get a good master' then they 'cannot do better' than a fisherman's life.

Such contradictory reporting encouraged a second Board of Trade inquiry. Conducted by Messrs Allen Stoneham and George Swanston, the enquiry led to the implementation of immediate safeguards, regulations to protect young apprentices and most importantly, the appointment of a Board of Trade superintendent to oversee the entire system. From now on, the Superintendent of Mercantile Marine was required to keep full records of each apprentice, noting their master, date of indenture, lodging address, and origin. The superintendent received complaints against masters, enforced discipline and requested that each apprentice reported twice a year to the Board of Trade for assessment of their general wellbeing. In 1880, the same year that the records began, the government passed the new Merchant Seamen Act. Section 10 of the act stated that seamen and apprentices were no longer liable to imprisonment for deserting a ship, removing the threat of gaol for the young apprentices. As a result they proceeded to break their engagements, much to the frustration of masters who found their apprentices were 'admonished and discharged' by magistrates.

For many ports the 1880 Act meant the beginning of the end for the apprentice system. However, figures show that in Grimsby it was largely circumvented. In 1882, two years after implementation, Grimsby magistrates sent 121 apprentices to prison. Hull magistrates committed three.

In 1882 the murder of 15 year old apprentice William Papper by his skipper Osmond Otto Brand caused national outrage. Reported in local and national press, the case revealed how Brand had grown angry when Papper lied about an alleged affair between Brand and Papper's sister. Brand began by thrashing the lad around the face with a metal-ended rope. The abuse that followed included Brand jumping on Papper's stomach, tying him to the stern, throwing stones and water at him, making him bathe on a freezing deck, pushing excrement into his mouth, locking him in the 'dill' – a small water-filled compartment at the bottom of the ship – and dragging him around the deck by a rope. Eventually, driven to exhaustion by continued ill-treatment and lack of food, Papper collapsed and died. His body was thrown overboard. Brand continued fishing, threatening his crew with a revolver to keep the true nature of the lad's death secret. Nevertheless, the offence came to court and after a long and complex trial Brand was charged with murder and hanged. In his written confession he continued to protest his innocence, claiming Papper had been mistreated by all of the crew.

When reports reached Parliament, President of the Board of Trade, Joseph Chamberlain, ordered a full enquiry into the regulations and customs of the fishing trade. The report that followed, outlined in the Merchant Shipping (Fishing Boats) Act, stated that skippers must take full responsibility for the safety of apprentices on board and protect them from the 'petty tyranny' of the crew. No boy under the age of 13 could be considered for apprenticeship and apprentices had to be over 16 to work on the larger trawlers. All indentures were to be strictly overseen by the Board of Trade and one month's trial at sea was compulsory before a lad signed on for a full indenture. The Superintendent of Mercantile Marine was given the power to act as guardian, to enquire into allegations of abuse and to provide sufficient protection. However, by the time these provisions were fully in place, Grimsby's apprentice system had entered its decline.

The increased social consciousness of the Edwardian era brought fresh attention to the plight of the remaining apprentices. In 1905 the *London Magazine* published a series of articles by Robert Sherard investigating the condition of pauperism in England and Scotland. In *The Child Slaves of Britain* he described Grimsby's apprentices as '... fine little fellows, each a slave with a hero in him, like Spartacus of yore'. Sherard wrote that trawler owners saw the lads as 'criminals or idiots', but he could find no concrete evidence of intentional abuse, only the treacherous natural conditions faced by apprentices and fishermen alike. One told him, 'We are the dirtiest men in the world and we are always the wettest and, in winter, we are the coldest. Our heads are under snow and the drenched waves... our hands are wounded by the passive defences of our prey. Our fingers are gashed and torn so there is suffering always.'

The First World War effectively marked the end for Grimsby's fishing apprentices. Many lads served in the armed forces rather than going to sea. Alfred Laurence, then 19 years old, was released from his master WW Crampin to join the army after serving four years of his indenture. Some lads became prisoners of war when their trawlers were caught by enemy ships. Apprentice William Boot spent three years at Ruhleben POW camp and was eventually released from his indenture as compensation upon his return to Grimsby. Other young fisher lads perished along with their masters and crew in trawlers blown up by enemy mines.

Even without the legitimised brutality that came to epitomise the apprentice system, a life at sea still held great danger. For Grimsby's fishermen this was viewed as an occupational hazard.

In the years between the wars, the industry continued to progress. With the advent of improved communications, larger trawlers and a new fish dock, opened in 1934, fishing could take place further from the home port. At the outbreak of the Second World War, a new set of dangers emerged. Bill Dillon's fishing career began in 1942. After a sailing from Milford Haven for a trip, Bill returned to Grimsby. His first ship was the *Irelands Eye*. Launched in 1891, the ship had been bought by the Loyal Steam Fishing Company during the war; the conditions on board would have been familiar to any apprentice from earlier generations.

Bill Dillon

'She had no electric lights. You had to use carbon lights. When we was hauling it was my job to get a big steel rod, wrap it with waste, fill it up with paraffin and light it, then go round lift the covers up and light these lights. When you went down the fish room, you had like a spike which you used to stick in the wood and it had a ring round it and you used to stick a candle in it. And that was your light in the fish room. You had a coal stove and when you came in dock if you wanted a wash and a shave you had to get hot water from the engine room. Or you got a big shackle, heated it up and dropped it in in a bucket of water. No toilets, you had to sit on the rail.'

Bill came into the industry at a time when the dangers of fishing were multiplied by the threat of enemy action and the ever-present menace of mines.

'I lost one or two mates, ships blown up and that. I lived with my mother - me father had got killed in 1940 so I really went to help her out. There was four of us, so I was like the bread winner. We scrapped and scraped and managed to get through it all. I started as a decky-learner, and then a decky. I never went higher, my son did, he finished up mate.'

As a lad, Bill was working long hours and 'time below' was always at the skipper's discretion, even if you were 14 years old and working an 18 hour shift.

17

'Some skippers'd let them work to say after tea, then say, "That's it go below till breakfast." Others would keep 'em up with you all the time. It all depended who you was with. They had it harder really 'cos they didn't know nothing. They'd make mistakes; say there was a sea coming, you would get out the way but it would maybe knock them over and they would get wet through. They stayed up as much as you did. Until the skipper said, "You go below son, you've had enough."'

Stanley Johnson's fishing life began on the docks just after the war. The family lived near Bainborough's cake shop in Rutland Street, one of a patchwork of narrow streets populated largely by fishing families a stone's throw from Grimsby docks. Like hundreds of other families, they made the best of tough times. With his father at sea, Stanley would accompany his mother to the pawn shop with his father's suit. The money would buy cheap vegetables and cuts of meat from Freeman Street Market. As soon as he was old enough, Stanley went to work on the docks.

'I was a barrow lad. When the fish merchant bought the fish, it was my job with another kid – used to be ten stone boxes a kit – we stacked them six on three, then another three. If we were on a pontoon, we had to take it from one end of the docks to the other, from the north end right round to the south end down these ramps. When it was filleted, our job was to pack it all up again and take it to railway wagons for London, Brighton, Peterborough – it was all chalked up on the railway lines. You got used to where they were because they never changed the wagons. We got fifteen bob a week.

'Everybody was looking for work after the war. That was the main thing, getting back on your feet. Work, work, work - that was why I thought I'd go decky-learner. I look back at my life and I don't think I could have done anything different. When I started off decky we got four pound ten a week. Shoremen weren't earning that. Mind you, your actual wage was two pound ten; the other two pound was risk money 'cos there was still a load of mines knocking about from the war. The *St. Oswald* hit one and blew up. Then the money went up to a fiver. You had to put a lot of work in to earn five pound a week ashore. Plus my mother knew for a fact that her lodge money was there every week when she used to get my wages. You always paid your mother half of what you was earning.'

Whilst many Grimsby fishermen were born into the industry, in the immediate post-war years the need for manpower to bring the fishing fleet back to full strength led trawler companies to recruit directly from men due for de-mob from the services. Harry Drinkell had joined the infantry in 1940. He had seen action in the Middle East and was still on active service in Greece in 1946. Knowing nothing of fishing or a life at sea mattered little at the time. When his commanding officer offered him the opportunity to return home to his wife and the daughter he had never seen, Harry took a chance.

'He said, "You come from Grimsby don't you?" He told me they were short of fishermen. I wasn't thinking of fishing, I was thinking of me wife and daughter see, so I said I'd do it. He said, "You've got a month's leave, then you'll have to report down the dock to a trawler company and if you don't stick it for two years you'll be called back into the army." So I went down to this trawler firm and the bloke said, "I'll put you down as deck hand trimmer." I said, "What's a deck hand trimmer?" He said, "Oh don't worry about that, there's another one aboard the ship, he'll show you what to do. You sail in the morning." I'd been in the Middle East, in the dessert. I'd been in Greece, all those hot countries…I'd only been home a month and I went straight to Iceland. I was seasick before we got out the Humber. We was away twenty-eight days and I was sick every day.'

In contrast to the harshest experiences of 19th century apprentices and fisher lads, the earliest experience of a life at sea for many boys was a 'pleasure trip' with fathers or uncles. Brothers Peter and David Coates sailed with their father as mate, then later as skipper. David would accompany his father to the docks early in the morning to see the fish landed before market. As he was to find out on his first pleasure trip, everyone on board had to earn their place.

'I had to sign on and got paid a shilling a day. I had to help the cook peel all the potatoes, then help the crew cleaning the fish and then I learned how to gut the fish. They took a lot of interest in us showing us how to mend nets, fill needles, then down the engine room getting the ashes into cans so you can hoick 'em up and throw them into the sea. You became part of the crew during the day, but dad wouldn't let us on the deck at night. You could be in the bridge or in the galley but not on the deck when they were working in the night.

'I thought the life itself was a good one until the last trip which was on the *Zephyr*.

David Coates (right) swilling the deck

From going out to landing we was twenty-two days and we only fished for four days, the rest of the time was on the end of the rope bobbing up and down while the wind was blowing and you couldn't fish because it was too windy. And that cured me wanting to go to sea.'

David's younger brother Peter also joined his father's crew for pleasure trips. Signed on and classed as 'super-cargo' for insurance purposes, David's first trip was as an 11 year old in the summer holiday just before his first year at senior school.

'I missed my first week 'cos I was still at sea with me dad. When I got back to school they were asking why I hadn't been there the first week. I said, "Well I was at sea with me dad," and it made me a bit of a celebrity.

'I loved going fishing, but I didn't love the sea sickness. That used to wipe me out for about three days. I felt so weak and all they kept saying was, "Son, keeping eating summat, you've gotta eat summat." And all I could eat was dry bread. It was horrendous, but once I got over that I was fine.

'They used to haul every three hours and they just kept working and working. If the ship's full of fish, they've gotta gut 'em, they've gotta get rid of it and they've gotta get it down the hole. That net went out and there was still fish in and I remember thinking, *hang about, when do they sleep?* But they didn't, they just kept going.'

For Peter, used to sailing in the summer, a trip at Easter time gave a taste of the unforgiving nature of the sea. Starting out, the sea had been calm. Peter was alerted when the crew started bringing the gear aboard. He asked his father, what was going on?

'He says, "We've had a weather warning, we're coming into some really bad weather so we're battening down the hatches." Every water tight door was shut and sure enough it started to blow. I thought it was like being on a big roller coaster, but then it really started. It was a gale force ten and we just had to batter into it. I was stood on the bridge watching the bow of the ship disappear, thinking, *Oh my God, is it coming up?* And the seas were way above everything, three storeys high, coming over the ship, it sort of thudded down, and then it comes up and you think, *Thank Christ for that.* All they do is steam into it, 'cos it's all they can do. Always go with it, never go against it. That was without doubt the most frightening experience of my life.

'Dad said to mam, "Get him into summat else he's not coming to sea." After the war there was that much fish and it kept coming in. But we'd had two cod wars since then and I'm pretty certain he knew. He could see the end of it. There was only Norman out of the four of us who went to sea. I would have gone, but where would I have been now?'

Graham Howard's first trip was as a galley boy, before becoming a decky-learner on the *Northern Gift*. A series of coincidences took him below decks following his father's footsteps as an engineer, later becoming chief engineer, also on the *Northern Gift*. If his mother and father had had their way, the 15 year old Graham wouldn't have been to sea at all.

'My dad was at work and my mam was out. I went down the docks and stood outside Consol's office. Mr Sutcliffe – they called him Sutty – came out and said, "What do you want son?" I told him I wanted go to sea. He said, "Do you mind going today?" I did what they called tide-jumping in the river, which meant the ship had gone to sea minus a crew member, which was a galley boy, and they wouldn't go any further without one. I had to go off as replacement. So I went straight from Consol's office to home, got some gear together, straight to the trawler and out to sea. And that was before me dad even came home from work. I was gone and that was it. We went into the river about April time and straight into a head-to-wind gale. I've never felt so bad in my whole life. There is no word to describe sea sickness, and I never went to sea in my life without feeling sick. Always. It was a terrible feeling.'

Graham Howard (second from right) with crew members

Jim Clark's family fishing history began further down the east coast in Lowestoft, where his mother's father had been a fishing smack skipper. Jim's uncles had been fishermen. On his father's side of the family, his grandfather had been an engineer. The advent of steam brought him to Grimsby and Consolidated Fisheries.

'He became Superintendent Engineer, went to Lowestoft to open up a new branch of Consol's and that's where my father met my mother. We moved back up here to Grimsby in 1948 and I started fishing in 1955. It was more by accident than anything. I left Grimsby Technical College when I was sixteen and went to the Merchant Navy school down at Sharpness near Gloucester, but I didn't stay the course. When I came back, my sister was nurse maid to Harry Crampin of Crampin's Steam Fishing Company and he asked if I would like to go on one of his trawlers to sea, to see what it was like. So I went on the *Bradman*. She was a bit more modern than some of the other trawlers. A lot of them sailing at that time had gone through the war, done their war service and been released back to the fleet.'

Mike Debnam was 15 when he passed his radio certificate, but couldn't legally sail until he was 16. After training as a radio operator, it was Mike's intention to go into the merchant fleet. Attending the Nautical College, he took a certificate for trawling. He just wanted to go to sea, but found leaving his family a wrench at first.

'When I was brought up, there was only me and my sister and the family. When you go away, you're on your own. It's a big responsibility. As you had to be sixteen to operate the wireless installation, I went on a pleasure trip with another operator and that was horrendous. We went down the river and I got as far as Spurn Point and I was seasick for two weeks. I couldn't get out my berth because I was that sick. Then I just got over it and enjoyed it from then on, really enjoyed it.

'Went I first got my wireless certificate I went down Fish Dock Road to Marconi's, the big radio place. I was politely told, "Yes you do have a certificate and you are a qualified radio operator, but come back when the ink is dry on it." I was lucky 'cos when I was coming back down Fish Dock Road, I called into Crampin's on the off chance and he wanted an operator for two trips. I explained the situation and he said it was no problem, so I sailed with them for that trip. We did really well but the boat had to be dry docked for a big survey and I was out of a boat. Then he said, "I can offer you a boat." I said yes and I never left that company. He only had five wireless operators. And they really looked after you. I worked for them for about ten years.'

Derek Grant came to the industry immediately on leaving school at 15. With his mind made up to follow in the family tradition, his education had extended only so far as the knowledge he'd need for a career at sea. With both grandfathers former skippers, right at the outset, Derek set his sights high.

'You was just expected to carry on in our family – my brother went to sea. Everything I was interested in at school at that age was fishing and trawling. I wasn't an artist but I'd got a picture pinned up of a trawler in bad weather – so it was always in my mind. I was in a C-class all the way through school because I just wasn't interested in anything unless it was to do with fishing. What I did do, which was a good thing, was maths. I liked maths as a lad at school. When I went to that nautical college, I got student of the year and that was maths, trigonometry, everything to do with angles, because we learnt to use a sextant and I came out on top.'

Jeff Beedham was one of many lads apprenticed to a trade allied to the fishing industry, in his case engineering. But as a Grimsby lad, his interest in trawlers and fishing started while he was at school when he'd go 'trawler spotting'.

'In Grimsby you had the herring quay that was doing a booming trade during the summer, so you got all the herring drifters coming in from Yarmouth and Lowestoft and places like that, plus occasionally you would get Lowestoft vessels on midnight landings on a Sunday. So you could see most of the Lowestoft fleet; the Aberdeen trawlers used to stop in as well because a lot of them had been seconded to Boston deep sea fishing.

Jeff Beedham (Top row, 2nd left) with engineering apprentices in front of Ross House Sept 1967

'The ship building industry training board was established to give a better apprenticeship for kids. In the first year, whether you were a fitter or a blacksmith, or a welder, a pipe fitter or a plumber or a shipwright, you all learnt a little bit of each other's trade. We all started off in the old engineering block at the college of technology which used to be on Laceby Road. We stayed for a year and in the holidays went back down the dock and they'd move you round into different departments to give you an overview of the whole set up.'

Thomas Green, known as 'Chukka', made the time-honoured trip from the North-east to become a Grimsby fisherman. Following his father down from Hartlepool and making his home in Grimsby

'Some did just a few [trips] a year down here and then went back home, and a few of 'em made their lives here and married here. Aye, Johnny Stringer God-bless-him, Kenny Green God-bless-him, old man Sandy; hell of a lot of

Grimsby lads, but every generation of Hartlepool fishermen, you know, fished out of GY. When I first left school I went fishing out of Hartlepool then when I was seventeen I got the train to Grimsby. At first I used to go home every trip, then every couple of trips, then in 1977 I came to Grimsby. I went to the FA Cup final when we beat Liverpool then I went to Denmark and stayed in Denmark for a year, came back to Grimsby and was away about two year that time. Ended up living with a Grimsby lass, and I'm still here.'

Richard Wright's entry to the fishing industry in the early 1950s has distinct echoes of the past. Richard was brought up in what was then known as 'need and care and protection'. His decision to go to sea was taken out of a need to escape an unhappy home life.

'My mother left when I was three, met and married a bloke in the war and buggered off with him, so I was put in need and care and protection you see. I wasn't very happy where I was living. I thought sod it, so I went to sea at fifteen on a trawler called the *Viola*. Oh it were bloody awful, used to treat you like bloody animals they did. I mean, not being nasty now, but if a bloke wants to pee he can pee any bloody where can't he? If you're working in an environment with just blokes, nobody bothers, do you know what I mean? So you don't clean your teeth, you don't get washed, because you ain't got the water to mess about with. If you cleaned your teeth on a trawler they thought you was homosexual.

'The crew, they knew I was pleasure tripping. I was away eleven days and they used to have a whip round and treat you, you only got a few quid like. And then I started decky-learning. I loved it; they were my family, d'you know what I mean? It was nice 'cos where I lived in lodgings I 'ad to be in bed by 'alf past ten, and if I wasn't in the 'ouse they used to charge me ten bob to open the door. It was bloody awful. If I got any letters, which was very few, she'd open them. You'd be sat at the table having yer meal and she'd say, '...and look at them sausages they was one and six a pound on the market' and I'd think, *Oh wonderful I'm really pleased yer tellin' me this*. I'd been to five schools never settled in any place, so I went to sea and made a life of it.'

2. McKenzie/Grant photo collection

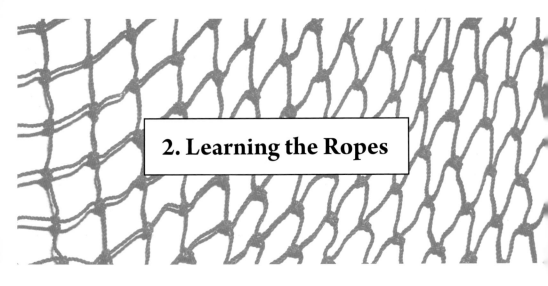

2. Learning the Ropes

*"…you may as well just throw your ticket away
if you're not gonna use it."*

The fishing industry always depended on a ready supply of workers prepared to pit themselves against the elements. For many years, the knowledge needed to bring home the catch could only be learned when lads joined a crew and followed the example of older, more experienced hands. Or, as in the case of fishermen like Michael Sparkes who first went to sea in the late 1950s, the skills were handed down from father to son. His grandfather had been one of the early cod fishermen, sailing to Greenland and longlining in a fishing smack. Michael's father followed, sailing for more than 30 years. When it was Michael's turn, nothing could quite have prepared him for the harsh reality of life at sea.

> 'Nobody came to you and said, I want to teach you this or I'm gonna teach you that. You learnt by the school of hard knocks. Everybody would be on your back until you got it right. You learn pretty quickly under them circumstances. It was a cruel way of learning but that's how you learnt stuff, trial and error.'

As the fishing industry entered its most productive period at the end of the 19th century, traditional ways of learning the trade were no longer considered adequate and in 1879 building work began on the new Fisherlads Institute. Situated on the corner of Tomline Street and Orwell Street on land donated by George Tomline Esq. and built at a cost of £3,500, the Institute included a gym, a reading and writing room and swimming pool, all intended for the recreation of young fishing apprentices. It was managed by men appointed by the Board of Trade who, responding to Baldwyn Fleming's 1873 report, sought to guard the moral welfare of fisher lads and young fishermen and to produce in them 'a robust and straightforward moral character'.

By 1907, with the apprentice system in decline, the Grimsby Education Committee had taken over a room at the Institute to provide lessons in navigation for fishermen of all ages. Part-time classes in seamanship followed shortly after. To fund the further expansion of the school, with the aim of teaching higher-grade navigation and seamanship, practical net-making and mending and sea-cookery, a grand county bazaar was held in Grimsby Town Hall. The final bill for extensions and modifications was around £4,500 with the Grimsby fishing trade contributing £1,000 and the remainder coming from proceeds of the bazaar.

Between 1907 and 1913 more than 4,000 students attended the school qualifying for 11,200 Board of Trade certificates.

By the end of the 1930s the Nautical School occupied the entire building, employing five full-time and three part-time teachers. A range of lessons covered all aspects of technical knowledge relating to the fishing industry as well as reading, writing and arithmetic.

The School was divided into five departments: Senior Navigation; Junior Nautical; Deep Sea Fishing; Marine Engineering and First Aid with Ship Surgery. In 1939 the school's Principal, Captain Townsend, claimed that 98% of students who presented themselves for examination were successful. The range of certificates awarded by the Grimsby Navigation Committee included: Skipper; Second Hand (mate); Third Hand (bosun); Deck Hand; First and Second Engineman; the London Saint John Ambulance Certificate for First Aid and Aircraft Navigation.

The Nautical School took on a fundamental training role during the Second World War. Fishermen were taught to operate the new motor minesweepers – skippers received a certificate exclusively for minesweeping services. The School also held classes for RAF personnel in navigation, wireless engineering, mathematics and science. Additional classes were held for army cooks. After the war, the armed services paid tribute to the contribution that Grimsby's Nautical School made to the war effort and in 1948 a plaque was unveiled by the Royal Navy to thank the school for the vital training of non-professional seamen for minesweepers. The Navy wished to record the bond that existed between itself and the Nautical School, and to commemorate the Grimsby fishermen who had worked alongside the Royal Navy.

The School continued to set high standards of teaching and in 1949 a Ministry of Education official noted that Grimsby's Nautical School was the only one in the country to receive complete co-operation from the fishing industry, with trawler owners taking an 'active interest in the education of their fishermen'. Attending a meeting in London with a national committee aiming to draw-up training schemes for the fishing industry, Captain Townsend confirmed that practically all of the proposed recommendations had been in force in Grimsby for many years.

By the 1950s, no newcomer to Grimsby's fishing industry, in any capacity, from galley-boy to skipper, could officially sail on a trawler without taking the appropriate qualification. This didn't mean that all fishermen were qualified as former fisherman Charlie Briggs remembers.

'I've never known a trawler go away a man short. It wouldn't matter who it was, whether it was a tramp off the quayside, they'd make the crew up and that was it.'

In 1950, the Grimsby Education Committee had relocated the Nautical School to the new College of Technology on Nuns Corner – the present site of Grimsby Institute of Further and Higher Education. The committee were criticised for not inviting the representatives of the fishing industry to discuss the proposed move. Many believed Grimsby's fishermen would cease to flourish in the new location and that the type of men who attended the Nautical School could only learn where they 'could see the masts of their ships'.

Concerns that the move away from Orwell Street to Nuns Corner would affect the learning of the fishermen certainly had some foundation, but for Arty Lea the tradition of gaining experience at sea was still the mainstay of his education.

'You still had to go to nautical school for your ticket, for six weeks or ten weeks, depending what the ticket was. I went third hand and mate. You did all the navigation, but that's all it was because your nets and deck work, you do that at sea. Old Wiggy Hardy said, get yourself to school and you can have a job. I did enjoy the studying and there was a lot of it. But it was experience at sea that counted, working in those weather conditions and you couldn't learn that at school.'

With fisherman taking time away from the sea to study, the disorganised timetabling at the new college was a cause of frustration for Arty Lea's class. A situation made worse because time ashore was time not earning.

'A load of people had come from overseas; Brazilians, Africans, all over. They kicked us out of the nautical classroom and we finished up in one where the bricklayers worked. We complained, we said. "We belong here; we live here and want to work here." We couldn't get any joy so we went to the Board of Trade down on the dock. A guy come from the Board of Trade, he sorted it out and we got put back in our classroom.'

Throughout the 1950s and 60s, the name Alf Hodson became synonymous with the teaching of fishing skills. Hodson came from one of Grimsby's most respected fishing families – his father, Skipper James Hodson, had eight sons, seven of whom also became Grimsby skippers. After his own time as a skipper and serving in Royal Navy Volunteer Reserve during the Second World War, Alf became head of the Nautical School, a post he held for 26 years. His aim was to ensure that young lads entering the industry were properly trained for the tasks that lay before them. The matter became of personal importance to Alf when his own son Michael was lost at sea, a memory which remains with Mike Debnam.

'I'd sailed with Alf's son, Mike, and we used to go out boozing. I went round and knocked on the door. I asked when Mike was due in. Alf told me to come in and sit down, and asked if I wanted a drink. I said I didn't. He said, "Have a dram." I asked him what was up and he told me Mike had died. See, when the trawl goes over the side there's a headline rope and he got behind it, and as they dropped this thing over it took him over the side. Never seen again, just taken straight to the bottom.'

Alf continued to educate and try to ensure the safety of all fishermen, becoming the author of two books on the practice of fishing. His manual for young learners, *Introduction to Trawling* set out a step-by-step guide to the technical demands of a Grimsby fisherman. The book was essential reading for students at the Nautical School and Hodson captured the enthusiasm with which many youngsters continued to enter the industry. As he attempted to demystify the dramatic pull of a life at sea, he described hauling in the net.

'To the fishermen in general, this procedure causes at all times an inward feeling of excitement, curiosity, and the hope that the haul will prove to be successful. Their

aching limbs are forgotten for the time being, and their thoughts visualise the sight when the cod ends are released, and the mass of dead and living matter, gleaming and slithering, spread in all directions in the fish pounds. With eyes staring, mouths gasping – it is all so strange the prey of the trawl – fish food.'

Irrespective of whether a fisherman received his training in the classroom at Orwell Street, Nuns Corner, or in the teeth of a North Sea gale, successfully bringing catch, crew and trawler home depended on each man's ability to do his job. A crew at sea operated with a clear system of authority and well-defined roles. The hierarchy was well-established, from galley boy to skipper. Jim Clark had been on a trip as a decky-learner on the *Bradman* in 1955, but went back to sea, sailing as galley boy.

'You had your own cabin and you didn't work such long hours. Galley boy was like a second cook; you did all the washing up, peeling potatoes, preparing meals and things like that. You received a weekly wage of about four pounds - a full deck hand would get six or seven. Then, when the ship came in you got a percentage of the catch, say six pounds in every thousand. Then you got perks like cod liver oil money. We saved the liver out the fish and then it was processed for cod liver oil tablets an' that. My father was a fully qualified engineer ashore, and he was bringing home between seven and eight pounds a week for a family. I would come in from sea with thirty to forty quid and blow it in two days.'

Although spending the majority of his career at sea as a chief engineer, Eddie Whyte started out as a galley boy at the age of 15. He spent two years at sea before joining the army on national service, signing on for an extra year to secure an overseas posting. On his return, he paid a visit to Northern Trawlers.

'They asked what I'd been doing in the army and I said I was a cook. They told me I could go cook on the trawlers, but I'd have to go galley boy first. You learn how to make bread and all that business. I finished up full cook for a year and a half. It was after that I thought I'd do summat else. I used to go down the engine room every night, and the chief engineer there used to show me bits and pieces, so I thought I'd go in the engine room.'

Finding yourself as the new lad on a ship with an established crew was never easy. Ray Powell recalls the bravado of decky-learners and a hollow confidence which didn't last long.

'They all thought they knew a lot more than you, knew everything there was to know, until it came to the actual doing of it. They always found it harder than they expected. There's nothing worse when you're feeling seasick when someone comes up and says you have to do something, but it was the only way to get somebody going, you've got to get up and work - that's what you're there for. You had to pull your weight and work as a team.'

As Derek Grant remembers, decky-learners didn't receive a lot of favours; they were the 'run-about' taking skipper's orders. And if there was fish to be gutted, they were there until it had been cleared.

'The only break we got was for meals; half an hour for breakfast, half an hour for dinner and half an hour for your tea, and that was it. Some of 'em just fell asleep at the table when there was really heavy fishing.'

The early years of Chukka Green's time at sea saw him sailing for three trips as the galley boy in *Lord Beattie*, then five trips decky-learner in the *Northern Chief* as a 'baby-decky' at the age of 18.

'You think you know everything but really you're just cannon fodder. Well you always got a couple of the older guys who took you under their wing; they'd show you and look after you, and you had a few that bullied you especially with being out of town and living in Hotel de Mish – the fisherman's mission. If you couldn't stand your ground, you was on the next train home. 'Cos you had the Grimsby lads, the locals that all went to sea and 'cos we was out-of-towners, all young lads, we were having a bit of a go, and if you couldn't stand your ground you was home. I knew it would be like that; it's a hostile environment out there and I wouldn't have missed it for the world.'

Whatever a crewman's place in the ship's hierarchy, there was potential for conflict. As an experienced deck hand, there came a time when you could carry out most, if not all, of the tasks of a third hand. Acting as the buffer between the skipper on the bridge, the mate on deck or in the fish room and the crew wasn't a responsibility all deck hands were willing to take on. Michael Sparkes had the knowhow to take the step up, but it wasn't until an accident to the regular bosun that he was given the opportunity, a move that created tension with some of the older hands.

'So the skipper says, "We're gonna have to take the ship back." He phoned the office back home and they said, "Put Sparky third hand." So the skipper comes to me and says, "Can you do it?" And I says, "Oh yeah, I can do it. I'd prefer to go home though." He said, "I'm not having that, they've asked if you'll do it." And it was like double poundage, more money. So I did it and that was the start of me going bosun. I was nineteen or twenty and all those old deckies were in their fifties and sixties. They said, "Do you know the job mate?" I said, "Yeah, I know the job." They said, "You'd better an' all, you'd better know it." But I shocked them 'cos I did know the job. I knew the trawl, how many meshes was in certain kinds of nets. I knew all the splices. I could net-mend, I could do virtually anything.'

Michael also had the necessary radar ticket and a detailed knowledge of the Decca Navigation System.

'It's a bit hard to explain, but the sea was in lanes on the map and there was stations at the top of these lanes. And it used to be red, purple, green, and we had a receiver aboard the ship which would give you the signals of all the different stations and you knew exactly where you was by the map of the lanes. It wasn't very reliable; often it would break down, but in those days I think the skippers and the mates were more experienced an' that. My father could take a ship to Iceland with a pencil and a ruler, you know, 'cos it was in the family you see.'

'The work was so hard that you just didn't have time for anybody or anything. It took you all your time looking after yourself. I've had people say to me that there was a comradeship aboard the trawlers… I don't know where they got that from, because I never found it. Okay, so you'd watch somebody's back and you'd help them, but when it come to doing your job, you had to know what you were doing.'

With the financial advantages that came from taking your ticket, moving up in rank and increasing your share of the catch, there were also additional pressures. When Stanley Johnson earned his ticket and became third hand and then mate, long-held friendships took second place to making certain the crew worked well under his supervision.

'You was alright as a decky amongst all your friends, but once you got your ticket you was above some of them lads, dishing out orders to your mates. That's when friendship ceased. Friendship ashore was great. I'd sit and 'ave a pint with them and a laugh and a yarn, but once we got on board the ship and got to sea, friendship ceased. The lads respected you for it. Otherwise you may as well just throw your ticket away if you're not gonna use it. Then the higher you got, the same thing again. A lot of them didn't bother about going for their tickets; they was quite happy being deckies. But once you got into that authority position at sea, if they made a mistake you had to tell 'em about it whether they liked it or whether they didn't. A lot of them knew the drill and accepted that they'd made a mistake. Once you got out there, you had a job to do and that was that.'

Graham Howard spent his early years working as a deck hand before eventually satisfying his interest in going below as an engineer. Graham's opportunity came about after a run in with the second engineer on board the *Vianova*.

'You could walk through the engine room, over the top of the engines to the bridge when you were steaming to and from the grounds. We was on the way home, about two days from Grimsby. The weather wasn't too kind and it was rolling a bit side to side, and I was going from the galley to the bridge. I had the ship's tin with a couple of pints of tea in it and she lurched so I spilt the tea on this pipe. The second engineer, a bloke called Al Sanford, came tearing up to the bridge, swearing and cursing and we got into a bit of an argument. I said, "It's alright for you, cushy down there." He said, "If you think it's cushy you should try it." I said, "It's a closed shop for you people, we never get to go down." So he told me if I ever sailed with him again, he'd show me if it was a cushy job or not. About two or three years later I sailed on the *Northern Gift*, and he was chief engineer. So I reminded him and he said, "If you think you're gonna come down to the engine room just to get off the deck that's no use for me. If you're gonna go for your tickets then you can come with me." So I said, "Right, you're on."

'After eighteen months, I'd got enough sea time in to go for me tickets. So I went to the college and I was towards the end when I saw this face looking through the classroom window and it was Al Sanford. He'd come down to ask if I could take my ticket early and go second engineer with him,

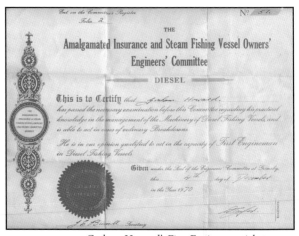

Graham Howard's First Engineman ticket

which I did. Then after a year of going as a second engineer, I went back to school to get my chief's ticket. Low and behold who comes tearing through the door again? It was Al. He wanted to stop at home for Christmas and recommended that I'd go chief engineer if I took my ticket. But when I went to sit for it, they said I hadn't really got enough time in; they'd pinched time here and pinched time there, but in the end he let me have it. I went engineer while Al had Christmas at home. The laugh about it was we made a real quick

Graham Howard takes a breather

trip and I was home for Christmas as well. So he really cursed.'

Graham's experience on deck and below deck gave him a unique perspective on the old adage that oil and water don't mix. It was true for the most part that engineers remained below, unless maintenance was needed to machinery on deck. It was also a cause for jealousy that engineers worked six hours on and six hours off while deck crew were often working 18 hours on and six hours off.

'Deckies assumed the engineers was lazy, idle, gits until they wanted something. Then it was, "Chief can you do this?" Or, "Chief can I hang me frocks in your engine room to dry?" With me having been on the deck I knew what the deck hands' problems were, so I'd say, "I'll unlock this area where you can hang your gear and dry it. But don't go anywhere else." I used to take a lot of pride in my engine room.

'Some skippers thought they knew best, but I'd never have a skipper interfere with the engine room. He caught the fish and my job was the engine and the running gear. If owt goes wrong with the running gear or the winch, they'd come to me and I would maintain it. If there was any complaint, complain at home. I fell out with a few, but I put 'em right.'

A significant source of resentment between deck hands and engineers was the disparity in pay. As an engineer Graham received a comparatively high basic wage, at least twice as much as anybody else on the ship. For the crew, whose income depended on the sale price of the catch, if one person failed to do his job, profits were at risk.

'When I stopped fishing I got like eighty pounds a week basic and something like ten pounds for every thousand pound the ship made. It all depended on the market. The art of being a top skipper was you caught fish when nobody else did. Same as the mate, it didn't matter how good he was as a person, if he turned out one trip of fish that didn't come up to spec and perhaps there was a few kits condemned, he would get the sack and would never get chance to go mate again. In some respects you felt a bit sorry if that happened, because the mate had to delegate one of the deckies to be his fish room man and treat that person out of his own pocket. He'd give him like twenty-five quid extra to make sure that his fish turned out alright. If he happened to pick the wrong guy, someone who didn't give a monkey's and his fish didn't turn out, it wouldn't have been that guy who got the blame. It was the mate who had to carry the can. He might make sure that bloke got the sack as well, but he had to take responsibility for it. It was a cut throat job it really was.'

Mike Debnam's position as a radio operator in a small firm gave him the opportunity to observe the workings of crews at close quarters. Mike found that rank, and the privileges that came with it, often put unnecessary barriers between crew members.

'Officers ate in a cabin, the crew ate in another quarter. We had butter, they had marge. On a Sunday we had bacon, they had cornflakes. In my opinion, it wasn't right. Most radio operators stayed on the bridge. They didn't do much else. I wasn't like that, so I said to the old man, "Can I learn to mend the nets?" And he said, "Of course you can." I went down and I learnt everything. When a ship went away shorthanded, if the crew was ten people, and you only had eight, they use to pay ten people and divide it up amongst the eight, so you all got shorthand money. I used to go on the deck, mend the nets, boil the livers, which was unheard off because operators never usually went on deck. If they was really shorthanded I use to go on the fore door with 'em. And you used to get the respect of the crew then, everyone joined in, but it was hard, really hard.'

Maintaining contact with the company and keeping track of weather reports was an important part of the radio operator's job. However, the competitive nature of the industry meant that following the fortunes of other ships made equal demands on Mike's time and ingenuity. Learning Morse code was essential.

'You have to take weather reports and keep in contact with your own company's ships at certain times of the day – ours was at eleven o'clock at night. One ship would take command and call up all the others and you would send your message. It usually involved the name of the boat, all in code, then your position, how much fish you'd caught for the day and what the weather was like. He would get all these messages together off the boats and send a telegram back to the company, who would know exactly where you were, how much you was catching and what the weather was like.

'I had to listen to other companies, where they was fishing and what they was

35

catching. Each firm had their own code. Me and the old man used to acquire the other firm's codes, by hook or by crook. When we was in the ship we used to put it on the chart table. Say it was Iceland, we'd put the big map of Iceland on the chart table and I use to stick these little pins in different places all around. The old man used to come in and look at the chart. "Is that where all the Northern boats are? And are they catching so and so…?" And that's where we would go. In the end they use to change their code regular, but if you had half a gram of intelligence, you could work it out. The first one was always the name of the boat, the second was the position, third was what he caught and then was the weather. The only one we couldn't get was how much they was catching. We did fathom that out eventually, but it was clever.'

For every man at sea, there were a dozen others ashore who were dependant on the success of each trip. The runners, or ships' husbands, were employed by companies to ensure each trawler had a full complement of men. Frequently this meant a hunt through the pubs of Freeman Street or an unwelcome knock-up in the small hours of the morning. Landing the fish were the lumpers and dockers, whose militancy often brought them into sharply opposing positions from trawler companies and the fishermen who went to sea. But as 'Chukka' Green recalls, there was a bond born out of shared experience between the men that went to sea.

'What we went through on them side trawlers and the conditions we worked under… I'm proud to say I'm a Hartlepool man, but very proud to be a Grimsby fisherman.'

3. McKenzie/Grant photo collection

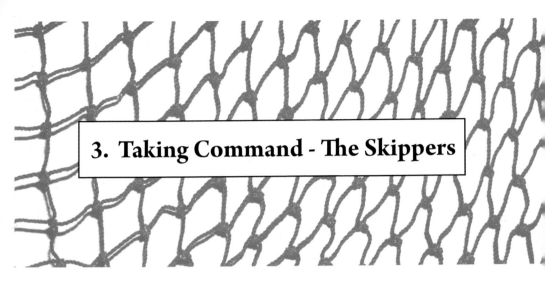

3. Taking Command - The Skippers

'The skipper was God and that was it.'

Becoming a skipper offered the greatest challenge for an ambitious fisherman. The process of earning your skipper's ticket and, more importantly keeping it, took skill, courage and the ability to command. The 1928 edition of *Olsen Fisherman's Nautical Almanac* describes the rigorous examination required to attain the elusive skipper's ticket:

> *'Skippers must not be less than twenty-one years old, and must have served five years at sea, of which one year must have been as a certified Second Hand on board a fishing vessel of twenty-five tonnes gross or upwards. He must pass a sight test and hold a valid first-aid certificate. For the Examination in Navigation, a Skipper must be able to work out sums in compound addition, subtraction, multiplication and division; to find the latitude by the Meridian Altitude of the Sun; to understand what is meant by Variation, Deviation and the local attraction of the compass, to find the deviation by bearings of the sun at noon, and approximately by the North Star.'*

A skipper was expected to have full knowledge of the Merchant Shipping Act, to understand procedures in the case of death, injury or ill-treatment, and to have a working knowledge of all regulations for accounts, wages and shares. Fishermen undertook many hours of study in order to sit their skipper's ticket and even then, there was no guarantee you'd be given a ship.

On a post-war side trawler the skipper was responsible for a mate and bosun, a chief and second engineer, two firemen, a radio operator, a cook and galley boy. The deck crew included up to eight spare hands and a young decky-learner. The skipper's commands were law and disobeying them at sea was a serious offence. As Jim Clark says, 'The skipper was God and that was it.'

George Nicholson was one of a crew who came up against George Burres, their skipper on the *Notts County* and faced the consequences.

'George was ready to go home, but wanted one more shoot up, y'know, cast 'em over. And we didn't want to. We jacked our hand in and said we weren't doing no more and we wanted to go home. That was it. We had to go in front of the trawler owners – used to call it kangaroo court – and we got suspended for twenty-eight or fifty-six days. That same ship went away next trip with a different crew, and she run ashore in Iceland. One bloke got lost and the skipper got frost bite.'

Skipper Tommy Spall (right)with WFS Letten of Atlas Steam Fishing Co September 1974

Whilst a successful skipper could reap large rewards, he had to keep ahead of the competition and make a name for himself. There were always more skippers than vessels and trawler owners, not noted for their sentiment, could pick and choose the men who performed highly and brought in the most profit.

Bill Dillon's first Grimsby skipper was a man named Woods. Bill then sailed with Eddie St Pierre, Mick George and Tommy Spall before finishing his time at sea with Ray Pepper on *The Black Watch*, a ship Pepper skippered between 1970 and 1976. Pepper looked to achieve a balance of youth and experience in his crew and avoid those he saw as weak links.

'You used to call them whifflers. They was whiffling, "Oh I can't do it, I can't do it. I'll have to roll in, I'm poorly." You sorted them out in different crews. Skippers got to know who they was. Tommy Spall always had a good crew. And Eddie St Pierre, he was so good people

Skipper Eddie St Pierre (left) being congratulated on a record-breaking trip by John Butt of British United Trawlers in August 1976.

wanted to get in with him 'cos he was such a gentleman, whereas Spall could lose his temper. Once you got a good crew you kept 'em. Peppy used to say to me, "You know what I do – I have so many your age, then the youngsters. The young uns can pull and out-work you, but you lot have got more brains then them - you know what to do. So when they're pulling, you can do the sorting out of the gear and that." When you weigh it up he was right really, when you were like me a forty-odd year old, you couldn't do what they were doing at twenty. But you had more knowledge of the trawler than they ever knew.'

Keeping a good crew whilst walking the line between no-nonsense command, good sense and affability, didn't come naturally to all who earned a skipper's ticket, but as Graham Howard remembers, all that most men expected was for their skipper to be fair.

'You didn't expect no favours and you didn't get any. There was the odd skipper you'd avoid 'cos they didn't give a damn for yer, but you was out to earn money. One of the top skippers I knew was old man Hardy, Billy Hardy, not young Billy, but his dad. He was top skipper at Consol's and he really was one of the fairest men you could ever wish to sail with. You knew you was gonna work hard, but if you were in bad weather, he would be on the bridge and if you couldn't sleep, he wouldn't sleep.'

Top skippers were tough, inventive and resourceful, willing to take risks to bring in a good catch. They relied on instinct, knowledge of seamanship and an almost sixth sense to locate fish others could not. Grimsby skippers had to act with a tinge of recklessness, and knowing the trawler was only making money when the net was over the side, there was always the temptation to keep working. Some would brave bad weather conditions and jeopardise crew safety to make that extra catch, or risk sailing through treacherous winds in anticipation of good payday at the fish market back in Grimsby.

Tom Smith spent the majority of his career at sea in middle-earning ships for the most part avoiding the top-earning skippers, a conscious decision as middle-earning ships usually had the best crews and were more likely to have easy-going skippers and mates.

'You had your top skippers and big ships, Snappers they called them, good fishing ships, catch plenty of fish but hard work. The crews were cliquey and the skippers were terrible to 'em at times, but they stuck it because of the money. I was asked to go. Two o'clock in the morning, I was in bed and one of the runners come round, knocking on the door – I was out of a ship. He says, "The *Ross Revenge* is in the river and we want a decky for her, is your Tommy there?" Me mother opened the door and said, "You're wanted on the *Ross Revenge*." I said, "Shut the door mum tell 'em to…" The calibre of crew on there would shock you; whatever you did was wrong if you were on that crew, they wanted to keep that job.

'Your next level of ship, still deep water, but always good fishing ships were the middle-earners. Whereas the big 'un would land three thousand kit and make this and that, you'd land two thousand kit and make a good living, never big money, but you had good crews and good skippers. If the weather got fairly bad our skippers would say, I think we'll pull the gear aboard now. Whereas they [the snappers] would carry on to the extreme when they actually couldn't even shoot the gear and get the cod ends over the side because the wind was blowing them back in.

'And then you had your ships further down the line, which were still deep water but never used to do much good – sometimes skippers that's been in trouble or gone walk-about, not very good at fishing. And you used to get a bit of riff raff, fishermen who didn't chuck their hands in or whatever.'

On occasion, Tom sailed in the so-called 'Silver Cod' ships. Between 1954 and 1968 the Silver Cod Trophy was awarded annually by the British Trawlers' Federation to the Hull vessel catching the largest amount of fish during the year. The work was relentless.

'There's only three hundred and sixty-five days of the year and some of them were spending three hundred and twenty-odd days at sea, so you can imagine how much time they was getting home. Some of the fish they was catching we'd normally dump, but as long as they filled the fish pounds and they went home with a great big catch, it all totted up at the end of the year. But we never had that kind of competition in Grimsby; there was no need for it.'

Until the industry went into decline, if a skipper made good money for the ship's owners, his job was relatively secure. A badly performing skipper could find himself out of ship and with his reputation tarnished. A skipper's income was often solely determined by a share of the profit of each voyage – the 'poundage'. The rest of the crew were paid a mixture of basic wage and poundage depending on their place in the ship's hierarchy. In Grimsby in 1946, a skipper would receive £9.10s for every £100 net profit. In the post-war boom conditions, some skippers were making £5,000 a year (around £115,000 by 2011 standards). These levels of profit continued well into the 1950s.

The dangers, pressures and risks did little to deter committed and ambitious new skippers. For a young and newly certificated skipper, taking that first trip could be a nerve-wracking experience, one which still holds vivid memories for Derek Grant. Derek was in his twenties, sailing as mate, but with a skipper's ticket.

Landing his catch, the head salesman for his owners, Consolidated Fisheries, 'wanted a word'.

FULL CERTIFICATE OF COMPETENCY
AS
SKIPPER

No. *29256*

Derek   Russell   Grant

having complied with the regulations under which Full Certificates of Competency are granted to Skippers of Fishing Boats :

This Certificate is to the effect that he is competent to act as Skipper of a Fishing Boat in all waters and authorizes him to act in that capacity.

SIGNED BY AUTHORITY OF THE MINISTER OF TRANSPORT and dated this *24th*
day of *July* 19*62*

Countersigned

Registrar General

A Deputy Secretary of the
Ministry of Transport

REGISTERED AT THE OFFICE OF THE REGISTRAR GENERAL OF SHIPPING AND SEAMEN.

'He told me when I went to settle, he wanted me up in the office. I thought, *What the hell have I done here?* I sat down and they started talking to me – nice trip, delighted with me – and then said, "How do you feel about taking your own ship?" How'd you *feel?* I said, "Yes, I like the idea of that." And they told me I was taking the *Real Madrid*. Anyway, we was in the dock and we let go, working away towards the lock pits, through the lock pits nicely, and then I get my hand on the telegraph and ring her on and I think – *hell, there's nobody up there to talk to.* 'Cos whatever you were, third hand, mate, if you didn't know something there was always somebody to ask, but I thought then, *you're it!* And as I went out into the Humber for the first time, I can remember thinking, *it's all on me now. I hope this goes right.*'

As a skipper, Derek had learned from experience how to get the best from a trip. Sometimes this meant taking a chance. If he'd had a reasonable trip, after a few days there would be the chance to explore new grounds.

'I would try to tow, monitoring positions on our radar screen all the time and marking it down, so if I got a clear two-hour run I'd know I'd picked a tow up that probably nobody else knew. So I'd mark it down on my private charts. You were fishing with all the charts for your areas, North Sea, Iceland, but you also had your private ones.'

A former Royal Marine with years of experience as a fisherman behind him, Ray Harries had also earned his skipper's ticket, but continued to work as mate with Grimsby skipper, Jimmy Nunn. Ray's opportunity came when Nunn wanted Christmas at home.

'He says, "Well Ray, much as I'd like you to take the ship away while I 'ave a trip off, it's not really fair to you 'cos you won't 'ave the experience. So I'm gonna 'ave t'get an experienced skipper to relieve me." We docked and the manager came aboard and I went on with me usual duties, making sure the crew was all off an' that. I said to the skipper, "I'm off now, it's all nice and tidy, all tied up." And he says, "Just a minute…" He come out on the bridge and they couldn't get an experienced skipper to come out for one trip, so he said, "What do you think, would you go?" And I said, "Yeah, I'll go." I was nervous taking her out, but we made a smashing trip - ten thousand pounds, which was a lot of money; the average trip was five or six, maybe seven thousand pounds.

'Jimmy says, "D'you want to go again?" I said, "I don't mind Jim." So he says, "Right, I'll 'ave another trip off." And that time it was shocking, fishing at Iceland; the weather was bad and the fishing was slack, but we still managed to make about seven and a half thousand pounds. There was ships that sailed with us that had gone down to five and six thousand.

'When we docked, Jimmy took his ship back and the boss of Boston's, Mr Fred Parkes, he called me into 'is office, and asked if I'd take another ship. He said, "She's never done any good. For twelve month, she's never done any more than five thousand. And we think there's something not being done right, so I wonder if you'd 'ave a go and see if you can find out."'

Ray may have proved himself with his first two trips, but it was typical of a newly qualified skipper to be given the chance to command an older vessel until he demonstrated himself worthy of a larger, newer or more powerful trawler. Before they reached the fishing grounds, Ray made an inspection of the ship.

'In the fore-peak right under the bows, one deck down, were all these iron bobbins. I thought that was making the ship tip forward in the water. So I got them to string 'em on a wire round the stern end of the ship out the way. And then when we were out on the fishing ground, we shot with two other ships and I got one, a middle class Northern boat – they were very good fishing ships – and I got 'im on me radar and followed to test me towing speed and we was overtaking him. So I got onto the engine room and knocked it down ten revs, then another ten revs until I got to the same towing speed as this good fishing ship. And we made a nice trip. She was smaller than Jimmy Nunn's ship, the *Oratava* – his ship was a hundred and seventy feet, while we were about a hundred and thirty-nine feet. When we docked, we docked at the same time as the *Oratava* and I thought I'd be going straight back [with

Jimmy] but the manager said, would I do another trip? I said, "I don't know, I'll 'ave t'speak to Jim. I don't want to lose my regular ship." But Jim said, "Go on, you go another one, Ray." So I went another one and we docked together again within a day and they asked me to go again. Jim said, "You go again, but I can't get a first class regular mate to come for odd trips." So I said I'd get that trip done and once again we made a good/average trip, which she hadn't done all year round and the boss wanted me to take a ship so I went to see Jim and yarned with him and he said, "When they offer you a ship, say you want the *Boston Weelsby*, the skipper's coming out and taking a brand new ship, it's being built in Poland, the *Boston Concord*." So I went on the *Boston Weelsby* and

Ray Harries with the *William Wilberforce* February 1970

I got me bonus every trip and a double bonus most trips, and then I got the chance to have another ship of the same class, an excellent ship, extra speed, extra beam on the ship, fish in any weather, and I 'ad to go and collect it from Fleetwood – *The Prince Philip*. And I was three years in that one.'

The relationship and understanding that developed between a skipper and his ship was a key element in the success of both. The difference between managing a ship well and bringing in a good catch was often the skipper's judgement as Ray proved when given command of the *William Wilberforce*, originally a Hull ship, and one that came with a poor reputation.

'They sent her to Grimsby and a skipper called Billy Balls, he took her away while he was waiting for a new ship to be built and he did no good. I said, "No, it's a bloody Jonah, that ship." These two managers said, "Ray, you'll take yer own luck." I said I'd go provided if I didn't do any good I'd get me *Prince Philip* back. And we shook hands on that. I went in the *Wilberforce* for four years. It was a similar story to that first ship. Not so much the angle she was at, more the speed she was towing the gear. The first time we got with a group of ships to compare what we're getting and what they're getting and we're getting maybe sixty or seventy baskets. And then the next tow, we'd maybe get two or three. We were too fast and the bobbins was jumping up and down instead of dragging on the bottom. We were skipping over the fish. So we slowed it down and slowed it down and in the end I used to shoot me gear away and maybe five-hundred fathom of warp away and with the last fifty fathom I'd bring her down to half speed and soon as I got the two warps in one single block on the stern, I used to stop the ship till I felt it tugging and I knew the gear was on the bottom, then I'd gradually build up speed, much slower. We finished up one of the slowest towing ships, but you need to get the right match between the ship and the gear.'

As Michael Sparkes remembers, skippers would often earn themselves a nickname. Behind every Burglar Bill, Non-stop Norman, Fire-bar Harry or Hurricane Hutch, there was a story.

'Non-stop Norman, he fished through any weather that there was. He'd fish in storms, gales, everything. He would never pay the gear aboard to lay, so they called him Non-stop Norman. Hurricane Hutch of course, it speaks for itself, but the worst one I sailed with was Ivan the Terrible, a Canadian. I'm sure he was an alcoholic. He was half alight all the time and he would take codeines. He didn't know whether it was morning, noon, or night. We was pulling the gear aboard one time, and the ship had rolled and pulled the net out. You had to be careful you didn't get your hand in it 'cos it'd take your fingers off. It pulled the net in and three or four of us went over the side with it 'cos we were stood on it. We weren't actually in the water but we was trying to scramble up and get back aboard. He says, "What's you three doing swimming when there's work to be done?" He was in a world of his own I think.'

Arty Lea's first skipper who had earned himself the nickname 'Comfortable Coddy' was known as a gentleman who put the welfare of his crew before the catch. Things changed when Arty switched to deep water trawling.

'He treated you as a man, as a son that Comfortable Coddy. Like in bad weather, he'd only fish up to a certain part, whereas some of 'em would fish until you nearly got washed off the deck. If anybody got hurt he'd come and talk to yer, not like most of them who'd send a mate or the bosun down. He had everybody's interests at heart. Whereas when I went deep water after about nine months, it was a different story. You could break your leg and they'd say, "What's he doing whiffling out?"'

'Then there was Mad Mac Mackenzie, a big red head. He was skipper and mate, but he didn't go skipper much. He was normally mate 'cos he could sort any crew out. You used to get some queer crews so you'd say, I know Mac's out of a ship, I'll get him to go with me and you didn't mess with Mac.'

It was not unusual for the pressure of skippering to take its toll. Poor results at sea or at market could mean a loss of command. But for some, no matter how they pursued the fish, their luck was out. Charlie Briggs remembers one 40-day trip with experienced skipper Charlie Major to the grand banks at Newfoundland.

'When we got back we was full up, but we'd run out of food and he wouldn't open up the fish room to get any fish out. He said, "You've got your bond, eat that." We all had bond, tins of chocolates, sweets, Dundee cake and biscuits. When we got back I met the ship's runner going over the Riby Street crossing and he said, "You've made a bomb." So when I went down I said, "What have we made?" He told me we'd made nineteen-hundred pounds on fish meal. I said, "You're joking." And he said, "Everything went to fish meal, we only made about thirty bob a kit."'

The additional pressure on Peter and David Coates' father was in full view once he became skipper. Suddenly the stakes were higher and the pleasure trips the lads had went on became more intense.

David Coates (right) with his dad, Sam.

'What a difference in a man, from being a mate to a skipper. I grew up very quick watching that. One trip we went out and both radios went down, so we came back into the river. They sent a boat with some Marconi engineers to sort the radios out. In between time one of the crew members had come up and said, "Skipper, I've got something in my eye?" So me dad had given him some Optrex or summat to clear it. We sailed again, went to shoot the first haul and the winch went, so they couldn't shoot. My dad's fuming now, two days he's lost. We've come back in the river, more guys have come aboard and sorted the winch out, and we sailed again. We started catching fish, now the decky that had come up earlier has come back up on the bridge and said, "Skipper, my eye's really bad, can you take me in?" Me dad turned around and said, "I couldn't give a fuck if your eye is on the end of your toe nail, there is no way

I am turning this ship round again." I'm a young kid thinking, *you bastard. How can you be like that?* When me dad was ashore he was a great guy, full of fun. But after he'd calmed down, he got on the radio to another ship in the same company who was coming back to Grimsby. What we did, which was an amazing feat of seamanship, these two boats come together in the middle of the North Sea, bobbing up and down, this crew member got on the bow with a couple of other guys with buoys there so the ships didn't crash together. I watched him step off one bow to the other bow to go home.'

Peter remembers his father, like many skippers, had an erratic relationship with his crew.

'He said, "Don't get too friendly with them bastards down below. Don't tell them anything you hear over this radio." Afterwards when I used to talk to the crew, they'd say, "Oh yeah your old man's all right, he's earned us some money, he's sound." They didn't give a damn as long as they earned. At the time they hated him though, "Fucking stormy bastard!" The slightest heavy weather the crew were hoping to turn in and he was saying, "Carry on, carry on."'

Some Grimsby skippers became household names thanks to their daring, life-saving or profit-making trips. Within the town's tight-knit fishing community a cult of personality could develop around a skipper, which in some cases brought them into the national spotlight.

One such skipper was John Hobbs. In 1950, as skipper of the trawler *Boston Fury*, Hobbs manoeuvred his vessel amongst floating wreckage to pick up the shipwrecked crew of Hull timber ship the *Fred Borchard* which had capsized during a storm off Norway's Lofoten Islands. The Daily Mirror described Hobbs' ability to pick up 'twenty-eight British seamen like a London taxi driver picking up fares in traffic.' In a sea littered with timber, five of Hobbs' men went into the cold water with lines around them to rescue 27 of the stranded crew. The rescue was considered 'one of the most brilliant' in the records of the Ministry of Transport. Skipper Hobbs was awarded an MBE in the Queen's Birthday Honours List in 1952. Five members of the crew were awarded the King's commendation for brave conduct, and Hobbs received a binocular glass from the then Minister of Transport, Mr Alfred Barnes. Hobbs also coined the nickname 'Parson' for his custom of gathering the crew together at the end of every working day for prayers on the deck.

Not all skippers' exploits were as commendable, although some were equally as daring. In 1936 George 'Dod' Black Orsborne, skipper of Grimsby vessel *Girl*

Pat, was arrested in Georgetown, British Guiana, after stealing his trawler and commencing a six week escapade, sailing 5,000 miles across the Atlantic with only a sixpenny school atlas for navigation.

On 1 April 1936, Orsborne, along with his brother James and a small crew, commandeered the *Girl Pat* and sailed south to Dover, arriving three days later on 3 April. The ship's engineer, a man named Jefferson was 'not in the know'. The crew plied Jefferson with drink and left him ashore as they continued their journey. Their aim was to sail along the African coast, trading en route, eventually reaching Florida, where they planned to sell the ship and share the profits. The crew painted over the ship's number and fishing letters, and had the whole vessel repainted in Tenerife. *Girl Pat's* owners, the Marstrand Fishing Company, believed it 'lost at sea' until bills for goods supplied to the vessel began to arrive at their offices. They traced the ship to Georgetown where Orsborne and his stowaway brother were arrested.

In a letter to his abandoned wife, sent from Georgetown Prison, dated 11 July 1936 a remorseful Orsborne writes:

> *'You must not believe what the press says Dear as I have no intention of leaving England without you but will talk that over when I get home, I hope all the children are well and tell them they will all go on a voyage with me the next time... I would have written you long before I arrived here, but I could not do what I did not allow the crew to do... '*

Orsborne's attempt at reconciliation continues:

> *'... Well Dear I get some awful stuff from the newspapers no doubt you get the same. I've no need to hunt for treasure as I've got plenty of that at home as you know very few have what we have. So keep smiling as I'll soon be home beside you and the kiddies and you remember I always said when I went out I'll be back... '*

Orsborne was brought back to England and tried at the Old Bailey in October 1936. A court report in The Daily Mirror describes the skipper/adventurer's departure from court on the first day of the trial having been granted £500 bail.

> *'Skipper George (Dod) Black Orsborne stood on the pavement outside the Old Bailey last night and roared "Ahoy!" A taxi cab driver fifty yards away heard his voice above the traffic and cruised to the kerb.'*

During the trial, Mr John Flowers KC for the defence claimed that the ship's owners had commissioned Orsborne to commandeer the ship to defraud the insurance company as the vessel was heavily mortgaged. However, on 23 October Orsborne was found guilty and sentenced to 18 months hard labour, with any alternative speculation quashed by the judge. Mrs Orsborne was photographed leaving the court in tears. Her husband was briefly famous and the *Girl Pat* was resurrected as a popular tourist attraction. The Daily Mirror reported that Skipper Orsborne and his crew were offered £200 a week for a tour of the music halls.

Taking crew and ship to the edge could make you a top skipper. It was possible, with daring and skill, to forge a highly successful living and make a good name, earning the respect of your peers and rewards to match. However, one Grimsby skipper in particular achieved notoriety. His name, more than forty years after his last exploits at sea, still elicits an extreme reaction from those who knew and sailed with him.

Bernard 'Bunny' Newton, also known as 'The Beast' is remembered as a skipper, club-owner and celebrity. Predominantly, Newton was a businessman. At sea it was his desire for wealth that drove him. He was single-minded and ruthless.

At the age of fourteen, Newton had cycled to London to seek his fortune, working as a hotel porter during the blitz. He returned to Grimsby to fulfil his ambition of becoming a fisherman, a course of action which set him against his father, John Newton, a former trawler skipper who had sworn than none of his children would ever go to sea. In the event, both Bunny and his brother Colin became fishermen. Bunny took a two week course at the Orwell Street Nautical School and in 1941 at the age of 16, he began sailing on the drifter *Silver Knight*.

John Newton lost his life serving with the Royal Navy in 1942. Bunny Newton was not deterred. By the age of 21 he had his second hand's ticket. At the age of 22 he became Grimsby's youngest skipper.

Newton spent 27 years as a fisherman. His crews were always hand-picked and his discipline so strict it earned him the nickname of 'The Beast'. It was also a reference to his large build and tremendous strength. Newton claimed his methods were a necessary by-product of his desire for profit. Tom Smith sailed as a decky-learner with Newton on the *Northern Eagle* and saw how Newton's discipline manifested itself at sea.

> 'To me he was absolutely frightening. We was hauling the gear and the cod ends were out, busted, we lost all the fish. 'Cos the third hand was there, and he [Newton] was ranting and raving on the bridge that the cods were out and it was blowing a gale. "I want you a minute!" He called the third hand on the bridge and then we heard such a commotion. We were waiting to shoot the

gear and the third hand comes down with his eyes blacked, nose bleeding. It wasn't his fault the cod ends were out, got caught on the bottom obviously, but he got the blame for it. I used to be terrified he'd come near me y'know. I only did the one trip with him and that was me out.'

Some skippers ran their ships to make a living for the crew and keep their owners in profit; Newton sought to 'make a killing every trip'. Derek Grant sailed with Newton and would become a successful skipper in his own right. He has an insight to Newton's success and its cost.

'He was a fantastic fisherman. Some people just run on an average, but we always earned a lot of money with him. He made big trips and we was always on big bonuses. There was no giving in with him at all; he was a terror you know, he had two overboard in one go. He was in one of those little ships before he took the *Lifeguard* and there was two lost in one go. And he just had a quick look round and right... [carry on].'

Derek Grant sailed with Newton during the first cod wars. The conflict brought the best and worst out of the reckless, battle-hardened skipper who would go to almost any lengths to keep his catch, his gear and avoid being caught. Whether this meant lining up distress rockets to fire at gunboats or taking more direct action, his crew were behind him.

'The little boats came alongside and they put a grapple aboard and what he did was pull the gunboat alongside – they weren't the big gun boats at that time – they was like a wooden trawler thing with a gun on, and everybody lined up on the port side with axe handles and you name it. They thought twice about it and didn't even attempt to come aboard 'cos we looked like a load of cut-throats. The funny thing about that was he came down and one decky had an ice axe what we used to have aboard. He said, "You idiot – what have I told you? I've told you to stun 'em not kill 'em." That was when he was making his name. He was the Beast and a brilliant fisherman.'

Even in his early years as a skipper Newton was making up to £12,000 a year by working in dangerous waters through terrible weather, risking the lives of the men sailing with him. Former Grimsby Skipper Don Lister spoke to the Grimsby Evening Telegraph in 1992.

'He was called The Beast because he was one at sea. I was a skipper myself for twenty years and never lost a man. Bunny lost many. He injured many.'

Newton bought his own trawler, the *Sletnes* in 1951, a former German gunboat, which he sailed for five years – in which time he was arrested by both the Russians and Norwegians for illegal fishing. Newton's brother Colin was mate in the *Sletnes*, but, as Arty Lea remembers, there were no favours.

'There was an argument. It was really blowing force eight or nine. Colin went on the bridge and Bunny kicked him off and he went down on to the casing, then he kicked him off the veranda, "Get down there and get the job done." That was his own brother! It was about four or five foot from the ground. And then you had another six or seven foot onto the deck.

'I did two trips with him. I was steering once – we was going to Faroe and he said, "Lea, do you know anyone called Teddy Lea?" I said, "Yeah he's my uncle." Well my Uncle Ted was about six foot seven and he'd jawed Bunny when he was a decky with him, flattened him. And he said, "Oh is he a big bloke with a big nose?" I said, "Yeah why?" Bunny punched me on the arm and I said to him, "You do that again and I'll get a spanner and I'll hit you with it." He let go of me and I moved, and the bridge on the *Isernia* was low and he hit a beam and he broke his finger. When I was on the deck the next day he come screaming down, 'cos he was always on the deck with yer even with seas coming over. Summats went wrong and the mate said something, so he flattened him and carried on getting the gear in in the mate's place. And he was absolutely drowning. I said to him, "You're a nutcase." He said, "After this I'm gonna give you a good hiding." When we got the net in he chased me forward. We had these big crocodile spanners for tightening nuts and bolts so I picked one up. I said, "Come another foot and I'll hit you." And he realised I would have done. 'Cos he was about six foot two, eighteen stone of solid muscle and he wasn't gonna get hold of me.'

Bunny's brother, Colin Newton became a highly respected skipper, held in great affection by his crews. He fished until the late 1970s using far less extreme methods. Although he did share his brother's legendary strength, reportedly pulling three crew men from the water on one occasion.

When he was 23, Bunny Newton was caught inside Russia's three mile limit and arrested for poaching in an area kept for manoeuvres by Russian Naval ships off the coast of Murmansk. He further defied the Norwegians by fishing inside their limits, yet claimed his crews were so well trained that they could stow the fishing gear inside the boat within five minutes. When Newton was eventually stopped by Norwegian gunboats there was no sign of fishing. It was a constant battle, fooling the authorities into believing he was not guilty of poaching. Newton once claimed, '…of course I was guilty as hell, but it was all part of the game.'

As Michael Sparkes remembers, this was just one of an array of tactics to keep the authorities at bay, often at the expense of older, slower ships.

'He had the *Northern Eagle* at the time and it was a fast ship. So often what he'd do, he'd go inside the Iceland limits, but he'd take a slower ship with him. Some of these other skippers would fall for it, thinking he knew where the fish was. If the gunboat come, he'd be gone and he'd leave you to face the music.'

In the years Charlie Briggs sailed as a regular member of Newton's crew, he experienced the skipper's extremes of behaviour. Keeping a crew working long shifts without breaks was a cause of many of the accidents that took place aboard all trawlers. Reflexes slowed and deck crews were vulnerable, none more so than when Newton's ship was in the fish.

'You never used to go to bed for forty-eight hours when you hit the fish. First thing he used to say was, "Bed watch." That was it, you didn't know when you was gonna go to bed. Then, he'd say, "Alright call 'em all out, we'll shoot away here." If the fish was there he wanted it. The sooner he got it aboard he could fill the ship up and he'd be on his way home and back again. That was his idea, money, money, money. But as soon as he'd say, "Righto, get 'em aboard we're goin' home," he'd change completely. Many a time the decks'd be full and we would be guttin' an' that and you'd hear somebody shout, "Catch!" as he slung a bottle of whiskey out the window or a bottle of rum and if you dropped it that was your bloody fault.'

Eddie Whyte was a greaser on the new ship, the *Victory* in 1965 when Newton's predilection for cutting corners backfired.

Newton on the *Brandur*

'The idea on them freezer trawlers was you freeze the fish for four hours, then put it in the fish room. And you've got to keep to that cycle. Four hours freeze, then in the fish room. And he must've thought - *I'm doing no good here, I'll make it two and a half hours, and get more fish*. So he throws the fish in the fish room after it'd only done two and a half hours in the freezer. When they defrosted it all, it was all rotten! All that fish, five-hundred ton it was. He tried to blame the engineers, said the freezing plant was no good. I was there when they sent the freezer chap to have a look at the freezing plant, and he couldn't find nothing wrong with it.'

Arguably, Newton's most notorious exploit as a skipper occurred in April 1967 when he was arrested for illegal fishing but decided to make his escape, taking two Icelandic policemen with him. His 760 ton trawler the *Brandur* was spotted by an Icelandic gunboat three and a half miles within Iceland's 12 mile limit. Bunny was arrested and the *Brandur* escorted back into Reykjavic harbour. In an extensive trial, Newton admitted to having been inside the limit but pleaded not guilty to illegal fishing.

The case was adjourned but Newton, concerned for his spoiling catch and impatient crew, decided to make a break for freedom. Under cover of darkness, he ordered his crew to repaint the ship's number, disguising the *Brandur* as a Hull trawler. Enticing the two Icelandic police officers charged with guarding the ship into his cabin with the promise of a cup of tea, Newton slammed the doors shut behind them and slipped out of the harbour. The infuriated policemen eventually managed to break through the cabin doors, by which time the *Brandur* was on its way to Faroe. Newton was once again caught by Icelandic gunboats, given a three month jail sentence and the ships owner's, Boston Deep Sea Fisheries, paid a £1,000 bail charge. From then on, Newton made a point of avoiding Icelandic fishing grounds.

Mike Debnam's skipper at Crampin's had run up against Newton. There was no love lost between them.

'Bunny had come on the radio and said, "Hey look at this what's coming in now? It's a little boat. Has it got any rowing oars on it?" The old man said, "Who's that?" I said, "Who do you think?" Newton says, "Little man, little boat." He was really the top man then was Bunny Newton. The old man said, "Well he'll alter course for me, won't he." So we were chugging along the same line. I was walking out the wireless room, "He's getting closer." "Is he? Good." I said, "Are we gonna alter?" Skipper says, "I ain't altering." I said, "He's awfully close." "He'll get a bit closer yet." Anyway he swung off and as he went away we hit him on the back, smashed his boat. Newton called him

hell. The old man made chicken noises, "Cluck, cluck, cluck," and then put the phone down.'

By the late 1960s Newton had been going to sea less and less, and eventually gave up seafaring life to pursue alternative business ventures on shore, including a laundrette, sweetshop, and bingo hall. His famous bingo hall was first located in Cleethorpes Pier, later moving to the former Royal Theatre in Grant Street, Cleethorpes, which Newton renamed The Clifton. Expanding his entertainment empire, Newton opened a club, Bunny's Place, in the top floor of the Clifton. A string of 1970s household names lined up to appear including Tommy Cooper, Cannon and Ball, and Charles Aznavour. The club's commercial success allowed Bunny to indulge his sense of showmanship, claiming he was responsible for finally putting Cleethorpes on the map. Newton spent his days wearing a diamond encrusted gold Rolex Watch and a diamond ring.

Newton was a larger than life character and it was perhaps inevitable that his death would be as dramatic as his life. In 1991, Newton was shot dead by his son Clifford after an argument at the family home. Clifford received a four year sentence. There were mitigating circumstances. His unsuccessful appeal, reported in The Independent newspaper in 1993, stated that, '…he had endured years of bullying, intimidation and violence culminating in a death threat from his father.'

Never far from controversy, there are many who praise Bunny Newton's skills as a skipper. In many ways he epitomised the lawless extremes of a life at sea, a fisherman-buccaneer whose exploits would not have been out of place in an earlier century. However, it is impossible to consider his achievements without acknowledging that there are many who suffered at his hand and who lost their lives as a result of his uncompromising approach as a skipper.

4. McKenzie/Grant photo collection

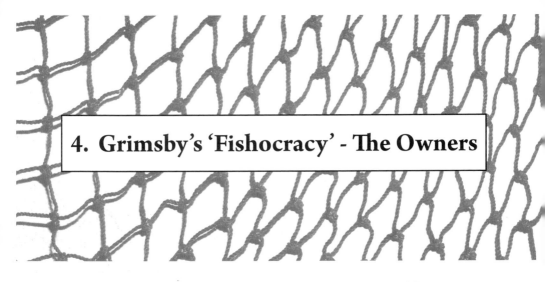

4. Grimsby's 'Fishocracy' - The Owners

*"I'll tell you now, I'd sack the lot of you if I could get
a crew to go tomorrow..."*

From the building of the first railway links to Grimsby in 1848, fishing smack owners were encouraged to migrate north to gain easier access to new fishing grounds in the North Sea. In 1857 the Manchester, Sheffield and Lincolnshire Railway (MSLR) financed construction of the first fish dock. The company anticipated a return from a prosperous local economy, higher rents and royalties, and increased traffic. The MSLR further assisted fishing-smack owners by building 25 houses especially for fishermen.

Over the years, further improvements to Grimsby's dock facilities enabled vessels to unload, re-provision and turn around faster, increasing productivity. Subsidiary markets grew though the development of specialised ship brokers, marine insurance agents and exchanges for hiring and selling ships. By 1889 there were 788 fishing vessels registered at Grimsby of which 760 were sailing craft, with the remainder steam driven vessels. In a single year 70,053 tonnes of fish was exported from Grimsby via the railway.

These early fishermen became self-made, prosperous owners. Their new wealth altered the social structure of Grimsby. They moved to large, comfortable houses on the outskirts of town. Many held public office and became town councillors. By 1880 it was difficult to find a magistrate not connected to the fishing industry and the town's businessmen were active in developing strong masonic links within the upper echelons of the fishing community.

In 1872 The Great Grimsby Coal, Salt and Tanning Co. Ltd was founded. Among its first directors were powerful leaders of the fishing industry. The company supplied the necessities of trawling, including sails, ropes, coal, salt, tar and tools. Eventually it took full control of fishing's ancillary industries. By 1889 the company's turnover had reached £100,000. In 1893 it opened a second branch in Aberdeen and by the 1920s had branches in every major fishing nation in the world. It was a shrewd business venture. The cost of provisions were subtracted from a crew member's wages for each trip

and paid back to the company, thereby returning additional profit to the pockets of the trawler owners.

As the powerful men of Grimsby consolidated their positions at the turn of the century, many became directors on numerous boards and most had several profitable interests. Mr Alfred Bannister, J.P became a trawler owner when he created the East Anglia and Forward Steam Fishing Companies. He was also chairman of the Steam Trawlers Mutual Insurance and Protection Co, chairman of the Steam Trawlers Coal and Trading Co., director of the Great Grimsby Coal, Salt and Tanning Co Ltd, the Grimsby Cordage Co, Grimsby Ice Co, and the president of the Grimsby Fishing Vessel Owners Exchange Co. From the outset, trawler owners looked after their own interests, forming co-operatives and subsidiaries which cemented the power relationship between themselves, the town and the men who went to sea.

The creation of the Grimsby and North Sea Steam Trawling Company in 1881 was an innovative venture which saw the advent of steam trawling effectively bring an end to the sail and smack fleet. When plans for the first steam trawler were put forward by Mr

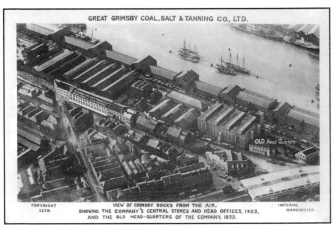

GREAT GRIMSBY COAL, SALT & TANNING CO., LTD.

COPYRIGHT 3238. VIEW OF GRIMSBY DOCKS FROM THE AIR. SHOWING THE COMPANY'S CENTRAL STORES AND HEAD OFFICES, 1923, AND THE OLD HEAD-QUARTERS OF THE COMPANY, 1873. IMPERIAL MANCHESTER.

Charles Jeffs, the idea had been dismissed but subsequently, Mr Alfred Cook, of Grimsby, agreed to join in the venture with a group of trawler owners including Mr JR Mackrill, Mr Walker Moody and Messrs James and George Alward. These steam trawling pioneers each subscribed £200 and the company was incorporated with a capital of £20,000. With their success in steam trawling, such men were to become shore capitalists, establishing once, and for as long as the industry thrived, the new Grimsby 'fishocracy'.

Norman Crampin is a descendant and former director of one of Grimsby's best known fishing families. Crampin's began as the boom of the late 19th century saw traditional owners consolidate their position within the town and its industry. He has maintained an extensive archive and detailed family history which begins with the three founders of the first Crampin company in 1897. Weston William Crampin (real name William Wesney Crampin) his brother Walter and his nephew, Norman's grandfather, Herbert George Crampin.

Weston William was self-educated, but Walter was unable to read or write. Norman picks up the story.

> 'Walter went into the National Provincial Bank in Riby Square. He went to the cashier and asked to open an account. The cashier produced a form, asked some questions and said, "Sign here". Uncle Walter put a cross, but the cashier told him he had to be able to sign his name to start a bank account. Walter went across the road to Boots, bought a big desk diary, took it home and said to his wife, "Write my name at the top of the first six pages." And he spent the afternoon filling the pages with his signature, then went back to the bank and said to the cashier, "I can write the bugger now give us that damn form."'

Weston William had owned two fishing smacks, but the family firm's first proper ship was the *Nellie Bruce,* a second-hand purchase. This was followed by the *Coningsburgh Castle,* the company's first new ship commissioned by WW Crampin.

In 1911 the Bunch Steam Fishing Company was formed by Isaac Bunch, Walter Crampin and Herbert George Crampin with WW Crampin mysteriously excluded from the second Crampin company's formation.

In 1920 as the Crampin brothers entered what were to be their final years, Herbert George became managing director of the company and his son HW Crampin, Norman's father, became company secretary. At this time Crampin's became well known for their 'cricket' trawlers, a collection of modern ships equipped to handle the worst weather in the North Atlantic. The fleet included the *Bradman,*

Hammond, Larwood, Hendren and *Leyland,* named after the cricketing heroes of the day. The best of the cricket fleet were wiped out in the Second World War whilst involved in Royal Naval operations in support of the ill-fated Norwegian campaign. In five vicious days in April 1940 the *Bradman, Hammond, Larwood* and *Jardine* were all lost.

After the War, only four cricket ships remained in operation. Crampin's commissioned the building of five new ships, the *Yardley,* a new *Bradman,* the *Trueman,* the *Statham* and the *Padgett.* The new *Yardley,* built just after the Second World War at Beverley, was chosen to represent Grimsby at the 1953 Royal Spithead Review. HW Crampin took a party of friends and colleagues – all fishing industry executives – to the Navy's royal day in the Solent.

When the *Trueman* was launched on 22 December 1960, Crampin proudly announced that, as the fastest middle water trawler in the fleet, it was named after England's fastest bowler, the irascible Yorkshireman, Freddie Trueman. 'Fiery Fred' attended the launch, along with his wife and was 'delighted' that the vessel had been named after him. The trawler was launched and christened by Trueman's wife – the famous fast bowler preferring to stay on dry land when offered a place on the ship's first trial trip. The *Trueman* sadly caught fire just two years after the famous launch with the loss of two crew members.

When HW Crampin became president of the Grimsby Trawler Owners Association, taking over from Sir Jack Croft-Baker, he created a reputation for solid business practice. As Peter Harrison remembers, in the Grimsby Vessel Owners Association the byword was 'No rubber stampin' with Crampin'. By 1970, Crampin's trawlers had disappeared from Grimsby, either sold or decommissioned as the industry declined. As Norman remembers, his father knew a small company wouldn't survive without being able to fish Iceland and offered them to John Bennett before finally selling the ships to The Ross Group

'He got out fairly smartly. Northern Trawlers, which

Mr J. Prior (centre) of the Ministry of Agriculture visits Grimsby fish market with members of the Fishing Vessel Owners Association September 1970

was the biggest distant water firm in Grimsby, their managing director was John Bennett and a few years before he'd said to my father, if ever you get into trouble, come to me first. Shortly after that John Bennett's father died – he was managing director of Imperial Fisheries and Food – and John had to go to London to take over. Two other small companies had already amalgamated into Northern's and their managers had taken his place jointly as Managing Director, that was Bill Letten and John Butt.'

Bill Letten had returned to Grimsby from Cambridge University with a degree in economics. His first move on taking over his own family's company, Letten Brothers, was a rationalisation of office structure to minimise overheads. For some companies, business practice had developed little since the industry's earliest days, a state of affairs borne out by Norman's own experience on joining Crampin's. Letten rented a small suite of offices above the old fish dock post office, sold all other company premises and cut back the shore establishment. Norman recognised the sense in Letten making the company more efficient.

'He made a deal with Cosalt that they'd get all their supplies through them. He got twelve and a half per-cent discount on everything he bought as long as he got everything from them, now that was pretty good, trawl nets, all the gear, everything.'

As Norman Crampin reflects on his family's role in the industry, there are two contrasting examples of how times changed and outmoded practices must have been experienced by the men who went to sea.

'My grandfather always said, "If you want them to work, you've gotta feed the buggers." We had a good name in my grandfather's time for provisioning ships. My grandfather wouldn't have anything inferior. The rest of the Grimsby fleet got their potatoes from one firm and they were just the scrapings of the barrel. My grandfather got them privately. It cost almost three times as much, but my father said you've got to what all the others do, you know its looks aloof to do anything different.

'One thing the crews liked about Crampin's was we had a cashier called Don Burnam. He was a nice bloke, brought up three girls on a cashier's pay. He used to come in on a bicycle wearing his flat cap, keep his bike clips on all day. The fisherman used to call him 'Dirt Track Rider' 'cos of his glasses. He gave every fisherman a settling sheet which showed them the advance they'd had and the bills they'd paid on ticket and what was left, which he paid them to the last penny.'

Mike Debnam was a one-firm-man, sailing with Crampin's from 1958 to 1969. He was happy working for a small firm.

'When I used to go in the bloke'd give me my wages and then he would give me two and tuppence. I'd say, "What's that for?" He said, "That's the price of the registered envelope." I'd say, "Yeah but I'm taking 'em." He'd say, "Yes but I would've had to pay that if I'd have sent them home to yer." That's how they was, they didn't cheat you.'

If the history of Grimsby's vessel owners was one of astute business practice, the creation of the Grimsby Fishing Vessel Owners Association was arguably its defining moment. The association ran as a co-operative, acting as a representative trade organisation for trawler owners. It lobbied from a position of power, negotiating with everyone from government departments, dock owners and trawler crews to lumpers who unloaded the ships, engineers who kept them running and their unions.

Peter Harrison's father had been a skipper. His involvement with the Grimsby Fishing Vessel Owners Association began in 1955 when he set up a statistical system to collect information on the amount, type, value and destination of fish brought into Grimsby. Ultimately, Peter became assistant to the Association's secretary.

Still involved more than 50 years later, Peter's knowledge of the Association and its origins gives an insight to the owners' governance of port matters.

'It was originally known as the Grimsby Trawler Owners Association. Basically it was all of the one-time trawler owners, then when the seine net vessels became more and more prominent, it became the Grimsby Fishing Vessel Owners Association. The owners of every fishing vessel in the port or the owner-managers of those vessels were members.

'A lot were family firms that had grown up over the years. They owned and operated trawlers. The ships came in and the owners would see to the provisioning, landing, fuelling, getting everybody back to sea, paying the crew and selling the fish. When the seine net vessels came into being, it wasn't just a question of the owner of the vessel, because in many cases a lot of the seine net vessels were skipper owned or half skipper owned. So the owner was in effect doing work on behalf of the skipper.'

Grimsby Fishing Vessel Owners Association also owned the Grimsby Exchange, a private company which dealt with financial and other practical aspects of the owners co-operative.

'As a trade union, the association couldn't have a financial trading company, so it had another company called the Grimsby Exchange Ltd which operated boxes for landing the fish, the baskets, the winches. All the landing equipment was operated by the company and was used by the ships and charged out to the owners. It was responsible for box washing, even for fuelling vessels. In the old days it would see the vessels were coaled and then it of course became diesel fuelled, heavy fuelled. They bought it from companies like Conoco or Shell, negotiated the contracts, then sold it out to the members. This is where the co-operative came in again.'

Peter Harrison at the Grimsby Exchange

The Exchange also ran the Official Credit List which listed Grimsby fish merchants who could be trusted to pay owners on credit at the time of sale at the fish market. The book also listed non-credited firms who had to pay cash on sale and who could not '…re-pack, remove or otherwise deal with the fish until the purchase is paid for'. Credited merchants were free to pay the owners for fish purchased on the Tuesday after the sale.

The Association required each owner to pay an annual subscription based on the number of vessels operating out of Grimsby. The larger ships paid a larger subscription than smaller ships and had more voting power.

Often on the agenda were landings and relations with port labour, controlled by the National Dock Labour Board. Lumpers were National Dock Labour Board employees hired out to members of the Association at a charging rate.

'Lots of the arguments originated from the order of the vessels being landed. There wasn't sufficient labour to land all the vessels at once and some were pushed over to the next day. There were discussions about increasing the labour force, so that was always on the cards. Then you had annual negotiations with fishermen and the unions. Deck crews were part of the Transport and

General Workers Union. The engineers had a separate union and the skippers and mates belonged to the Trawlers Officers Guild. Other arguments were with the Associated British Ports (ABP) on dock charges. Whenever ships came in they had to pay wharfage, dock dues. There was always an argument with ABP over charges.'

The Association also had a formal disciplinary committee set up at the instigation of trades unions. Just one of a number of groupings in a complex committee structure that included a port committee, near, middle, distant water and seine net committees, each dealing with their own sized vessels.

'The association was controlled by an overall council, which all members had some representation on. They didn't want to get involved in discussing everything. The meetings would start at two-fifteen on the first Tuesday of the month and could go on until six-fifteen, and that was only dealing with matters and reports from other committees. So they didn't get involved in the actual negotiations. If there was a big dispute then the council were involved, but in the main there were sub-committees.'

The establishment of the Trawler Owners' Club in Fish Dock Road in 1947 had been a sign of an industry whose owners were confident of their position. The club's boardroom had capacity to accommodate up to 40 people around its table, but it wasn't all about work; the club had its own restaurant.

'The canteen did meals for staff, but then at the forward part was the trawler owners club and they would have silver service at lunchtime. They could come in at any time during the lunch period. And of course there was there was a bar. If there was a VIP visit, a member of parliament or whatever, then they would use the facilities of the trawler owners club to provide meals, or bring in outside caterers and use the board room. That was on the third floor, the second floor was the offices of the chairman and secretary.

'The chairmen of the association were all the top trawlermen, Sir Jack Croft-Baker was one. WFS Letten and Sir John D Marsden-Bartley were chairmen over the years. They were strong resolute people who had grown up in the industry.'

For the owners, the relationship between their representative on the docks and their skippers was fundamental, the link between business ashore and at sea. The arbitrary nature of markets made a lucky skipper as valuable an asset as a competent one as Stanley Johnson remembers.

'What the gaffer was concerned about was your fish. You had to be down dock at six o'clock in the morning on that pontoon to see your fish out. When you landed, your fish was laid out, two-hundred boxes to a square, and Mr McCormack the health man used to be round with his white coat and he used to smell your fish and examine it. He had a book full of little squares of paper with writing on it – *unfit for human consumption*. If there were one or two bad boxes, the whole two-hundred went. Many a time when a mate hasn't put enough ice amongst his fish, or he hasn't put a lot of boards on to take the weight and it's crushed 'em, it's cost him his job, 'cos when the gaffer comes down and sees them white bits of paper on top, everyone knows what they are. Even the buyers, once they see that they walk on and start buying fish off the next ship. The biggest responsibility of a mate was to look after the fish. If you turned in top quality stuff and it fetched good prices you'd done a good job, because then everyone was earning money. But if you neglected down that fish room, the skipper didn't want yer and the firm didn't want yer.

'The gaffers used to come down just before seven and have a look themselves. If they see they boxes condemned you knew for a fact you were ready for the ol' sack. They might even give it you there. But the other way round you got a nice handshake and a pat on the back and, "Well done Mr Johnson, very nice trip, well turned out." You felt on top of the world and you knew your job was safe. And you knew the lads was gonna make a good trip, because your fish was selling well and everyone got paid. Everyone was happy.'

The vessel owners 'having it both ways' was a practice not lost on men like Pete Woods. Buying his gear from dock-based outlets, for which he paid from later earnings, he was never completely sure where his money had gone.

'If I went to sea, I would need oilskins, sea boots, gutting knives, gutting gloves, all that stuff, and we had to buy it all from the owners' shops. The prices were way above what anybody else would pay. And we had to get it on credit, so when we landed they would take this money off us for gear we'd bought. But we never knew how much it was 'cos it'd just say, *store gear* or summat like that. The owners was milking us for the gear we needed to work on *their* ships.'

Grimsby's trawler owners were also key stakeholders in the Lincolnshire Steam Trawlers Mutual Insurance and Protecting Co. Ltd. As well as providing collective insurance cover in the event of a lost ship, the company safeguarded Grimsby owners' interests. In 1956 the Mutual Insurance and Protecting Co. received a letter from the Grimsby Exchange in which they listed the names of fishermen their medical officer recommended should under no circumstances be signed on by trawler owners. It was generally thought that, as well as attaining the required Board of Trade 'ticket,' fishermen in Grimsby had to receive a separate certificate of competence from the Mutual Insurance and Protecting Co. Without it fishermen could not work with any owner in the co-operative. The certificate could also be withdrawn as a method of discipline.

Grimsby was a unique port with its own ways of working. In 1958, the owners' United Navigation Committee requested that the Mutual Insurance and Protecting Co. inform them of owners intending to employ any skipper from outside of Grimsby to command a Grimsby vessel. The committee wished to interview the skipper before he sailed to advise him of the 'rules and procedures applicable to Grimsby'. The committee felt that skippers should be fully advised of the '…local rules and requirements particular to this port'.

For working fishermen, the owners were distant figures whose only link to the crews was through the ship's skipper. Bill Dillon met Bill Letten, then owner of the Atlas Steam Fishing Company, when he was one of a crew that refused to sail.

'He had us all in his office. I will give him his due, he said what he wanted then let us speak. We said, "The thing is, we get the least time in dock. We're the first out the dock and the last in. There isn't a ship that goes out before we do, and there isn't a ship that comes in after us 'cos we're always the last." He said, "Look at it my way, every day in the dock costs me six or seven hundred pounds. I'm looking at it as a business." We said, "We're looking at it as our view." He said, "I'll tell you now, I'd sack the lot of you if I could get a crew to go tomorrow, but I can't get no engineers so I'll give you the extra day in dock." He tried to say, "Come in next trip and I'll give you an extra day next trip." But we said no, we'd fallen for that too many times. So he gave us the extra day. In fairness, every day *was* money to him and when we was in the dock he wasn't getting any profit.'

The sense for Bill Dillon that owners had little consideration for his well-being was reinforced when he faced a family emergency and needed to get home.

'My brother was in Boston's and he got a wire that me mam had died. They put him in at Norway and flew him home. I got a telegram. Luckily we were going home that night. I thought, *fair enough, I can get home in time.* On the third night, one of my pals said, "Hey Bill, d'you know he's eased the ship in?" I went up and said, "Either you take me in and let me fly home or you go full speed home." He said, "Okay then." I said, "I've got to be there." So the office rang the operator, they said, "Tell Mr Dillon, that the tug'll take him straight off and we'll have a taxi waiting to get him home." We got in the river, dropped the anchor, but no tug. I had to ring and a tug come. There was no taxi. I had to walk to Riby Square and get a taxi. I got in about eleven o'clock in the morning and I was burying my mother at two o'clock. I went straight to my mam's to see her in the coffin. I got washed and changed and went to the funeral. My brother had been home thirty-six hours. If I'd flown home I would have to have paid for it myself. Outside work they wasn't interested in you. They were millionaires let's face it. What was a few hundred pounds to them?'

Richard Wright was another fisherman who felt let down by his company when he had an accident on board and found himself in hospital in Denmark.

'Nobody had even been in touch with my missus, she didn't even know. It was only the fact that there's a bloke down our street from Hesburg and his wife was in Hesburg when I got put ashore there. It was in their paper about me getting smashed up, and I was gonna lose my leg and all of it, and she thought, *bloody hell I know that bloke*, and came to see me in hospital and told my missus. When the trawler people came to see me, I said, "I wanna use a phone. All I've got on is a pair of Danish underpants and me false teeth, so where's me money?"'

Whilst companies like Crampin's typify traditional family run fishing firms with

Mr J Carl Ross laying the foundation stone of the new Hope Street Mission 16th July 1966

their roots in the Victorian 'fishocracy', J Carl Ross stands out as a 20th century pioneer, a progressive owner whose reputation outshines his contemporaries.

A native of Grimsby, educated at Wintringham School, Ross built the town's most diverse and, ultimately, successful business. Trained as an accountant before buying a fifth share of his father's fish merchant business in 1919, by 1929 he was in overall charge of the business. In 1934 Ross bought the *British Columbia*, the first diesel vessel of its size registered in Grimsby.

The *British Guiana* and the *British Honduras* followed. As well as purchasing nine trawlers from Sir Alec Black, Ross took over a controlling interest in Trawlers Grimsby Ltd and, in 1956, took over G. F. Sleight's trawling business.

Ross was acutely aware of the threat to deep-water fishing and as early as 1949 expressed concerns about over-fishing in the northern waters, writing that, 'many seem to assume that Providence will provide the fish ad infinitum.' He believed the fishing business would result in survival of the fittest, declaring '…that is what we intend to be.'

Ross Group built a well-balanced fleet of distant, middle and near water vessels that could land a variety of fish. Seven middle water 'Kelly' ships were built, followed by the famous fleet of Ross 'cat' ships, and finally a number of larger distant water vessels named after battleships. The group led the industry in developing modern freezer trawlers for fishing the North Atlantic. In each new Ross ship, special attention was given to methods of working, deck layout and improving conditions under which fishermen lived and worked.

When Ross obtained the rights from America to manufacture and use fast-freezing apparatus, stores were built and equipped to hold stocks of frozen fish, potatoes and vegetables. Frozen food production was soon a key part of the Ross Group. Ross also extended his interests in shipbuilding, printing, road haulage, catering and wholesale and retail distribution of frozen seafood, poultry, fruit and vegetables. At its height, 248 companies came under Ross Group control. In 1955 the company had an annual turnover of £7m and employed 2,000 people. By 1965, turnover had increased to £76m with 13,500 employees in total. Trawling, fish merchanting, shipbuilding and engineering divisions accounted for 25% of the group's profit. Ross Group would not be dependent on the fishing industry.

In his memoirs, Ron Reynolds remembers Ross as an approachable man, standing apart from the general sum of owners around the fish dock. Reynolds remembers being offered a lift from Ross in his Rolls Royce, even though he was walking home in smelly clothes from work on the fish docks.

In 1966 Ross Group reported that fish-related industries had reduced to 21% of the group's profit, of which trawling contributed less than 10%. The outlook for Ross trawlers worsened. After four years of steady expansion Ross Group's profit fell by more than a third in the year ending September 1967. As fish prices fell, operating costs climbed and Ross Group began to reduce the size of their fleet. Five vessels were scrapped, five sold, five transferred abroad and three withdrawn from service. The company also suffered the loss of the *Ross Cleveland*, sunk whilst sheltering from bad weather in Isafjordur with the tragic loss of 16 crew members. The only new vessel bought by Ross in the year was the *Ross Impeccable*, a freezer trawler to produce more frozen-at-sea fish for marketing under the 'Ross Valiant' frozen food brand. The group received a 40% grant from the White Fish Authority and a 55% loan under the Shipbuilding Industry Act to launch the *Ross Impeccable*.

It was clear that lack of support, indecision, and changes of policy at government level were signs of a declining industry. The UK market was open to landings of foreign caught fish. Limits were needed in the interests of a secure industry and a healthy economy for trawler owners. However, inter-relationships between the British Trawlers Federation, the White Fish Authority and the fisheries department of the Ministry of Agriculture, Fisheries and Food and the Treasury were chaotic. J Carl Ross retired in 1968 and in 1969 the Ross Group formally became part of the Great Imperial Tobacco Company.

*

In 1980, the managing director of one of Grimsby's oldest trawler owners, Consolidated Fisheries, took a £5,000 pay cut, claiming he did not believe in asking people to do things he would not do himself. Inflation-related cost increases and lower fish prices were making the post cod-wars situation impossible for the fishing industry. By 1980 there had been no settlement of the Common Fisheries Policy, designed to manage and limit fishing of European Union member states.

Consolidated Fisheries hoped that a slimmer operation would safeguard them against liquidation. They closed their engineering yard at Riby Square, sublet their premises and shut down all servicing departments with staff made redundant. By 1981, eight of the company's older vessels were sold, the workforce reduced to nine and the company offices at Auckland Road closed. The company was left operating a small fleet of seine netters.

Announcing closure in 1982, Consolidated blamed a shortage of cash, lack of government help, the failure of a take-over bid and the refusal of bankers to extend borrowing facilities. Fishermen were laid off and the company's remaining ships sold or scrapped.

British United Trawlers (BUT) was one of the last large vessel owners to fish from Grimsby. In 1984 the company operated eleven trawlers, all former Ross 'cat' boats built before 1960. BUT had provided minimal upkeep, allowing the ships to fall into disrepair. The chairman's report of March 1985 announced that BUT would keep the vessels fishing only as long as it was economically feasible. A proposal was made by CAM Shipping Ltd to convert the vessels to standby boats for the oil industry. The board believed this was in the best interests of the company. Contracts were exchanged as early as January 1985, but it was not until July 1985 that the trawler crews were alerted to the situation. The *Ross Jackal* returned to Grimsby and the crew was signed off for the last time – the first information they had been given of their redundancy. The crew received their regular pay for the trip. A similar situation occurred when the *Ross Cougar* landed some days later, marking the virtual end of deep-sea fishing in Grimsby.

Before selling to CAM Shipping, BUT formally decommissioned the vessels. As a result, the Ministry of Agriculture, Fisheries and Food paid BUT grants of £400 per registered (gross) ton of vessel. MAFF figures show that between 1984 and 1986, payments of £1,389,236 were made for decommissioning of Grimsby fishing vessels, with a clear majority paid to British United Trawlers.

The 1986 Annual Report of Associated Fisheries – BUT's parent company – states that the company received a total of £927,000 for decommissioning as well as unspecified profit from vessels sold to CAM Shipping Ltd. Associated Fisheries invested more than £6 million on cold storage, distribution, engineering, food processing and a restaurant business. Any money remaining in fishing was invested in fishing vessels in Scotland.

The fact that trawler owners received decommissioning grants and the sale price of vessels whilst redundant fishermen received little or nothing was a harsh reality. Some trawler owners demonstrated a startling lack of foresight, abandoning the industry rather than diversifying for the good of Grimsby's economy.

The owners of the 1960-1980s were not public benefactors. They extracted the town's wealth, leaving the fish docks to dereliction. Whilst there had traditionally been a degree of respect for the trawler owners, the way the 'gaffers' who remained profited from the industry's demise leaves fishermen like Richard Wright disillusioned.

> 'They just walked away from it. They scrapped all the ships. We felt like the least they could've done was make an effort but they didn't. In the end it was just money; it was just a number. Board of Trade acquaintances they used to call us. You got this money, they used to call it the easy six or the easy nine, nine pound a week that's what you got, bloody pathetic.'

5. McKenzie/Grant photo collection

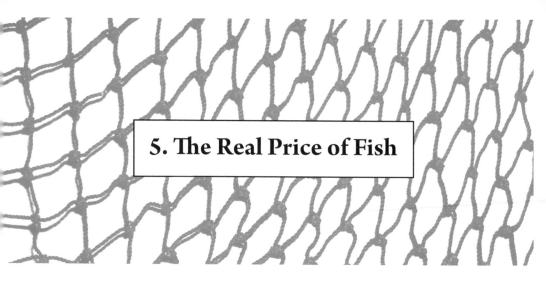

5. The Real Price of Fish

'Someone says, "Do you believe in hell?" I says, "Yeah, I've been."'

For many years, the constant dangers of a life at sea were accepted as 'part of the job'. Whilst health and safety as a concept did not enter many shore-based workplaces until the mid-1970s and the introduction of the 1974 Health and Safety at Work Act, the situation did at least begin to improve. A fisherman's well-being on the high seas was always beyond the reach of legislation, remaining in the hands of the skipper, the crew and the sea.

The attritional nature of the work in long shifts – men could work for 48 hours straight with minimal breaks – made even the toughest deckhand tire eventually. Mistakes were inevitable. Once a trawler hit the fishing grounds it became a working factory, with men operating unguarded industrial machinery on a shifting deck in all weather. The ship earned its keep against the clock and the tides, with each trip placing a pressure on the skipper and crew.

Responsibility for the seaworthiness of ships sailing form Grimsby lay with the Board of Trade's Safety Department and the Chief Maritime Surveyor, for many years the well-respected Captain Millward. Sheila Crampin worked for Captain Millward, a man with the power to prevent any ship going to sea.

'Captain Milward used to go around the docks every morning – he had his ear to the ground. He could check the safety equipment and go on a ship and say, "Right, we're having lifeboat drills now." He was a small, quiet gentleman. When I first went there he used to stand up when I went into his office. He had a lot of respect around the docks, definitely.'

71

Losses at sea occurred in Britain's fishing communities with alarming regularity, but perhaps the darkest time for the port of Grimsby came between February 1953 to February 1954. In a single year, five vessels were lost, taking the lives of 55 fishermen. The year began with the worst North Sea gale in living memory.

The first reports concerning the steam trawler *Sheldon* began to arrive in Grimsby on 11 February 1953. *Grimsby Evening Telegraph* ran the headline, 'Anxiety Over Silent Grimsby Ship'. There had been no news of the vessel for 12 days. The *Sheldon's* owners believed the ship's wireless might have been out of action and that she could be sailing off the west coast of Scotland. An international appeal was broadcast by the BBC and the Fisheries Ministry put out a general appeal to all ships at sea for news of the trawler. The *Coquette*, a Fisheries Protection vessel, began a search of the area and aircraft from the Scottish Command patrolled the sea around the Orkneys. On 18 February the owners abandoned hope of finding the vessel. A week later a lifebuoy from the *Sheldon* was picked up in the Shetlands.

Fisherman's Bethel, Tiverton Street

Port Missioner Mr Albert Broughton broke the news to the families of 14 men. A memorial service was held at the Fisherman's Bethel in Tiverton Street, Cleethorpes. A full Board of Trade inquiry followed. It was concluded that the *Sheldon* had in all likelihood sailed into the worst of the gale in the early hours of 31 January and was sunk after being overcome by a huge wall of water amidships. The true fate of the *Sheldon* remains unknown.

In the early hours of 22 March 1953, the *Leicester City* was returning to Grimsby after a successful trip in Icelandic fishing grounds. As they passed the Orkneys in darkness, a thick fog descended. The *Leicester City* crashed into the rocks, developing a heavy list to the starboard side. Skipper Osmond Johansen gave the order to abandon ship. He claimed later, "I told them it was every man for himself."

The crew shot flares into the darkness, spotted by crofters on Hoy who alerted Stromness and Thursoe lifeboats. The skipper and nine crew members took to the ship's small lifeboat which overturned in the rough sea, leaving the men clinging desperately to the upturned craft. Mate Edward Young, the strongest swimmer, attempted to swim for help. He was found later, killed by a combination of cold and exhaustion. The skipper and men, still clinging the lifeboat, eventually drifted to shore. The remaining crew members clung to rafts that were swept away from them by the rough seas. Two hours after the first flare, the Stromness lifeboat picked up four exhausted men clinging to a raft in Hoy Sound, one of whom died on the lifeboat. At daybreak the lifeboats resumed their search for survivors. The last man found was the 26 year old wireless operator, Michael Dimopoulous, whose body was picked up by the Thursoe lifeboat.

The following day, the *Leicester City* was still floating on the rocks. It appeared to have righted itself and was standing on an even keel. Skipper Johansen realised that had he not given the order to abandon ship, the crew could have been taken off by lifeboat in daylight without difficulty. Instead, seven of the *Leicester City's* crew lost their lives.

The sinking of the *Riviere* after a collision off Flamborough head brought the third tragedy of the year when, on 10 June, the 226 tonne trawler collided with a 2,841 tonne steamer, the *Firelight*. The damage was so severe that she sank just minutes later. Ten of the crew were lost, with just three survivors – a fireman and two deck hands.

September brought more loss of life when the *Hassett*, a 152 tonne vessel belonging to the Perihelion Steam Fishing Company ran aground some ten miles from Wick on the rocks at Auckingill. At around midnight on 18 September 1953, the crew reported feeling a heavy crash as the vessel hit the rocks. The engines stopped. The ship's telegraph was ringing full astern as she remained bumping and shuddering on the rocks, being overcome by mast-high waves breaking over the boat deck. The mate, Malcolm Smith, ordered the men to gather on the bridge, the safest part of the sinking vessel, but the starboard side windows had smashed and the bridge was filling with water. Men clung to the rigging as they attempted to make their way across the ship to the bridge. Within seconds the huge waves had dragged them into the water. Five men lost their lives in the grounding, including the chief and second engineer, two deck hands and a trimmer.

The *Hassett* on the rocks at Auckingill

One of those lost on the *Hassett* was a deck hand named Thompson. The Thompson family were to face another tragedy when just a few months later Mr Thompson's brother Christopher was lost on board the *Laforey*. The *Laforey*, a modern, oil-fired 609 ton vessel was five years old when she capsized and sank after hitting a reef in heavy seas near the coastal city of Florø in Norway. The entire 20 man crew were lost in the disaster including Skipper William Mogg, who was preparing for a new role ashore at the Ross Group head office, and was commanding the *Laforey* for his final voyage. His wife, Millicent, not only lost her husband but also her son and brother. The couple's son, Kenneth Mogg, was the ship's mate and had been sailing with his father since he left school. Kenneth had been married just six months before the disaster. Millicent's brother, Jack Powley, was also lost.

The *Laforey* lost off the Norwegian Coast in February 1954

On 3 September 2010, more than 56 years after the tragedy, the *Grimsby Telegraph* reported that the wreck of the *Laforey* had been

74

discovered. A team of Norwegian divers found the ship after working to locate it for many years, a task made more difficult by rough seas and strong undercurrents. The discovery made headline news in Norway. The team managed to film part of the wreckage, showing both the engine and the front of the vessel still intact. The divers left the fishermen's grave undisturbed, but hoped to bring the ship's bell, engraved with the words, *LAFOREY 1949* home to Grimsby.

Even without loss of life, making a living at sea involved making sacrifices. Safety, security and home comforts were left far behind each time a ship sailed through the lock pits. For Harry Drinkell the years away from his family bring a measure of regret.

'I never even dreamt of fishing, the life I had, it was a terrible life. You got two days in, so I seen less of my wife. I wish I'd have known then, I wish I'd have changed my mind, waited for me release and got a job somewhere ashore. I never ever earnt any money, it was a hard life. We lost many ships. I used to kiss my wife you know and wonder if I was ever going to get back.

'I lost me wife, she died sudden, within twenty-four hours she'd gone with her heart. She was my sweetheart. I married her when I came home on leave from Italy during the war. We got married in 1944 and back I went. I think of the years I lost at war, the years I lost at sea and I look back at those times and wish I'd had them with her.'

Graham Howard acknowledges conditions at sea did improve over the years, albeit slowly. The Ross 'cat' trawlers were an improvement compared to Graham's early experiences of going to sea and washing in a bucket of water.

'The accommodation on the *Ross Tiger* was wonderful, bathrooms, plenty of fresh water and you could chuck it away. On steam trawlers the water was precious, it was needed it for the engines. They couldn't afford it for you. From a deck hand's point of view, because diesel engines don't take as much space, they don't need as much fuel. So you got all the space of the steam room, massive boiler, massive bunkers to carry oil and all that space could be turned into the crew accommodation. No need to sleep forward end of the ship, everybody could come to the stern. And that left under the whaleback as room to keep spare nets and things like that. But those older ships, there wasn't much joy on them, I tell yer!'

Dealing with the cold in places like the Barents Sea, Bear Island and Russia was a constant battle. On open decks in black frost, fishing through temperatures of 20 or 30 degrees below zero, men's oilskins would crack with the cold. Flatfish hauled up would freeze as they hit the deck. It was no place for the faint-hearted. In the aftermath of a series of tragic losses in winter months, parts of the North Cape of Iceland were declared off limits. Michael Sparkes has vivid memories of fishing in Iceland on deep-water ships in the worst weather.

'I hated that place. Someone says, "Do you believe in hell?" I says, "Yeah, I've been." If there's a hell on earth, that's it. Later on at the North Cape of Iceland they banned it in December, January and February. You weren't supposed to fish there them months 'cos there was so many ships getting lost and men getting lost over the side. There was all sorts of accidents. But before that, I mean we'd been going to the North Cape of Iceland for years.

'It was so cold up there in the black frost, I've seen people with their noses bleeding. They were breathing in ice cold air and it could make your nose bleed. The mate used to come along and say, "Right, I want somebody to be a winch man this trip." And they used to disappear, because shooting away the trawl you had to stand behind your winch, paying away, but it was done more or less head to wind. You'd put your head down with your sou'wester on and you'd be paying the warps away and when you come off deck you'd have an icicle on your sou'wester. They'd say, "Look at Sparky's icicle!"

'We used to say it was a place where angels fear to tread. You'd get seas like mountains. Come night time you couldn't see 'em coming. On the ships under the wheelhouse there used to be some bars welded – we'd call them monkey bars – and the skipper would be on the bridge looking out and he'd have the searchlight on the water; he'd see the water coming and give you a shout. You'd jump up and grab the monkey bars quick 'cos the water came aboard, you'd put your feet up and hang on the wet bar and that was the only safety you had when you were hauling and shooting away. After eighteen hours on the deck you can imagine how tired you was to keep trying to do that. 'Cos your faculties aren't all there. I think I was only seventeen or eighteen year old, I must have been an idiot.'

There was little protection for men on board ship in bad weather. Richard Wright had been badly injured at sea and found himself in hospital in Iceland.

'I had to go from Iceland to Greenland with my leg in plaster and I'm on a stretcher in the airport, and there's this great big bloody Icelander there, built like a bloody shed he was. And I said, "I'd like to go to the toilet for a wee." I'm not being funny now, but have you ever tried lying on your back having a pee? If you're a bloke... You can't do it. So they bought me a fruit tin to pee in. Can you believe that? In full view of everybody and I said, "You're takin' the complete piss." Can you imagine trying to go? It was very embarrassing.'

Years later, the injuries suffered at sea still take their toll. For Richard, with a family to support, the only option was to take legal action. He had been put ashore in July and was back at sea by December.

'They was going to take this leg off, I've had eight operations and there's still a good chance I'm gonna lose it, cos they've given me two new hips but I've got arthritis causing this lot and they told me that they'd give me a new knee. Well I went last July and Mr Robins said, "If we start messing about you're going to lose that leg 'cos there's nothing to work with." So I said I'll keep my knee, 'cos you know what happens, you ain't got a leg to stand on have ya.

'I got six pound a week the first time and the second time I was a married man with two kids and I got nine pounds. And when they told me I couldn't go back to sea, they gave me nine hundred pound and said, "If you come back to sea you'll have to give us this money back." I got bugger all mate. I said, "How am I gonna survive? I've got a house, two kids, no job, what's me prospects, not good are they?" So I had to take 'em to court.'

Bill Dillon's skipper would usually have a medical box on board with basic first aid equipment and painkillers. Given the seriousness of the accidents likely to occur at sea, it was barely adequate. Complications were often made worse by the distance from help.

'I was in a ship with Snowy Robinson, he'd just got out of the Navy. I think it was his first trip. He said, "I've just trapped me hand Bill." He took his mitten off and his fingers was in his mitten. I'd never seen owt like it. So we shouted the skipper and he said, "Get the fish gutted first and then we'll take him in." We said, "No we'll swill the fish away, take him in." The cook stuck his fingers into a bag of flour and bandaged them up. There was no medical aid. I mean you broke your leg or owt you had to lay there till they took you in, maybe two or three hundred miles away.'

Distance from help played a part in the series of factors which led to the tragic accident on board the *Trueman*. Mike Debnam was the radio operator.

'We had a spare skipper with us. We introduced ourselves to him and he said, "What kind of sea ship is it?" I said, "It's a good 'un." I took the weather forecast that night, went through to him and said, "You're not going to like this. It's a severe storm, possibly a hurricane in the North Sea, they've advised every boat in the area to make for safety." Where was we? Right in the middle of the

North Sea. We couldn't do anything, so he said, "You sure it's a good sea ship?" I said, "Oh yeah." I went to bed that night and I finished up laid with the bunk on the wall.

'To open a door up that's got an angle on it, you've got to jump up and I'm trying to swing the handle, but my weight wouldn't turn it. Eventually the door came in and all that came through was sea water. I was sixteen years old so you can imagine what I felt like. I hauled myself up, got my arms up and climbed the ladder to the bridge; it was that way up, because the ship was on its side. I crawled onto the bridge and she was really suffering. The two blokes that were on watch were injured; the old man was injured.'

'The next day the weather was lovely, flat, calm water. I went down and was talking to the cook, and I said, "What we having cookie?" He said, "We are having the biggest piece of roast pork you have ever seen with all the trimmings." Next minute – fire! They all come up. She'd caught fire below in the accommodation. The electric wiring had got that badly wet it had shorted out and caught fire. We went down, my mate he stood at the back, he was a skipper, Pulfrey. He went down and his hair caught fire, they had to bring him out. The old man said, "I think you're going to have to send a distress signal out." When you're training, a distress signal is the one thing you learn you have to do. But when the time comes you have to do it, you freeze. If you can imagine a radio station going off, it sounds like budgies chirping, and the minute you send that distress signal it dies. It's like nobody is there. And then you get a reply from somebody answering your distress call, normally a station based around the coast. He takes charge, gets your position, gets you sorted out, and asks you what the problem is. They put me in touch with a Norwegian radio station who sent a tug to us, took us in to Harstad. They couldn't put the fire out; they actually sank the boat to put the fire out, that's how bad it was. When they pumped the boat out, they found the second engineer dead in his bunk and another chap who had tried to get out. He'd just got engaged and his father was the chief engineer of the boat. We came home in her. There was nothing in the deck below; it was completely gutted. We left Norway in a storm. Nobody went to sleep. She was taken to Hull to be repaired. I went back to sea in her again and then I signed off. It wasn't the same boat.'

With the unpredictability of the sea, the process of getting the gear over and returning the catch to the ship was never without its dangers. In high seas it was barely possible to hear commands and much depended on the understanding between the deck crew. The fishing operation called for split second timing. Graham Hobson was close by when the dangers of operating heavy machinery in rough seas were brought home.

'One of me friends lost his arm through the warps. The ship rolled and he put his arm out to save himself, but it went between the ballast and the wall, then the splice caught his jumper and dragged him through the bottom roller and chopped his arm straight through. We was about eight hours trying to get him in to Isafjordur. We was about two hundred miles off, but we had to get him in. There was no first aid. They had a morphine tablet. They put a red cross on his head to let them know that he'd had morphine.'

Most fishermen were hard-working men used to long hours. Invariably, it was the conditions that made the work unbearable. 'One hand for yourself and one for the ship' was good advice, but not possible when you were working on deck. Chukka Green was fishing in bad weather in Greenland when he was washed overboard.

'Imagine what a fifty foot wave weighs. It's like getting slammed in the back by a steam roller. We was all waiting for the doors to come up. And

Deck hand Mick Creegan chopping ice away from rigging - believed to be on board the trawler *Northern Chief*

she just took a hell of a sea and the next thing I was down the ramp. People say you see your life flashing between before your eyes and that, personally, I didn't. I was freezing in about minus twenty or something plus the shock of the water nearly give me a heart attack. She dipped her arse and as she come back up again, the same one that took me down the ramp got me bull's-eye and shot me straight back up the ramp. As I was flying up the deck in about six foot of water I thought, *You're gonna hurt yourself.*

'You just go back to work don't you; they don't give you time off. The only time I got time off was when I got catapulted once, 'cos the mate, he heaved when he should have lowered, and I was sat on the dividers on the trawl, and it shot up and twanged me on the arse. It was comical actually, smacked me on the arse and shot me onto the hydraulic pipes on the deck head. Aye, I'd've laughed if it hadn't been me.

'This doctor doom, he was chief engineer and medical bloke and he said, "You'll need stitches in that." So they called one of the standby ships that took me alongside this oil rig – this is when the scary stuff started. They lowered this dalek thing down, put me inside it and the next thing I'm up like two-hundred foot in the air like. And one of the medics on this oil rig he stitched me up and give me a sick note for twenty-four hours off in case of concussion! I said, "Oh nice one mate, I'll have a day off with this." I gave it to the skipper, Johnny Simpson. He said, "You can wipe your arse with it." And ripped it up, "It's only stitches and a black eye, it's nowt."'

Richard Wright was on board the *Lifeguard* with skipper Johnny Linford at Bear Island when the skipper's quick thinking saved the life of the third hand, a Polish fisherman who had been washed overboard.

'We was catching this real heavy stuff and you had to put a rope round it, then we all had to hold on while he took the rope off. Anyway, he's using what they call a fanny, it's a wire thing with the hook on it, heaving up, and it parted. Well he went straight underwater, you didn't see him. You're frightened to death, 'cos it's bloody freezing. The skipper jumped off the bridge onto the deck in his slippers and he got this rope, heaved it up, and there he was, hanging on the net like that. And he's going, "I'll be alright Skipper, I'll be alright!" He was wet through. We got him on board, pleased to hell. The skipper had to tell him to go get off the deck and get changed. He was going, "I'll be alright Skipper, I'll be alright!" Johnny said, "You bloody well won't be alright, get outta here you silly old sod."'

'I went over the side once, trying to be smart. In the summer we used to race each other. The doors come up, you chuck a chain round it, hook it on, they slack it off. Well I always tried to be quick, I've always tried to beat that bugger. Well I dived on and I missed it and went over the side and pirouetted straight in the water. I heard 'em all going, "Yeah!" Pissing freezing I was, there's all these blokes trying to grab me out the water with a bit of stick with a hook on the end. Course your boots fill with water, you lose them otherwise you're going down with 'em, so it in't much fun and you don't realise how far you are in the water, how far you are from the ship. You think you're just gonna jump aboard but it ain't like that.'

Time at sea and the pressures associated with the work took their toll. For some the battle was psychological. Richard Wright recalls the story of a young hand on the *Ross Renown*.

'He was gutting, having a fag, and all of a sudden he got his cutting knife, stuck in the wooden stanchion, went, "See ya lads," and jumped straight over the side. Never seen him again. They all thought he was larking about and he just jumped. You're going at three mile an hour but there's nothing you can do. You can't stop the ship 'cos you've got all your gear out. You've gotta haul your gear up, go round, and by the time you've got all that done it's too late. He just jumped. No one knew. People's minds go or summat don't they, I don't know.'

Sheila Crampin's work for the Board of Trade in Grimsby gave her a unique perspective. One of her duties was to write reports and type statements from fishermen following accidents or losses at sea. With a death at sea, as soon as the trawler returned the crew were interviewed.

'They'd lost a colleague or a friend, so they were very always respectful. It was a statement, but they weren't public inquiries.

'If they got badly injured, often they'd just bleed to death. When you're out there in the fishing grounds miles from anywhere and they can't stop the bleeding, and of course the warps when they're hauling in the net, it was a dangerous thing if they got caught up in that. I can even remember one accident when a chap had fallen on his gutting knife and cut a main artery. I mean if you're at sea and can't stop the bleeding often they were lost. They knew basics [of first aid], some of the skippers, but I don't think there was a lot they could do. Death from an accident on the ship was as frequent as a loss overboard, I thought so. Sometimes we'd have two in a week, then we'd go for two or three weeks without any.

'I can remember this inquiry – I think it was the third hand got caught up in the net as it was going over and he went overboard, this young deck hand grabbed a life ring round him and jumped overboard to try and get him. In those seas you've not got many minutes, it's so cold, and he managed to get to this third hand, but he struggled to bring him to the side so he could put a ring around him. This lad was losing consciousness, and the skipper thought, I'm going to lose two men here and he dragged this man back.

'I think most of them [skippers] were concerned with safety, but the money was important. And if they didn't bring the big catches in then they'd be let go, so I think there were a few that carried on fishing maybe when the weather was a bit too rough. I don't know, when they get a freezing icy deck, gutting knives, it's not the easiest of situations. I can tell you the price of fishing and it's not in pounds and shillings.'

For every fisherman who sailed there is at least one story of a near miss, an instance where a split second decision was the difference between life and death. Tom Smith has graphic recollections of his time aboard *The Bombardier*. On the coast of Norway in worsening weather one winter night early in 1968, the ship found itself in serious trouble.

'It was freshening all the time, so we were gonna dodge head to wind and get the gear aboard. Everybody was laying in the focsle. There was a few of us still awake, and all of sudden she went up, we felt her lift out of the water, then she went down with a crash, and just seemed to go down deeper and deeper, I thought, *What's that?* Then you heard all this noise and we thought, *Christ it were the sea.* The focsle led to the alleyway, the crew panicked and the first thing they did was jump out of their bunks and open the door which leads on to the foredeck. All I could see was this wall of water come down the alleyway, course by the time everyone shouted it was too late it was already in. It flooded all the focsle down below the other side. Nothing we could do, but you could feel the vibrations, so obviously she had her engine running.

'The skipper had just happened to walk on the bridge at the time, and the third hand was up there and a chap called 'Bib' on the wheel (Bear Island Bennett that was what his name was). It being dark, they just see it go darker and it was a wall of water, not the sea because you would have seen the white top. It just dropped on the ship, pulled her right down, put all the windows in, the bridge, the lot. Like I said, we was forward and there was nowt we could do. When she cleared of water you could see it just pouring over the rails, that's how deep she was. So literally we were under the water except for the foredeck and bridge, but she came up because the skipper had rung on the telegraph for full

The trawler *Isernia* head to wind in bad weather

82

speed. Fortunately an engineer was stood next to the telegraph and put her on full speed straight away, so as she went down she was already entering with speed which brought her up again.

'When she'd cleared I looked on deck and everything had gone – fish washer, pound boards, all the spare warps, trawl doors. All washed away. All the bridge windows were in, radar scanners had gone and the two inflatable life rafts had disappeared as well, galley funnel, everything gone. We managed to get some gear on, go on the deck, make sure everything was alright, still dodging head to wind.

'It was becoming daylight then so you could see all the damage. I've never seen owt like it if I'm honest with ya. I mean she was six hundred and sixty ton, that's a big ship, but well known for being a bad sea ship. It was the design of it, there was that many trawlers with all the different designs you know, some were good sea ships some wasn't. And another factor was we'd only had a bit of fish in, we never had much in the fish room, so all that buoyancy in the fish room helped her to come up.

'I went on the bridge checking round the ship and everything had just gone. And the life rafts which were on the deck aft had been sat on cradles – the cradles, life rafts had all just been ripped out the deck. The ship that picked them up was the *Ross Cleveland*. She escorted us into Harstad in Norway.

'It was the worst I've had at sea. I think it was about a force nine storm, ten at the time. But during the night when the wind had dropped a bit, the swell was still running and it was just a dead sea; they call it rogue seas nowadays, it'd just come up and dropped on top of the ship. If another one had come along and landed again it would have just put her down and that would have been it. Even the radars that were on the bridge, the telegraphs, the starboard side radar and port side radar were on the veranda outside the bridge, the impact had shot them of the pedestals and shot 'em through the door. The clear view screen you used to have on the trawlers, that had come out and shot across the back of the bridge and embedded itself in the bulkhead behind the man who was on the wheel. If Benny hadn't turned at the right time it would've taken his head off.

'While we were being escorted in, it was still bad weather. We was changing watches, doing an hour, there was just a steering wheel, no compass, no radar. The water had got into the bridge and the radio operator he got flung against this table. The trawl had gone through the bridge window and it was hung up on there like a big cobweb at the back of the bridge, 'cos all the wires were down and bridge all exposed – the electrics you know. The water had gone into the cabin behind the bridge, where there was a bunk and the bond locker. Of course the skipper was busy enough, talking to the operator, he said, "Clear that bond locker out there's water in there." When he opened it water flooded out with cigarettes, 'bacca, all the rum and beer. Course the operator not thinking stuck it all on the spare bunk. As we were changing watches steaming into Harstad, they all noticed it. Oh aye. You've never seen people walk so funny in yer life when they were going back to the focsle. I did it myself, bottle of rum in each pocket. Watch keeper's saying, "What's going on?" We managed to move most of the bond forward to where we slept. By the time we got into Harstad, the mate come forward, "Alright lads we're tying up, where you lot been? Where's all the cans and bottles come from?" The skipper found out in the end didn't he? But he said, "Alright it's my own fault" And that was the end of that, he just charged the minimum in the bond.

'We was eight days in Harstad while we got a temporary compass put in, temporary radar, a couple of life rafts and that was it. We was sent back home through the south fjords. But the impact, how bad it was, I mean people didn't realise. It's a big ship, but when it went down you had all your nets and bobbin bins down the fore hold. Well the woodwork just shattered like matchsticks and everything fell out into the lobbies. I've never seen woodwork like that, big pieces of wood just collapse in the middle.

'Yeah it was a bad trip, and it was badly damaged that ship. She got scrapped later in '68. When they got her in, she had boiler trouble as well, they reckoned it had actually moved her bridge backwards an inch and a half, the actual structure had moved with the force of the sea hitting it and they didn't think it was worth repairing.'

The Hull ship *Ross Cleveland* that had found the *Bombardier*'s life rafts and escorted her into port was herself lost later in February 1968. On this occasion, Tom Smith was in the nearby trawler *Lord Willoughby*.

'Everybody knew this forecast was coming and all the men got the gear in and made a run for the fjords. By the time we got there we was dodging head to wind. That was in a decent ship, but the engine was going full to keep us head to wind, that's how strong the wind was to push her off course.

'We was dodging all night. The skipper said, "This is no good the way she's icing up." He told us all to move outside, so we went out and we were changing watches accordingly. When I went on watch to do the steering I'd never seen seas like it. To see these big white things just rolling up, but the ice was worst because from our bridge right down to the whale back it was completely covered; couldn't see the winch, fish washer, pounds nothing – just one sheet of ice. It was a few hours later when the *Cleveland* went. She was trying to get in the fjord, but when she turned, she turned a bit too hard and course the weight of ice just tipped her. There was eighteen died on there. Harry Eddom, the mate, he was the only survivor and he just happened to have his gear on as he was clearing the ice off the radar. Two of the crew had managed to launch a life raft as she laid over but they had no gear on, so they got into the life raft and drifted off as she went down. They found the life raft with the two bodies in it, these two lads. Harry was found wandering the shore. That put us all off that winter, even the family at the time said, "You're not going back are you?" But it's a job int it?'

Graham Howard was also at sea in the winter of 1968. These were the worst conditions he or anybody else had witnessed.

'The water was just blowing flat with the wind. We was under protection of the land, we got two anchors down, we got our engine going and we were still struggling to hold against the wind. Never seen owt like that., but it was part and parcel of the job and you knew that when you went. We always knew. When you see freezing conditions, it's always at the back of your mind, *let's hope it changes quick.* I can't think of anything worse than what happened to them on the *Cleveland*, the *St Romanus* and the *Peridot*.

'They was head to wind and it started to ice up, the weather was too bad for them to turn round, else they'd have turned over. All they could do is keep going head to wind, very slow. Dodging we call it. They knew the ice was gonna build up. They were praying that the weather would change, but it didn't. You think about it, every time that ship rolled, little bit that way, a little bit the other way, each time further and further and you're just wondering when it's gonna happen. There's nowt you could do. It hurt us too when they were lost, it really did.'

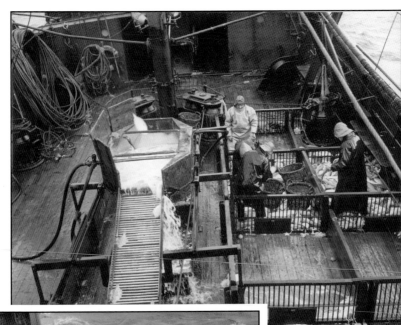

6. McKenzie/Grant photo collection

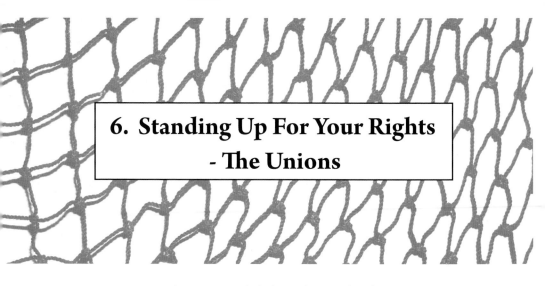

6. Standing Up For Your Rights - The Unions

'...we just didn't stick together.'

Fishermen were rarely able to come together with any degree of unity. Scattered across the sea working different shifts for different companies, on board any one ship crew members could be represented by four or five separate trades unions or guilds, often with competing interests. For some men it was more important to make the best of their brief time ashore than plan for the future. Others were reluctant to spark conflict and earn a reputation with employers as they tried to climb the ranks. The lack of industrial unity often meant that men received a raw deal from owners who, for the most part, were able to exert control over fishermen entirely dependent on them for their living.

In spite of the challenges to effective industrial action, there were examples of lines being drawn. Often it was the courage of a small collective of fishermen who brought about mass action.

The earliest recorded protests took place in the 1880s when fishermen rallied against the practice of winter fleeting. To compete with the new steam vessels, large smack fleets were staying at sea for up to six weeks at a time and transferring their catches to 'mother ships', fast steam carriers which brought the catches into port. Fishermen remained at sea on ships, often with no sanitation and rotting supplies, for up to eight weeks. They were exposed to considerable danger with almost 50 smacks fishing together in a small area. The transfer of fish from the smacks to larger steam carriers was highly dangerous. Tough in summer, 'fleeting' became unendurable in the harsh winter months.

The catalyst for the fishermen's strike against 'winter fleeting' was the so-called 'gum slip' issue. Trawler owners stuck a gum slip onto the fishermen's official Board of Trade engagement forms which listed the deductions made to their share of the profit from each voyage. This covered an extensive list of provisions including food, nets, fish boxes and related gear. Fishermen were infuriated to be paying so extensively whilst trawler owners made maximum profit. Every trawler firm had individual service departments that were expected to make a good profit supplying their vessels by buying poor quality items and charging the fishermen a high rate.

The biggest culprit was the Grimsby Ice Company, who had built up a smack fleet of over 100 vessels and tried to enforce winter fleeting. The Trawl Fishermen's Society who had gathered over 1,000 members in Grimsby, moved to strike action in September 1880 with the initial 250 strikers soon joined by many more men as their ships landed in dock. The strike lasted three weeks and eventually the government intervened, demanding an enquiry under the Secretary of the Board of Trade, which decided that winter fleeting was to be completely suspended and the 'gum-slips' removed.

The issue of charging the fishermen for their own supplies was brought to light again in the 1901 Lock Out. On this occasion, demoralised by hunger and intimidated by the admiralty, men agreed to return to sea pending an official enquiry by the Board of Trade to decide on the issue of pay and poundage. The enquiry subsequently took the view of the owners and enforced the poundage system.

It was not until 1961 that Grimsby witnessed its next major strike. This time the action of Grimsby's fishermen was to have international consequences. The

strike of trawler officers in 1961 was a protest against the landings of fresh and frozen fish from Icelandic trawlers in retaliation to the first Anglo-Icelandic 'cod war' agreement, which through extension of Icelandic fishing limits, began the swift decline of Grimsby's fishing industry.

The forming of the new United Fisherman's Union (UFU) by Grimsby skipper Charles Chapple and a handful of dissenting deck hands in 1961 was the first significant step to providing effective representation for Grimsby's fishermen. The UFU harnessed the atmosphere of discontent spreading from a recent trawler officers strike to create a new grassroots union which would represent an increasing majority of ordinary deck crew. Chapple tramped the docks to recruit members, successfully increasing the membership of the union to 2,000 members in Grimsby and Hull. The UFU battled with the trawler owners, arguing the case for better pay and conditions for fishermen, and regularly proposed ideas for trawl improvement. Chapple reportedly used his own house as security to help fund the UFU and, although he took the role of president, he strictly refused a salary for the position.

Richard Wright joined the Union but, in his experience, at the outset their informal approach to resolving disagreements stalled at the first hurdle.

> 'They'd come aboard the ship, the skipper would give them two or three drams of rum and they'd come off saying, "I've sorted it lads!" Bloody rubbish it was. So it wasn't like the proper unions, bloody cowboys they was. They never did get looked after the fishermen; they were their own worst enemies.

> 'When they went on strike, it'd be about 1961, and it was the UFU United Fisheries Union – me and my mate we decided to we'd had enough so we buggered off and joined the Merchant Navy. They barricaded the fish docks with seine netters and they couldn't get out, so what they did, they crewed them [the ships] and went into the south quay on the Royal Dock and sailed from there. They come on buses and allsorts that's what it was like. See, people don't always stick together.'

Despite Chapple's attempt to gain grass roots support, the UFU was represented negatively in the press and by the trawler owners, largely due to 'aggressive tactics'. In May 1961, during the Trawler Officers strike, which had now spread to the deck hands, UFU members prevented crews from signing on in Grimsby by picketing the dock and threatening the fishermen wanting to cross the picket line and sail.

As a result the trawler *Chrysolite*, owned by Alfred Bannister (Trawlers) Ltd, did not leave the dock despite a significant number of skippers and crew telling the owner that they agreed to sail. The firm claimed that the many deck hands who had been eager to go to sea were reluctant to do so for fear of reprisals upon their return. It was reported that a further 200 fishermen were outside the offices of the Ross Group on 11 May ready to sign on, but they also left the docks after being approached by the UFU pickets.

Owners would offer incentives to any man willing to break the strike and go to sea. With increased hardships, as Michael Sparkes remembers, it seemed an invitation too good to turn down with fishermen ashore and the docks off limits.

'I'd been ashore about four weeks and there was a knock at me door and it was a runner and he says, "Do you fancy going away – blackleg?" I says, "You're joking, I wouldn't sail out of Grimsby, I'd get mobbed!" He says, "We're gonna sail from Immingham, We'll take you in a taxi, and off you go in a tug and get on the ship, it's already in the river." He says, "We'll gi' ya a week's wages and a ten pound sub an' all, we'll buy your tobacco, your cigarettes."

'He come and picked me up at two in the morning. And he got a crew, and we went, and we was glad to get away to be honest with you, 'cos it was crippling us this strike. We weren't getting any money from anywhere, no benefits or anything.

'It was to do with the deck hands pay. It was the UFU, which was a new union what had set up and called a strike. We started to be members of it and everybody come on shore on strike. I couldn't get a penny from anywhere. An' me father was a fisherman, he could only just get enough, just a very pittance for me mother, so I couldn't pay me lodging or anything, know what I mean? So it was putting hardship on everybody. In the end I took this blackleg thing, I went. I was only away about sixteen days, something like that, went somewhere like West'ard or Faroe and when we came in it was over. But by did they cane us when we landed. We would have made around about four thousand pounds. Four thousand pound in the early sixties was a lot of money. We only made about two thousand five hundred. So all this, what they'd paid us, to get us to sea, all those perks, they took it all back when we landed. They didn't really give us anything, they robbed it back off the trip.'

By 1962 the UFU claimed a membership of 2,300 fishermen, 90% of the port's deck hands, and decided to apply for affiliation with the Trades Union Congress (TUC). They were rejected. The TUC accused the UFU of poaching members from recognised unions, and assured the union's officials that 'there is not the slightest possibility of the union being accepted into affiliation with the Congress.' The UFU was further deterred when the National Joint Industrial Council rejected a third application from the union to place a representative on their board to negotiate on behalf of its members. The

Transport and General Workers Union (TGWU) who did hold a seat on the National Joint Industrial Council board, stood in the way of the UFU, claiming they were dishonest and using destructive tactics.

Despite the United Fishermen's Union having far more members amongst the fishing community than the TGWU, they were never represented on the National Joint Industrial Council or the Grimsby Port Committee. It became clear to Chapple that the only way to secure formal representation was to officially incorporate his popular movement into the official, though arguably less affective, TGWU. Despite the strained relationship between the two organisations, the amalgamation of the UFU with the TGWU in January 1966 brought better representation for Grimsby's fishermen. What began as a genuine grass roots movement had in a few short years became one of the most forceful unions the fishing industry had ever seen.

Jim Clark remembers paying union subscriptions. As ever, for many fishermen ashore for only a few days, the money was paid over without question. Once back at sea, different rules applied.

> 'This woman use to come around, she was a barmaid and what she would do was come around the pubs to get the fees; she knew where we were when we was in dock. I probably paid ten years union in one month. She'd say, "You owe money." And you'd pay your union fees and all that. But once you got out that dock it was his [the skipper's] word and that was it. They could throw mutiny at you and everything. If you were heavy fishing they would break a watch so you would work twenty-four or thirty-six hours and they'd use the safety of the ship [as an excuse] because the ship was overloaded with fish, so they could break a watch so you could work whatever.'

The fast turnaround for ships became a contentious issue and the root cause for industrial action with men like Bill Dillon.

> 'Say you came in Wednesday night about teatime. You would land the next day, then you'd be away the next day. Till we got a bit of union and started complaining and then they altered it so you had two days of landing. Which was a godsend to us. But at one time you would come in and the next day you would be away again.

> 'We started one [a union just for fisherman] but we could never get them all to keep together. The last strike we had, we all come out and said, "Right that's it, we've had enough. We're not going." But there was three or four who I knew, pals of mine. And I went out on the North wall and they were letting the

trawlers go and they're stood there. I said, "What are you doing going to sea?" They said, "We haven't any money." I said, "Well we aint!" They said, "Yeah, but we'll come out on strike when we get back." I said, "You will do because you're hoping to get a bloody good trip out of it." Well they went. And I never got on with them anymore. To me they sold us down the line. I mean nobody knew who they was till they let go. We was lucky 'cos we got on the North wall where the police were trying to stop yer. We sneaked on and see 'em. And that was why you never did no good with the union because they wouldn't stick together.

Arty Lea worked nine months in the North Sea. Starting at Butts' on deep water ships and then to Northern Trawlers. From Northern Trawlers he moved to British United Trawlers (BUTs) but fell out of a job after a dispute.

'I got thrown out of British United Trawlers. Three or four lads, we went down on the wall one day when we was supposed to be sailing. We said, "No, we're not sailing under these conditions." What we was after was a rise in our poundage, because there was more fish going over to the Pyewipe factory when they couldn't sell owt and we weren't getting money out of it. We were going to sea and only picking up two or three pound after twenty-two days. We decided, they're not going to change it. Skippers, you couldn't talk to them, so we went down and started a strike. That didn't come to much. In the end we had a big strike, but that was because everybody realised we were all going the same way. Even the skippers realised their money was going down. So in the end we got our way but BUTs kicked me out. The next day a runner who used to be a taxi driver, George Chase, he come round and said, "Do you want a ship?" So I went to Consol's. It never worried me.

'I went to court three times and got fined seven pounds for missing a ship because of some argument we had. Me and a kid called Brian Turrell. Me, him and Barry we got fined seven pound for missing this ship because they wanted us to sail one man less and we said, "No we're not going." We had an argument and in the end I said we'd sail in the morning. So we showed up in the morning but come the afternoon we were told, "You three aren't sailing." So we got taken to court. This was because Croft Baker was a trawler owner, the Croft Bakers, you didn't mess with them, any trawler owner at all. You knew you were going in front of Croft Baker, but it was about a fortnight before they took us to court. They made sure you had your week ashore so you were hard up and then we got fined our seven pounds.'

As David Rimmer recalls, the relative power of shore-based trades' unions and sea-going engineers gave them a distinct advantage over fishermen, but there was little in the way of solidarity with fishermen.

'The engineers' union never went on strike 'cos we used to get what we wanted. Near enough ninety-nine per-cent of engineers were in the union. If we'd have said we were on strike, that was it, the ships wouldn't have been able to move. They can't move without the engineers. Same with the skippers, they couldn't move without the skippers. But the deckies there was only so many in the union and so many wasn't. When they had that strike we had a bloke with us who said, "That's it I'm not going I'm on strike, so he jumped ashore." One of the pickets walked across to the stores, picked his bag up and come aboard with us as a tide jump.'

Even without industrial action men would often be out of work when a ship came in for a re-fit. It could be anything up to ten weeks and, as Charlie Briggs remembers, you couldn't afford to not be earning.

'During that ten weeks you couldn't do labouring or anything like that. You went to the labour exchange and were told you couldn't sign on, because, "... you're not out of work". Well you *was* out of work but still employed with the company. But nobody paid you. I mean if we did ten weeks fit-out, I used to get myself a job at Dunlop making bike pedals until the ship was ready. Or if there was another ship, I'd go off in another ship until our ship was ready and pick it up when we came back.'

Peter Harrison remembers the owners' perspective on dealing with trades unions on the docks and the differences in organisation and influence between shore-based unions and the fishermen's unions.

'In 1967 the new Dock Labour Scheme was evolved by the Labour government which drove the owners into employing the lumpers directly. But they were still under the control of the National Dock Labour Board. It was difficult because as the [vessel owners'] Association negotiated direct with them on terms and conditions and the new agreements and the rest of it, all the companies had to be taken over by a permanent employer, whether it be Liverpool, London Docks, whatever the case may be. They had to take over a whole dock labour force and they couldn't dismiss them.

'In 1971 there was a big London strike and there was the Jones-Arlington Report which basically gave a docker a job for life. The only way you could get rid of him was for discipline. If he stole fish, you'd say, "Right, back to the National Dock Labour Board." You didn't dismiss him you just returned him. And then the National Dock Labour Board could hear his case and decide whether they would take him off the register or reinstate him to the employer. Nine times out of ten there was reinstatement.

'The dockers were organised because they had always been in the unions in the forties and fifties when the Dock Labour Scheme was evolved. They were controlled by the National Dock Labour Board and all that had happened was they were allocated to a fishing vessel owner to land a ship and then they were returned. But the system was a bit iffy, because there was a lot of favouritism. The foreman lumper for the owner could say, "I want you, you, you and you, but I'm not bothered about you." That's why they had this reorganisation of the whole Dock Labour Scheme in 1967. That's when I was appointed manager of the Grimsby Landing Company to control the lumpers which I handled for nineteen years until Maggie Thatcher closed the scheme down and we all became redundant.'

When a fisherman was out of a ship, the most important man was the runner. As Eddie Whyte remembers, there were runners who weren't averse to taking a bribe from a man in need of a ship. It was even worse for men who found themselves with a troublesome reputation.

'The runner would say, "Have you got a match?" You'd say, "Yeah I've got a match for ya." You'd put two pound in this matchbox and hand it over. So next thing you know, he says, "Here's a job for ya." 'Cos he's got his two pound hasn't he. Everybody knew it went on. It was illegal, but everybody did it you know. Used to down in Northern Trawlers, even when I was cook, y'know. Down the fish docks, we used to stand there nine in the morning, might be twenty of you and all of a sudden the runner's come forward and picked you out. You might have stood there till twelve o'clock, then they'd come out, no more jobs today, come back tomorrow. Then it'd all go on again. This is how it went on, all the time. That's the only way we got a job.

'When I got to the engineering side, we didn't so that. They said, right we'll look after you and you'll never be never outta work. But the deck hands and that and the galley boys and cooks, and if you'd been a naughty boy you could stand there for days. If you missed a ship, you wouldn't get a job. You could stand there forever. Used to knock at the window. It's embarrassing innit, but that's how they did it y'see. And that's how you went back and got your job.

'The regular deck hands, the good ones, they was alright. If you were a good worker, you'd always get a job. But these people who'd go from company to company to company, who would like their drink, they'd have hell of a life. They could make it really hard and you'd never get a job in Grimsby.'

Ray Walker 'did a promise' as a deck hand trimmer in return for a trip on a deep sea trawler. The promise was never honoured. As Ray remembers, '…they would always promise you anything those runners'. Jim Clark remembers some runners operating a tidy line in loan-sharking.

> 'Some of 'em were a bit corrupt. You could borrow money off 'em, say a pound or two, but they would want five shilling in the pound interest. What some crews would do was borrow the money 'cos if you owed the runner money he would keep you in a ship.'

Improvements in conditions were gradually introduced. Much of this was due to better ships and a more progressive attitude from a few owners. The TGWU appointed Barry Cooper as a full time district organiser for the union, with special responsibilities for fishing. Cooper reported in 1970 that the TGWU had 1,000 members from the fishing community and were recruiting at a rate of 75 per month. Cooper helped to win a £4 a week pay rise, and secured fishermen free protective clothing and bedding. However, the bedding allowance consisted of one flock bed, one pillow, two blankets but no sheets. Men only received the bedding if they filled out an application form, provided proof of an up-to-date log book of three years, and held a medical certificate. Only one set of bedding was issued per year and it had to be taken home to be cleaned. When Cooper left his position after two years, he claimed there was 'a lot more to be done, particularly from an organisation point of view and in improving wages and conditions'. Cooper was not able to rally the fishermen and fishermen had failed to back the call for strike action in support of their pay claim. Cooper said, 'I shall never understand why a group of men, in a secret ballot, voted for a strike then ran away from it, when the time came'.

Graham Hobson remembers how having to find work during periods of industrial action was a necessity. In his case this meant working at a 'fish house' to 'fetch some money in'.

> 'You daren't go to sea 'cos you'd get called a scab. So I got a job on the North Wall. Once the strike was over I packed my job in and went back to sea. It was like a magnet, it used to draw you back to it. My brother in law was the mate of the *Boston Halifax* and I went down in my car one Saturday morning to see

him off about lunch time, and I never come ashore again till three weeks later. They had one or two cans of beer with them and they was one man short, so he shouted, "Cast off we've got a spare decky here." I lost my job over that, where I was working at the time. The wife wondered where I was. Made a phone call to my sister, my brother-in-law's wife, and she had to tell her that I'd gone to sea again, then the crew rigged me out with gear.'

The last and most memorable protest by fishermen in Grimsby and Hull was facilitated by the South Humberside Share Fisherman's Association in 1975. Like the events of the 1960s, the strike was a protest against imports of foreign fish. In this case the British government was held responsible. The British fish market was flooded with cheap imports of frozen Norwegian cod fillets which were subsidised by the British government. The imports undercut prices of home producers and reduced the demand for Grimsby caught fish. Norwegian cod was underselling British cod by approximately £120 a tonne. On 23 March 1975, the small trawlers and seine netters from Grimsby docks blocked the entrance of the lock pit of the Royal Dock. Learning from previous strikes, a further 20 vessels sailed to Immingham where they sealed off the dock, crowding into the approach channels.

March 1975, Skipper Dennis McKenny and Skipper John Abbott heading to London to discuss seine netter strike

The strikers were led by Skipper Dennis McKenny who described the blockade as a move of desperation. He was prompted into action when he was unable to sell his quality catch due to undercutting by foreign fish, and subsequently sent it to the fish meal factory. The blockade lasted for 12 days, during which time the fishermen lived permanently on their unmoving ships, whilst some fisherman's wives began to picket local frozen fish factories that were using imported cod in their products. The strike was cut short when the British Transport Docks obtained a high court injunction ordering the ships to move, backed by a threat to send in the Royal Navy if they refused. Despite their actions, the pluckiness of the small fishing boats was almost forgotten when the third cod war and its aftermath effectively brought an end to the fishing industry.

7. McKenzie/Grant photo collection

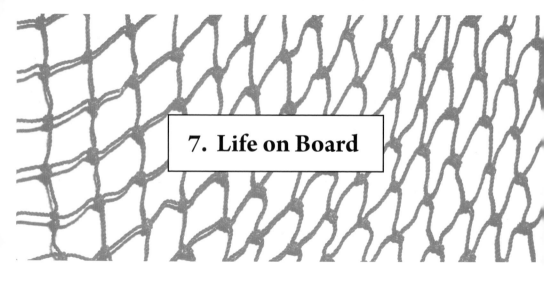

7. Life on Board

"Can I have me eight bottles and a case for in morning?"

In the aftermath of the Second World War, the majority of trawlers, including all of Grimsby's distant water vessels, were coal fired. Many owners joined co-operatives which bought, supplied and traded in coal, yet it was still in short supply and expensive compared to oil. It became profitable to convert the more modern coal burning vessels into oil burners. In November 1946, the *Northern Duke* owned by Northern Trawlers was the first Grimsby vessel to undergo conversion from coal to oil. Another 19 vessels were converted by 1950.

The first new oil burning trawler was the *Rinovia*, which sailed on her maiden voyage in January 1948. Built for the Rinovia Steam Fishing Company, the *Rinovia* was equipped with the most up to date accommodation and equipment of its time, including showers for crews and a record player with loud speakers. It was also the first British trawler to be equipped with radar. In 1964 the *Rinova* underwent another major re-fit, re-entering service as a diesel powered vessel with the Ross Group. In 1966, she was renamed the *Ross Revolution.*

As a shore-based engineer, Jeff Beedham was one of a team responsible for the maintenance of Grimsby's trawlers.

'Gradually after the war, oil fired trawlers came in and they was more economical, atomising oil into a boiler and burning it. The room where you'd had the coal bunker holding a hundred ton of coal could be turned over to fish. Then during the 1950s any coal burning trawlers that were in any sort of good condition were converted as oil burners. All you had to do was convert the boiler side from coal to using oil, putting tanks in, putting all the atomising gear in the end of the boiler. Then you had the modern diesel engines, you see, post war they were bigger than previous; the technology had moved on. Grimsby had motor trawlers in the 1930s but they were only North Sea trawlers; they only had smaller engines. After the Second World War, they built bigger trawlers with bigger engines.'

Harry Drinkell worked as a deck hand trimmer on coal burning trawlers directly after the Second World War. In order to carry sufficient fuel to last the trip, every available space was given over to coal including the fish room and deck space. Dragging baskets of coal through to the engine room was a relentless task.

'The old coal trimmers it was a horrible job. This bunker's in the middle of the trawler, it's all coal and you have to climb through this little hole in the middle of the engine room into the coal bunker with a little carbide lamp, then build this great big wall of coal and shovel down and over the top so you built it up to last for so long. If the other trimmer didn't do his job and fill that up as far as he could, it would be left to me.'

Harry's work didn't end there, he was also a part of the deck crew.

'Many a time the chief engineer or second engineer has been in and said, "Harry you'll have to hurry up mate, they're gonna haul in quarter of an hour." I've had to come out of the bunker into the engine room, get a bucket of cold water, put a steam pipe in it and use a sweat rag to wash all the coal dust off, squeeze the sweat rag out and dry myself with it, put me sea gear on and be out on deck. I didn't think about it, I just took it in my stride that was my job.'

Graham Hobson also began his life at sea as a deck hand trimmer on coal-burning trawlers. Lack of basic amenities meant that even a trip to the toilet had its hazards.

'Some of the North Sea ships I went on when I first started never had a toilet on them at all; you had to go over the side, hanging on, or go down to engine room and shovel it in to the fire. When we went to the

Graham Hobson

Faroes in the steam ships, I went trimmer-fireman, that's trimming the coal itself and firing the ship. Then when you got down to the fishing ground I would become a deck hand. I was seventeen or eighteen then, that was the hardest time of my life.'

In 1950, the Board of Trade ruled that all fishing vessels were required to have a toilet on board, yet many trawler owners responded by simply cutting a hole through the boat, covered by a hood, and passing it off as a working toilet. As negative publicity over ship sanitation increased, trawler owners began fitting their ships with flushing toilets and baths, in which water had to be pumped in and heated using a steam hose.

On board any trawler, the relationship between chief engineer and skipper was crucial. The 'chief' was effectively in charge of his own department. Even skippers tended not to enter the engine room without permission. The task of the engineers on board was to keep engines and machinery working. Including winches used to lower the nets to the bottom of the sea and return them with the catch. Graham Howard spent half his life at sea on deck before moving below to the engine room.

'You work six on and six off from the engine room; there was a chief and a second engineer, and on the steam ships there were a fireman for each engineer. On the diesel ships, especially the smaller ones, there was a chief engineer, second engineer and one greaser. By then the ships was bridge controlled, which meant the skipper could control the engines from the bridge by means of the telegraph. In the old ships, the engineers had to stop, start and reverse whatever.'

As Arty Lea explains, each trip had its routine, a timeline that crews familiar with each other and their ship would fall into. It began once the crew came together in dock.

'You'd have some guys come from home after two or three days on the booze. We used to sail in the night time then. Later on you could only sail on one tide a day, but when I first sailed you could pick either the morning or the afternoon. The first two days you'd be steaming down getting your gear ready and all that down in the fish rooms. But it was mostly two-and-a-half or three days before you was fishing. You'd be taking watches, working on the deck, one full day on the deck, then you'd take every third watch, so like every four or eight hours you had your watches.'

Once the ship reached the fishing grounds for ten or twelve days fishing, the shift patterns changed with the skipper pushing the crew to the limit of their endurance. Notionally the shifts were 18 hours on and six off, but when Arty Lea started fishing, 20 hour shifts were common.

'If you got any fish, the skipper would say he wanted to pinch an hour, so you did twenty-one and got three hours sleep, so you'd get the fish off the deck. When we started fishing until we finished fishing, we were living like animals. We never got time to have a wash or owt, or we'd get washed after ten or twelve days. It was atrocious. There was a lad called Alf Hewson, and when he first come decky-learner – it was in a Northern boat and they were still sailing with no showers or baths – and he said, "Where do I get a bath?" So I said, "In a bucket." And he said, "I can't get in a bucket!" A bit slow, but a smashing kid.

'There was one kid I asked, "What you doing?" He just couldn't be bothered to wash, because time below, that was your time for sleeping. He said he liked a five minute read, but he had the book upside down, he couldn't read. I said it would be easier if he turned the book the other way up and he told me off. You're sleeping in a place as big as this room, you've got twelve blokes living in this thing, with a coal bunker in the middle, and a coal fire. That was my first deep water ship and I was in her fifteen months. And you'd have nine on deck and three trying to sleep.'

As Jim Clark remembers, the easiest time aboard was the journey out to the fishing grounds with the crew split into three watches.

'You had three steaming watches, a skipper's watch, third hand's watch and the mate's watch and then you had what they called day men. They got the trawl ready and the ship ready for fishing. It could take you up to four days to go down like Bear Island, Russian Coast. Iceland with good weather you could do maybe two and half to three days.'

With long watches and extended shifts, tiredness would take its toll. On one occasion, Jim's night wanderings almost had lethal consequences.

'I went to get me head down and the next thing I can remember, I saw the mate paying away the warps and these warps ran through bollards and when they were going if you touched one it would whip you straight through the thing. And I'd sleep- walked – I did as a child – and I come to and I heard the mate shout. I was just going to put my hands on the wire to get over and he shouted, so I sorta woke up, turned around and went back. Every time after that they use to tie me feet together. If I'd have touched that wire I'd have shot right through the block, I wouldn't have sleep-walked after that.'

A quick dram and then back to work

Most fishermen liked a drink and it was customary to take a bottle of rum and a case of beer aboard. Often, as Graham Nicholson remembers, that would have been well on its way before the ship left the docks.

'We'd get started as soon as we got on board, had a dram. When you let go we were still having a dram. You knew you were gonna get your head down, you weren't working unless you was on the watch. You had day men; they wasn't going to start working while next day – that was getting the trawler ready. But you had to go on watch with the skipper or the third hand, and you'd have to take your turn on the wheel. But you used to be sober that night anyway. You only had that drink, you'd get your head down and then they'd call you out for your watch.

'Then the booze you bought to take to sea, always a case of beer, you used to get that from the Humber [pub]. And you didn't pay for it until next trip. "Can I have me eight bottles and a case for in morning? I'm going to sea." This was at like two in the morning, used to give it you it the night before to take home. You had to take it on credit, pay when you come in on landing day.'

Once the crews had seen off the beer and rum they'd taken aboard, the only other alcohol came from the ship's bond store. One skipper believed in getting the drink out of the way.

'It was relentless, "Get it down you." After it was gone, then it was hangover time, but sometimes we'd get a nasty surprise when we realised we'd caught over a thousand kit without knowing it, nobody knew much about it. On the other hand, once we went to shoot the gear, shot the gear over the side and forgot to make it past one of the bobbins so we lost a trawl. Stripped it away.'

As Jim Clark remembers, access to the bond – items kept on board exempt from UK Duty – was one of the perks of the job. Fishermen taking more than their allowance ashore could find themselves in trouble with HM Customs.

'We got cheap cigarettes – fifteen shillings for a carton of two-hundred cigarettes; Tins of tobacco – Old Friends would be about ten shillings. When we came in, customs would be waiting, so if you tried to take more than you was allowed ashore they would take it off yer. The Customs and Excise people also had what they call a 'black gang' and they would hit a boat if it looked like the bond bill was high. You thought you could hide stuff, but they knew every place on that ship. They're all in these black overalls, and they can strip a ship. They have sniffer dogs, sticks with mirrors and they can look under stuff.'

Once a trawler was at work, the smooth running depended on the understanding built up between a crew. As Charlie Briggs pointedly says, '…everyone had a job to do, if one of those jobs was neglected, it cost a man his fingers or arm or worse. You had to have confidence in your crew doing the job they was paid to do'.

Often the nature of the fishing community with its close-knit relations and word of mouth opportunities meant that family members sailed together. Some skippers preferred to keep only one member of a family in a crew, an understandably pragmatic approach in case the ship was lost. Robert Atmore sailed with his brother.

'Me brother used to wake us up, because we used to work during the day going down to the fishing ground, what you called day workers. Sometimes we used to be playing cards all night. "Come on you lads. It's time to get up." That's how he used to call us. I got the sack on one ship, because the skipper didn't like relatives sailing together. Tommy Brightmore, Harold was his dad, he was the third hand so me and him got the sack. Mark Bradley had eleven kids, Midgey Grant had eleven, Harold had eleven and his wife was expecting. Our Ron had five, I had five and someone else had five. Then you had ones and twos.

'I was winch-man and Ron was mate. We was both on the winch and it was blowing and it was cold. It was freezing up. I couldn't hold the brake, but we managed y'know. He went on the bridge and got a bottle of rum, a nightly tot. He come in the galley and said, "I'm telling me mam on you." Then I said "Well I'm gonna tell me mam on you because of you getting onto me." He went skipper of that ship and he were brilliant. I mean if it got too bad, we used to lay because of the bad weather. But when he was mate… he lost two of his fingers and had stitches all down his hand.'

With men living and working in close proximity, it was inevitable that from time to time there would be friction. Disagreements could spill over and there was always the old tensions between deck crew and engineers. Relations weren't always rosy between members of the deck crew either. Arty Lea witnessed a few punch-ups. For the most part hard feelings tended to be kept away from the ship. But there were some differences of opinion that wouldn't wait.

'There was blokes from all walks of life. We had a horse dealer with us, he used to live in Spilsby and he went bust. Big Ted they used to call him and he never said a word to anybody until a bloke upset him one day. He picked him up by the scruff of the neck and he carried him the full length of the deck and he was gonna drop him over the arse end. He said, "Next time you argue with me you're going over there." Then he just put him down and never said n'more about it.

'It was people like that who made the job interesting. I got on with that guy and sailed with him for nine month and you couldn't meet a finer fella. You had people from all works of life. Like Mad Joe Harris who was skipper in Consol's, he had two with him once – the bosun with him that trip was Keith Mussel – and Joe was shouting these two blokes and one of 'em just said, "Who's he shouting at?" So Keith said, "He's the skipper." But these blokes'd come out of jail – one of 'em had done nine years for manslaughter and the other one was a murderer. They couldn't get a job, so the probation service had sent them to Grimsby! Course at Consol's then, they would sign anybody on.'

Robert Atmore's experience of clashes between crew members as the industry entered its later years was markedly different from earlier days with regular crews.

'You used to argue, but you all took it in good part. Towards the end you couldn't do nothing like that. One bloke got stabbed. I was on the bridge and I went to get a cup of tea. The one who got stabbed come on the bridge and his shirt looked just like someone had thrown a load of jam at him. That's how it was. I thought, *Blimey, what's happening?* We went into Aberdeen; the one who did the stabbing he got locked up. They give the bloke that was stabbed two pints of blood. They wanted to keep him in, but he said, "I'm not staying."'

Emotions could run high for all sorts of reasons, one way to guarantee low morale in a ship's crew was poor quality food. Fishermen at sea needed to be well fed. The energy required to work long gruelling shifts came from three good meals a day. Breakfast, dinner and tea were the means by which men measured their days and weeks. Sunday's bacon and egg breakfast was a highlight and there was plenty of fresh fish. The cook was usually a new fisherman starting out or an older fisherman moving below decks and assisted by a galley boy – often the first job for lads on board a trawler. From baking fresh bread to preparing a sweet or savoury 'duff' or keeping fresh butter for Sunday tea, the cooks had their work cut out. As a cook on Grimsby trawlers, Ray Powell's shifts would start around 6am.

'I had a couple of hours off after dinner and I was always finished by about seven at night. My galley was like a house, you could always find work to do. The firm put a statutory amount of food aboard and there was certain things you had to order: flour, potatoes, vegetables, that sort of thing. But all the meat and the good stuff – eggs, bacon that sort of thing, they put it aboard automatically. You had a certain amount and that had to last you for twenty-four days. The first ships I went to sea in – the *Northern Pride* was one of them – had no fridge at all. So all the meat was stored in ice and after about eight or nine days it'd smell. So we used to salt it and put it in casks on the boat deck in salt/brine water so after about ten days you was working on salt meat. But of course as things got better you got better ships with refrigerators, things last forever in them … well, almost.

'We made our own bread as we needed it. I used to do it every day so you had fresh bread. It was made in the morning, when I got up in the afternoon, about three o'clock, I would put it straight in the oven and by half-past four it was out and I started with my evening meal. We had all that to do, you had to use your imagination with what you'd got at hand and you did get a reputation. I was classed as one of the better cooks. The better blokes could make bread, a lot couldn't. I could make pastry quite well, but I couldn't make a cake if you paid me a thousand pounds.

'In the kitchen everything was pot, all except the pans. They were big, metal pans. But, you could put them on the stove and clamp them down. Yer frying pan was about two-foot square and had a division in the middle so the fat wouldn't go over the edge, so I'd do fish in one side and chips in the other. Nowadays they use oil, but, then we'd use fat. Once that started splashing about it made a bit of a mess.

'The table was divided up into sections with boards, every man had eighteen inches and your plate and cup would just fit in there. When it was bad weather we used to wet the tablecloth then the plates would stick to it, otherwise they'd slide about. And that was the galley boy's job, keep the tables clean, keep the mess rooms clean. There were two mess rooms; one for the crew and one down below for the officers: skipper, mate, third help, chief engineer, second engineer, oh and me. I dined with the officers, some of them. That was your place, down there with the officers. That's if it was down below, if it was like the *Northern Chief*, that was all on one level. You didn't go down except to sleep.'

Mike Debnam remembers one voyage with cook 'Chippy' Walker.

'So I asked him, "What they call yer Chippy Walker for?"
He said, "They've always called me Chippy Walker."

I said, "What we having for dinner?"

"Chips."

"Tea?"

"Chips."

That's why they called him Chippy Walker.'

'This one used to make like a big suet pudding, sometimes in the pudding there would be meat or it would be an onion duff – they call it a duff. It used to be on the range in the galley, a big square thing full of water and the thing was on the top, they used to put these duffs in it to steam. So I come down to have a drink like, I walked in to the galley and the mate was there. I said, "What's the duff?" He said, "I don't know but I ain't having none." I said, "Why?" He got this big spoon and lifted the top off the pan and in this bowl of water was the cooks underwear, boiling away!

'At night they used to put loads of bread on the table, big slabs of cheese and tins of corn beef and that was your supper. You helped yourself to that. When you got to the fishing ground you lived off fish for your breakfast. The meals were good. You used to have two sittings, it wasn't what was left over from the first for the second, always fresh. You used to get meat pies, Desperate Dan meat pies we used to call them. You had soup, a main meal and a sweet. But the favourite used to be fish in batter. I mean everybody loves fish in batter. You could have as much fish as you wanted as long as you cleaned it and brought it for the cook to do himself. It must have been a terrible job, because from leaving the dock to coming back to dock he had to feed yer. What was on the boat they had to eek it out.

'They used to get big joints of pork, big joints of beef and everything. I thought, *what's he doing with it*? They had big wooden barrels on deck, big beer barrels, filled it up with water, saltpetre and all sorts in it. Chucked the meat in, put the cowhide over the top, make it tight, put a big lid on it and leave it. It used to be in there for twelve/ thirteen days. When they took it out, it was a cream colour. They use to boil it and it was lovely. Use to slice it and it was like proper silverside, I used to take some home with me, it was lovely. Everybody enjoyed it, they all looked forward to it, but it was the way it was made. There was no fridges like I say so it had to be done.'

With rationing still in force after the war, the food fishermen had at sea was better quality – and there was more of it. Ray Walker remembers his first white bread after the war.

'Throughout the war you got this awful brown bread. The first trip I went on

106

we got white bread and to me it looked like snow. We was out ten days and when we came home, the cook did a batch of bread and everybody got a loaf to take home with 'em. Now when you put it on the table, the rationing was still on, compared to brown bread it was beautiful.'

Opportunities for leisure time were scarce once the ship hit fishing grounds. Most trawlers had few amenities beyond a pack of cards, but when Arty Lea first went fishing with his cousin, there was a record player on-board with a few well-worn records.

'You'd be halfway through a record and all of a sudden she'd roll and there'd be a big screech. When we run out of needles, those 'red fish' they had a spiny back and we used to take one of these spines out and put it in! You'd get two lines, then a screech, then another bit. You just used to screw them in, put them in the turntable. But it worked.

'As I was the youngest I was the disc jockey and if it went wrong they'd throw a boot at me. They liked country and western and all that, ballads, all that stuff. When we was around Iceland and we had the radio on you'd get all the things we wouldn't get around here like Boxcar Willy. I wished we could have recorded because it used to be murder at sea. With all the different channels, somebody would have Boxcar Willy on one, Jim Reeves on another and all the top records from Yankee radio stations. Even when you was on the deck if the skipper felt nice he'd say, "Do you want a bit of music lads?" And he'd put them on. Lovely, it cheered everybody up because everybody used to sing.

'When we got the bond, we'd have a little party. It was surprising how many guys would sing, especially when we were steaming down to the fishing grounds and there was a case of beer open, and a party after tea when we weren't on watch.

'You always got a singer, I've heard some brilliant voices, get a few cans and a case down and they'd all start singing There was lad called 'Snowy' Green, he'd always sing songs about your mother, a couple of country and western ones and he was really good at it and he'd used to have everybody in tears just singing. It was just like a party at 'ome.'

Charlie Briggs remembers the skipper of one ship taking a cat to sea, not a popular addition to the crew.

'On the *Bombardier* the skipper, Brennan, used to have bloody cats, well I don't think there was a fishermen who could stand a bloody cat. And one day it was bad weather and it was blowing and somebody said, "Listen." I said, "What?" "Listen to that it's that bloody cat." It was sat on top of the mast. So Jasper said, "Come on then, somebody go and get that cat." We all told him to piss off. He said, "I'll give you two or three drams of whisky." I said, "If I go up there for that cat it's coming down faster than I get up there." In the end he made the mate go up there and get it.'

*

The Sea Fishing Industry Act in 1951 attempted to regulate accommodation on board fishing vessels, making it compulsory for all new trawlers to have crew accommodation built in the more comfortable aft section. Largely ignored until 1959 when the Ministry of Transport finally used their influence to enforce the Act, it ruled that new ships should provide a separate cabin for the engineers and firemen, the skipper, mate, bosun, cook and wireless operator on the starboard side.

In later years, on the larger freezer trawlers with up to 25 men away for six weeks at a time, accommodation and facilities aboard improved beyond recognition. The Grimsby ship *Victory* had two-berth cabins and a recreation room with darts and dominoes. Skipper Tommy Spall would make regular inspections to ensure the ship was kept in good order. For Eddie Whyte, life on board was a world away from the older vessels.

'You had no oilskins in your accommodation, you put them in the proper drying room. Didn't take long to dry. 'Cos on them old ships they used to hang them in the engine room, anywhere, to try and get the clothes dry. You could even have a film on, but you had to ask the skipper. You know what I mean? It was different times.'

With skippers and mates taking a percentage of the net profit as their sole payment, the risks of a market flooded with fish were all too real. Lower ranks fared little better once the basic pay allowance collected by wives or mothers at home had been deducted from the settlings. A poor market or a condemned catch meant the crew remained in debt. The bond bill went unpaid, any goods bought on credit, supplies from Cosalt or any of the other company shops added up to lines of red ink on a fisherman's settling sheet. The pressure would build on the next trip to be successful. But even the trips when everything seemed to fall into place, when the weather was kind and the fish found the net, you couldn't guarantee a profit. Jim Clark remembers a trip to Bear Island in 1957.

'We hit what we called a *fish shop*. There was fish everywhere. You couldn't

108

actually pay your nets away without moving for somebody else. And as it happened two Hull trawlers, one was going home, one was paying away, and it cut right through and sunk the *Saint Crispin*. And we'd just come into these life rafts, you never had life rafts, big inflatables and the story was there was nineteen of the crew in one, and the skipper in one on his own! We came up with nearly three-thousand kit of best cod and we made nineteen hundred pounds and settled in debt. By the time they took our bits out we finished with up with nothing.'

In the years after the war when the fishing was good, the pontoons at Grimsby were full of fish. Charlie Briggs remembers how, when so much was destined for fish meal, the temptation to make a few quid on the side created a substantial black market.

Grimsby fish market - unsold fish was destined for fish meal

'You used to have ten stone in a kit, and the kits would be in four high and packed all the way down. And tons and tons and tons of it went to fish meal. It was a real shame. My father used to land at midnight and go down at three in the morning to patrol the docks. They always used to say there was a ghost train as so much fish used to vanish. Nobody ever knew where it went. It just used to vanish into thin air, and they called it the ghost train. It went on for years. They always said the trawler owners had a lot to do with it, but they couldn't prove anything, because nobody could ever find it. Four thousand, five thousand kit at a time used to vanish. Nobody ever got paid for it, 'cos no-one knew where it went. But it was sold somewhere, someone was getting it.'

'Chukka' Green remembers one occasion when he'd been beam-trawling from Holland and took advantage of the local conditions to make a few pounds extra.

'We was wedging loads of money off, 'cos basically if we had three hundred boxes in, we was doing like a hundred boxes for the office, and two-hundred boxes going in our arse pockets. Easy. Just give the auction master a few quid. Stock up money, it was part of the trade, stock up money that's what you called it. When you went in surrounded full of boats, you always used to have a few boxes.

'Say like if you was in a seine netter, no matter where you landed, say you had two hundred boxes in, depending on who you were with, some of them would just put a few boxes away, but if you was with a good skipper he'd put a few more. But when we was in that beamer, oh, we put we put lots away. Basically was like legalised larceny actually. Every time you went into a foreign boat you always had a bit away, it was like expected. Same as when you came here, what they called the ghost train.'

There were good trips, times when the catch and the market came together to make the kind of money most shore workers could only dream of. Stanley Johnson was known as Leo when he sailed as mate with Skipper Bill Hodson on the *Ross Tiger*.

'We got fishing in the North Sea and Sunday morning we come out the fish room as we was coming on to land, Bill Hodson said, "Leo, we're gonna haul." I said, "Well I'm shot, put the gear down I'm gonna have a nap." I'd been up half the night. "No," he said, "There's plenty of fish marks." The echo sound was goin' all the time, telling you the depth of the water and sometimes groups of fish show. It was there in black blobs, it could be food, it could be fish. I said, "Alright then, go on." The lads were gonna roll in you see, so they wasn't very pleased; you can imagine the atmosphere. Anyway the trawl was absolutely full of cod. We got it all on board and it filled the deck. We shot the gear away again, he said, "Don't gut 'em Leo, just throw 'em the other side, because we're goin' through all these marks again and I'm gonna haul shortly." So instead of gutting we all had to stand there and fill the port side up. When we hauled it was the same again. And that's all we was doing, and we had another haul after that. Sunday dinner was the last time, because the deck, from the winch right the way forward, going onto the whaleback, there was nothing else but cod. He looked down and he said, "Will that fill her up Leo?" I said. "Yeah, definitely." "Right then we'll go home," he said. Well we couldn't go full speed because she would start rocking and rolling and the fish would slide over the rail so we had to go slow speed, nice and steady. We dropped anchor in the river at seven o'clock at night and we was gutting all night. It was half-past eleven the next morning when I come out the fish room and all the fish was put away. I'd been up all that time. I was that tired, I got the requisition book ('cos it was the mate's job to order things for next trip) and I gets me pencil and fell asleep, great big pencil line across the page. I'd just bobbed off.

'I reported one thousand, two-hundred and fifty boxes full up, single tiered cod. It was a lovely sight on the pontoons. So when I goes down six o'clock the next morning the lumpers were moaning and bloody groaning. And one of them said to me, "Are you the mate? Can you bloody count? You turned out over fourteen hundred and fifty bloody kit!" When you report into the boss like I did, they only hire enough lumpers to handle twelve hundred and fifty kit. But if they knew it would've been fourteen hundred and odd there'd have normally been another ten men working. It looked smashing, even the gaffer said what a sight. I made nearly ten thousand pound for that catch, it was a good trip and only seven days.'

The fishing industry operated complimentary groups of trawlers: the distant, middle and near water, and inshore fishing fleets. The distant water fleet was comprised of freezer vessels which fished the North-West and North-East Arctic waters, and wet fish (or fresher) vessels which fished mainly in the Faroes, off the north-west coasts of Norway, and in Icelandic waters.

The tug *Brenda Fisher*

The middle and near water fleets were comprised of smaller vessels below 135 feet, and operated around central and north-western areas of the North Sea, the northern coast of Scotland and the eastern coastline. Inshore fishermen generally operated in coastal waters but some ventured further afield catching a wider variety of fish, including whiting and shell fish.

With ships only able to enter harbour on the tide – two hours before and two hours after high tide, the competition to be first in and unloaded was fierce. The tug *Brenda Fisher* would sail out into the river and give each ship a 'section number'. This dictated the order in which they'd arrived in the Humber and the order in which labour would be allocated to unload the ship. With the dockside workforce of dockers and lumpers whose job it was to unload the fish – lumpers were employed by the Grimsby Landing Company, an associated company of the Grimsby Fishing Vessel Owners Association – as Peter Harrison remembers the landing sequence was rigidly applied.

'They would come in that section number order which they'd been given, then berth in that particular order on the south market. There were eight vessels on the south market and so many on the west wall and they would berth as they go round, in their sections. The distant waters always had it first, then the middle waters, then the near waters, then the seine net vessels right at the end.

It was all controlled by this tug and there were rules laid down about method of allocation and the labour was quite strict. That was a matter of negotiation through the Vessel Owners Association and its members.'

Ensuring the company knew when you were due to arrive back in port came as a result of far better communications between ship and shore. In the aftermath of the tragedies in 1958, ships were required to report in regularly. Basic messages gave owners the size of catch and estimated time of arrival. In later years, the advent of Global Positioning Systems (GPS) could track ships remotely.

The role of the radio operator on board was fundamental. He would operate and service the equipment, usually located in a room at the back of the bridge. After 1960, trawlers carried as much equipment as a merchant ship, including short-wave radio to send and receive messages from the home port, as well as a radio telephone used to speak to other ships in the vicinity. Trawlers also carried advanced equipment to aid the search for fish, including radar and echo sounding-machines, essentially doing away with 'skipper's intuition' as the main means of locating fish. Typically, the proximity of the workspace and the relationship between skipper and radio operator had the knock-on effect of isolating the radio-op from the deck crew. They were well trained specialists but, as Mike Debnam found out, you could find yourself in a potentially compromising situation.

'You had to sign the official secrets act, but when somebody would come up and say, "Can you send me a telegram?" If the person he was sending it to was the wife of the bloke stood on the bridge, I couldn't tell him what was going on. The old man used to know. He said, "Is er...?" I said, "Oh yeah, it's still going on." I don't know how he got away with it. Everybody knew, everybody.'

Eddie Whyte's telegram home

For many years, the main method of communication with the shore for most fishermen was the telegram. Remembering anniversaries, birthdays and family events at home and ensuring your thoughts were passed on was an essential link to life at home. Telegram delivery boys would buzz around town on red motorbikes. At a cost of a shilling a word, it was important to use as few words as possible, so fishermen bought simple code books. At home, the family would de-code the simple message often simply to say they were coming home.

The return trip gave crews time to clean the ship. As Chukka Green remembers, it became a matter of pride to make sure the ship came home in good order.

'The cabin itself you keep clean, and when you come in dock it was spotless, 'cos you took pride in the ship. If people come down your cabin and see a scruffy cabin, that reflects on you. And he [the skipper] knew where to look for the muck. And if another skipper comes down and your cabin is not up to his standard, then you know you won't be getting a job with him. You'd be in the second and third division ships. Some of the lads were cleaner and more hygienic than some housewives would be. And that's the way it should be. That's why lads showed respect in the ships. When we come in dock and parked up alongside some other ship or something we'd say, "D'you never clean that bastard down or what?"

'Once fishing's done, you swill the deck down. But with them having sheltered decks and whalebacks now, you don't go down the cabin so much with your rubber gear on, or if you do you take your rubber gear off at the top of the ladders and go down the cabin just with like your dry clothes on. Every day you used to take your mats up, give 'em a shake, and sweep the cabin floor, it's just part of the process. The *Sorrento*, she was a lovely ship. I used to love that cabin, I used to polish the woodwork religiously. It's your home isn't it.'

Fishermen like Arty Lea would take a big bag of gear to sea. As men were frequently unable to wash, a change of clothes was as good as it got.

'Most of us took four changes of gear, but whether you changed four times or not it depended on what kind of trip you were having. If you were having a tough trip, you might only get changed once. If you wasn't catching that many fish, you'd get changed as many times as you could. But if you were *really* fishing and working hard all the time, by the time you got to your bunk, you didn't feel like it. You'd just want to climb in, shut your eyes and that was it.

'The only smells you got was from the docks because the ships were spotless. You could call a fishermen what you like but when they left a ship they cleaned it. It smelt like a new one when they come in. And normally when you went away, unless it had been fitting out and that. The older ships did smell because they'd been fishing years and years and there was some stuff on deck you could never get rid of. That had a fishy smell, a dock smell. But most of the ships were clean.'

For most fishermen, sea-sickness faded after the first few trips. For some each trip brought a new bout on the way to the fishing grounds, but there were a few, like Graham Hobson whose sickness came closer to home on the return journey.

'I was never sick going away after I'd been at sea a few years but as soon as we saw Whitby Head coming down the coast home and the water used to change from blue to brown, that's when I use to be sick, right up till we come in the dock. Sick for thinking we're going to get home like.'

The working life of a fishermen with its danger and uncertainty took its toll. For some, as Pete Woods says, the routine of three weeks at sea and three days ashore could make for an unsettled existence.

'There was something I learnt about fishermen, they was never good people ashore. They was always odds if you know what I mean. Something about the real world that we didn't quite gel with. If things was going bad at sea, sometimes you think, *My God I wish I was at home*. But when we was at home, if we'd been at home two or three days more than usual, you'd think, *Oh God I wish I was back at sea*. Because suddenly you start being at odds with everything.

'You can't settle; it's a life of wishing. I mean the winters are awful out there. When you go on the deck you don't know if it's gonna be the last time you go on the deck. And even when it's really bad, it could be chopping ice up, seas coming over and all that, while that's going on, you don't actually think, I can't do this anymore. It's when you come off the deck. I must have heard it a hundred times every trip, *I ain't coming back, this is my last trip*. Those words, "this is my last trip" is probably the most said thing ever. But, when the old man says, "Right, last haul, that's it," and you're on your way home, no matter what's happened that trip, it's forgotten. You're on your way home, as soon as you see the Spurn Lighthouse, the adrenaline really starts. I mean some people'd actually get physically sick coming home. Soon as we get to Bridlington or Flamborough Head.'

For a fisherman to take a long break from the sea was rare. There were regular maintenance checks which would see the ships laid up. A re-fit could take six weeks, sometimes longer, during which time the crew either found other ships or were laid off and on the dole. There was no retainer from the company and men wouldn't be paid until they sailed again. However, there were other options for fishermen. Out of a ship in the mid-1960s, George Nicholson joined an Icelandic vessel. The working practices were something of a contrast to those he was used to.

'The best time in my life fishing was when I joined this Icelandic ship. It was a big freezer like the *Ross Revenge* – a big green one. It was a lot easier, six hours on, six off compared to eighteen and six on the English. There was two Canadians aboard, I was the only Englishman. These Icelanders, they're good workers I will say that for them. We used to be away fifty-six days. We would land in Reykjavik, all the fish was headed, we used to head it so we could carry more fish, chop the heads off see. Flatfish, which is prime, we were dumping that, we had ten to fifteen baskets of plaice and that, waste and all that, wasn't in the contract. Now that *was* good money, fifty-six days away going to Greenland.

'The skipper loved me he did. I used to learn me Icelandic, but it was all swear words. The food was lovely and we had a coffee break! Everybody drops everything, gear off, you go aft, bread, cakes, supper… coffee break, never heard of it on the English trawlers, where we did eighteen hours on deck, you were never allowed to go aft for a drink.

'After that, when it finished here, I went seine netting on the little wooden ships, but I didn't think much to that. Then I went to Spain – I lived at the seaman's mission – a lot of blokes was going to Spain. You used to be towing for five or six hours, then haul the gear, change your nets and haul again. But the fish you was catching was like that small you couldn't make a fishfinger with it!'

8. McKenzie/Grant photo collection

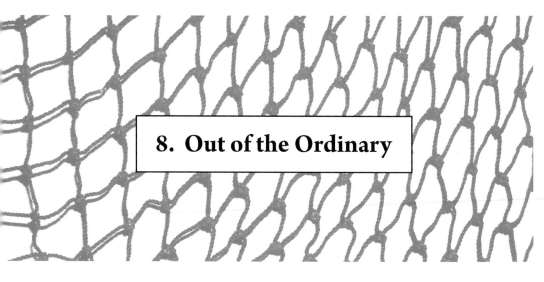

8. Out of the Ordinary

"You don't really want to know, Dave…"

A fisherman's days at sea were usually filled with routine and non-stop work. Trips merged together and a fisherman would be hard-pressed to remember one over another. An event out of the ordinary would stand out years later. Many fishermen recall strange catches, unusual objects which found their way into the nets. After dragging their trawl for miles along the sea bed, they could never be entirely certain what the catch would contain.

It was once reported that a Spanish cargo vessel hit trouble in a storm off the Humber bank whilst carrying a cargo of Seville oranges destined for Ticklers jam factory in Grimsby. In the weeks following the disaster a number of trawler fishermen described finding a 'good catch of oranges' in their nets.

But while trawlers picked up unwanted catches regularly – sharks would often find their way into the net – Richard Wright recalls an incident where a crew picked up more than they bargained for.

> '…In the fifties there was a Hull trawler fishing off the Norwegian coast. They got the gear aboard, dropped it down, and inside this cod bag was a walrus, still alive, and this walrus was unhappy. Very unhappy. The skipper looks out the wheel 'ouse and everything's alright, then he goes in the wheel 'ouse to speak to somebody. When he comes out again there wasn't a single person on deck only this walrus smashing the ship up. It was goin' berserk and course everybody run for their life. When the skipper saw it he's telling all these men, "Come and get it!" In the end they got a big plank and they shooed this thing onto it and it went over the side.'

Another unexpected catch which has passed into the Grimsby fishing folklore is the story of a floundering whale which found itself on the deck of the trawler *Olympia*, almost sinking the vessel as it fished off the Faroe banks. The crew were used to large catches in the Faroes, where legend had it that 'haddocks were as big as cods, and cods as big as men'. But nothing prepared the crew for their unusual trawl, as they heaved what they believed to be a large catch, to see a giant tail shooting out of the water. As the crew hauled, the whale's head and shoulders were still in the water whilst its body and tail were entwined in the net's cod end bobbing above the deck. The crew attempted to free the wires, hoping the whale would slip over the side and drop free of the ship. But it fell straddling the ship, with

David Coates with a sizeable catch

its head on the starboard side and its tail flopped over the port bow rail. The only way to remove the whale was for the crew to slaughter it using large knives, ice choppers and axes to cut through the thick layer of blubber.

Jim Clark recalls the extensive cleaning process that would take place with such catches.

'You'd drag dead whales up and you never ever got rid of the smell. Or somebody would drop a trawl full of fish, and you'd pick that up. You wouldn't think that it would rot in there but, oh God it did smell, it really did smell. We used to have tins of what they called chlorid lime and you spread that down and scrubbed it in.'

Animals were not the only unwanted catches. Anchors of numerous shapes and sizes, rusted iron from ship walls, or waterlogged timber from wrecked smacks would often be brought up from the deep. Some catches were far more disturbing. Harry Drinkell remembers one such incident.

'It was a lovely day this day, we was pulling in the nets and there was a horrible

118

smell. I said to the crew, "Bloody hell I don't know about a cod end full of fish, more like bodies if you ask me owt." Anyway I cut the cod end and went down into the fish pounds, 'cos you're up to waist height with fish and we was gutting away there and I got hold of a hand. I looked and there was a body there. A naked man with no identification or anything. But you could smell he'd been in the water a long time. So I shouted to the skipper that we'd got a body in the pound and he said, "Any identification?" I said, "No, none at all." Anyway we put him back into the sea. The smell was around for days. Just some poor devil had got lost.'

This was not an isolated incident. As a young lad on a pleasure trip with his father, David Coates narrowly avoided sight of a body at first hand.

'Fortunately it was night time so we weren't there [on deck] but you could smell it on the ship when we got up the next morning. I said to one of the crew, "What's that smell?" And he said, "You don't really want to know, Dave. But if you do ask your dad." So I went to ask him and he said, "We had a bit of a bad do, we picked up part of a fighter plane with a body in it." I think they'd looked to see if there was any identification, they said a prayer and put it back in the water.'

The sea bed was a graveyard for world war wreckage. In places it was littered with downed aircraft and shipping sunk by torpedo, mine or in direct naval engagements. During the First and Second World War, Grimsby's trawlers were bought or requisitioned by the Admiralty and converted for use as minesweepers to trawl for mines and torpedoes lying on the sea bed. When the First World War broke out in 1914, of the 700 stream trawlers in the port of Grimsby, 600 were requisitioned

"I'm not going to wait about any longer, John . . . before we can go out and fish peacefully we've got to clean up the seas . . . you can't put landlubbers in the Royal Naval Patrol Service—it's a seaman's job—so I'm going"

They do not serve who only stand and wait . . .

This man realizes the stark fact that the sooner this war is cleaned up the better...standing about or walking up and down the quay won't help . . . there's work to be done. Seamen, Second-hands, Enginemen, Stokers and Cooks (age 18 to 55) are wanted now. Come along and join the other fishermen who are doing a fine job. There are also a number of vacancies for men age 35 upwards to volunteer for the Boom Defence Service. Your local Registrar, R.N.R., at the Mercantile Marine Office, Custom House or Fishery Officer will give you full particulars, including rates of pay, allowances, etc.

and manned by more than 6,000 volunteer fishermen. In the first year of World War One, over 40 of Grimsby's vessels were blown up by enemy mines, resulting in the loss of approximately 300 men. Mines in the North Sea became such a danger that no men were obliged to sail for fish. Any ship that left the dock was manned voluntarily by fishermen determined to provide fish for the home front.

During the Second World War, trawlers were again requisitioned as minesweepers, this time as part of a more efficiently organised military operation. Losses of Grimsby fishermen were more severe, with 119 of Grimsby's vessels lost taking with them the lives of 600 fishermen. The risk from U-boats and enemy torpedoes increased. Throughout the war, convoys bound for Russia sailed around Iceland,

Aircraft wreckage recovered February 1940

passing close to Bear Island and across the Barents Sea on their way to Murmansk and Archangel. En-route they were open to submarine and aircraft attack, but not all torpedoes hit their targets. Those that missed would continue on their trajectory until the motor ran down and they sunk to the sea bed, to lay with the thousands of mines also waiting there.

When Ray Walker first sailed, the North Sea was full of aircraft.

'We used to fetch up parts of planes shot down in the war. We used to stack it all, and then we came to the Humber lightship we'd dump it. Everything we used to pick up it's still there. We also picked mines up, only once we picked a mine up and it had a small hole in. But once you pick anything up that's been in the sea, it starts to get hot – it starts steaming. If you pick a bomb up and you fetch it up on deck it starts to sweat. I was a bit young and ready to go in to the lifeboat, but that was a waste of time 'cos your lifeboat served as a potato locker! We just pushed the mine over the side, and the third hand cut the ropes away and she went to the bottom.'

Once a mine was on the deck of a trawler, fishermen were advised to contact a coast station by radio and wait for a team of naval experts to be dispatched. They would remove the detonator and render the mine harmless. For crews fishing in distant water, it could take disposal squads over a day to reach the vessel. In bad weather a rolling deck could trigger the mine at any moment. Many crews took matters into their own hands and removed the deadly catch from the deck themselves. Mike Debnam recalls an occasion on the trawler *Trueman* when the trawl was caught fast, anchored to the sea bed.

'I'm on the bridge with the old man. He brought the bag up off the sea bed, it came under and swung, then what they used to do was undo it and the fish would come out. He stood there and clapped his hands. "Got a mine." I'm not kidding you, I run. He said, "It's no good running, if that goes we're all gone." So I come back and we discussed what we were going to do with it. He said, "Right, we're going to lower it on to the deck, take the trawl off it and see what it's like." It was grey with a big red band around it. He said, "That's not very old." They were all looking at it and I'm out smoking, the old man is walking up and down. I said, "What're we going to do?" He said, "We're going to lift it up and put the other rope on it. And as the boat rolls it will swing out board. I'll shout let go, we'll let go of the rope and it'll drop over the side." So they're all ready, everybody is shaking. He said, "Where's the trimmer?" He was right aft. He said, "Get up here. I want you up here, right up the front." So he could see what he was doing. "Now when I shout let go, let go." Everyone is sweating and frightened to death. Well she rolled and it swung out. He shouted, "Let go!" The trimmer stammered, "Le... Le... Le..." The boat went back, he let go of the rope. It came back hit the rail and bounced back on board. All the skipper said was, "It's a dud."

For those fishing in foreign waters, the political relationship between cold war antagonists often made encounters between the two unpredictable. Whilst there are stories of trawlers used as spyships, or reporting sightings of Soviet vessels back in port, chance meetings tended to be amicable. Mike Debnam was a radio operator sailing three miles off the Russian coast when communications began with a Russian station.

'I was sat in the wireless room and the skipper said, "I want you a minute. There's a light flashing over there, what's it saying?" I said, "I don't know." He said, "Well you're the operator." I said, "Well I do the di di di's, you do the flash flash flash." He said, "Will you do it for me?" So I answered the light. It was a Russian station that wanted to know where we was and what we was doing. We answered him - gave the name of the ship, the registration and everything else. Every night he used to come on and [the skipper] used to say, "Is your mate Ivan on?" This particular night the skipper said, "Your mate's late. Ah no, he's here look, he has a different coloured light tonight, it's a red one," I said, "What do you mean a red one?" I picked the lamp up, put it on the side of the bridge, turned it on, dropped it and run. He said, "What's up?" I went, "You want to see what is out there..." It was a Russian naval ship, and I mean a big 'un.

'They came across in a motor boat from this warship. There was two officers and some sailors with guns that came aboard to inspect everything. They couldn't speak much English and we couldn't speak Russian. They came aboard and they was talking. "So, you wanna fag?" So one of the officers gave me a Russian fag. It was a little bit of tobacco in the back, like a hollow tube. We got talking and everything. And we had chocolate, so we gave them some chocolate to take back with them. They went all around the ship and they all had little bags of buns that the cook had baked. Everything was all friendly. The officers were really smart and they inspected everything. The skipper said, "Would you like some fish?" So they took some fish back in the boat. The skipper said, "Thank God they've gone." I said, "They're coming back." He said, "Oh they're not." They came back again. They brought a case of vodka as a thank you. When we came out of Russian waters, we was escorted by a Norwegian submarine back into the Fjord.

'When we got home, we got a radio message saying none of the crew was to leave the boat, we was all to stay on board. We had to come in to the dock and go into a special area, where we would be met. Naval Intelligence officers came aboard and they wanted to know what this boat was that we had seen. God knows how they knew. The crew said that I was the only one who actually saw it. So I went into his berth and he brought this book out and it was all silhouettes of boats, like you've seen in war films. I said it had three funnels. And they were all looking at each other. So he got this other book out and turned it over. "That's it," I said. "It can't be. That boat is near Australia," he said. "Well if it is it's taken a short cut 'cos that's where it was." The intelligence was all wrong. You get a lot of people saying about boats spying, but I never knew anything about any trawlers that spied at all. I know they used to send 'weather reports' but we never got involved in it.'

Bill Dillon's experience of meeting Russians was similar. Whilst the fishermen found the Russians professional they suffered no ill treatment, in contrast to the picture that the British Press painted, maximising the propaganda value of the encounter.

'We had an accident. Tommy Spall was skipper, we had to take this bloke in and we had to get permission from the Russians. He nigh chopped his thumb off. They wanted to go to Murmansk and Tommy Spall said no, we're not going to Murmansk because it was a big naval place and it was a bit dodgy them days. So we went to a place called Teriberka. And they come up in a tug, they all had guns and they was immaculately dressed. Better uniforms than our soldiers. And there was women stood with these guns. They didn't threaten us or owt, but they had their guns there. They took him ashore, they wouldn't let us tie up or owt like that, we had to drop the anchor. They took him to the hospital and they made a marvellous job of it. He come back and when he got in he went to the hospital to have a check-up. They couldn't believe what they had done to him and how good it was. That was the Russians. We all had to line up to see how many [of us] there was. "You got any passports?" They was strict. A Sunday paper got hold of it and said they were armed and holding guns to our heads and it was a load of bull. Even Stroudy said, "Guns at me head? All they did was the guard sat outside while they took me in. I come out, come back and went straight to the ship." One of them gave him one of them red stars as he was going, put it in his hand, a little red star off one of their uniforms. But when we was going home somebody was coming out and they was talking to the skipper they said, "By 'eck you had a rough time didn't yer? All those Russians with tommy guns." He said, "I don't know what yer talking about." He sent a wire to the paper and they said sorry, but they'd got the wrong information. It was a story, that was it. They got a good story out of it and sold more papers.'

For many fishermen, working away from home with their mates, sharing laughs and tough times made the trip memorable. After the hours of hard graft, fishermen turned to each other. Pulling each other's leg and giving new lads a rough time was part of the job. Robert Atmore remembers playing tricks on an Australian cook.

'He had a habit of jumping out of his bunk into his shoes and off. All in one movement. So one of the crew nailed his shoes to the floor. This bloke Jim Hawkins, he wasn't much of a cook. So one of the crew he got this seagull which had got trapped in the trawl and put it in the oven. The cook used to get up in the mornings, poke the fire and open the oven door. It was his routine. So when Jim got out of his bunk "FIRE!" And it exploded as he opened the oven door.'

Young, inexperienced crew members were an easy target for jokes as they were still finding their feet at sea. Mike Debnam remembers how they were always 'yanking the chain' of David, a young galley boy.

'He was slow, really slow. He came into the galley. I said to the cook, "Is he alright?" The cook said, "Well you know when we finish the meal I get

123

everything in the big pan and we dump it over the side. I said, "Dump that David." And he come back and I said, "Well where's the pan?" He dumped that over the side too!"

'David came on the bridge and said, "Can I ask you a question Mike, you know when you send a message, what happens?" Well of course they'd all wound him up. One of them said, "Take this up to Mike. It's a telegram I want sending to Alsons on the North Wall. I've split my sea boots and I want a brand new pair." So he said, "Will you do it?" I said, "Yeah." He came back a few hours later and I had a pair of boots waiting. I said, "Here, take them down." He said, "How did you get 'em?" I said, "They come through the air."'

Mike recalls one joke in particular which backfired on the crew when the skipper decided enough was enough.

'This particular day I was sat in the wireless room with my feet up reading a book and the door opened. The skipper went, "You. Get your backside down there. Get your suit on, get your tie on." I said, "Why?" He said, "Oh you'll see." Well we'd wound David up by saying that every Sunday morning we had a church service on the boat deck. And he'd got all dressed up, gone to the skipper and said, "Nobody's on the back end up there for the church service." Skipper said, "They will be David, don't worry." So he made everyone change in to their shore clothes and stand on the boat deck and have a service. He said, "That will teach you bloody lot." We were stood there, it was raining, it was cold. It was horrible! And the old man was stood there with 'the book' and a big smile on his face.'

Jokes were usually nothing more than good natured banter between the crew and trainees. Mike and the rest of the crew developed a close relationship with David. He was one of them, naïve and good natured. In turn, the crew were protective of him.

'We'd had a really good trip, and well, you was a millionaire at that age. When we went away the next trip, I said, "Well how did you get on David? Did you get plenty of money saved?" He said, "Yeah. But my dad, he had a good time. He bought loads of beer." His dad had literally taken the money off him. Well next trip when we came in and settled up, his dad was with him, but his dad didn't finish up with it. The crew all got rid of him. They took David down Freeman Street, which really was *Freeman Street* back then: it had a John Colliers and an Alexander's in there, and they got him a suit, got him all done up. He got a girlfriend and everything. But his mum and dad really milked him, the poor bugger.'

When Derek Grant first started going to sea, his frustration with one man in particular led him to play a joke on the crew which left him branded 'The Bogeyman'.

'I was sat on the forward arch, feeling sorry for myself you know... all my mates ashore. I looked up and saw the mate – oh he led me a dog's life. Oh course he'd tell you he was battering me into shape but he wasn't, he never left me alone for a minute. And that ship it had like a veranda around the front, he was watching and he had his head out the window. It was that calm that you're nearly caught nodding off, you know, daydreaming. Well my mother she used to put this white blanket in my kit bag and I mean I daren't even take it out, you couldn't be seen with a blanket on board a trawler. Anyway, I went down into the focsle and some white sea boots come out, tie boots, when they'd worn them a bit you used to cut them down, and make 'clumpers', they're like your slippers. Just something to walk about in. But all these tops used to be hanging about. I cut up across, and I cut in eyes and nose and mouth and I got this white blanket. I looked and he was still there, so I crept up and I put this thing on my head, and I went, "Bruurggh!" He gave such a scream, went off like hell you know. And I run off onto the boat deck and I took it off and put it all into the life boat then went into the galley.

'I thought well that went alright. And I let it die off a bit then I thought right, let's have a look down the engine room. So I went along the casing and I looked down and there was the engineer and the fireman, pulling the furnaces, they were coal burners you see in them days. So I got all my kit out, just dressed myself up, and there was like iron steps down the bunker fronts and I crept down, 'cos they was that busy you know sweating and pulling the fire… So I put it on and I just tapped them both on the shoulder and the chief engineer went, "Ooh!" I was out that engine room like a flash. He kept it quiet like, 'cos I didn't know, but apparently he had a problem with his heart. But he was alright.

'My brother had just got out the Navy and he joined our crew. I didn't tell anybody who it was 'cos they was like, "Who was it?" And you know all through the trip, all the fishing and everything: "Who was it?" Anyhow, Pete said to me, "It was you wasn't it?" I said, "Yeah." So he was laughing. But he must have told his watch mate. Then it got around like tom-toms. It was the only time I've had the sack. Oh, we used to get up to all sorts of things.'

9. McKenzie/Grant photo collection

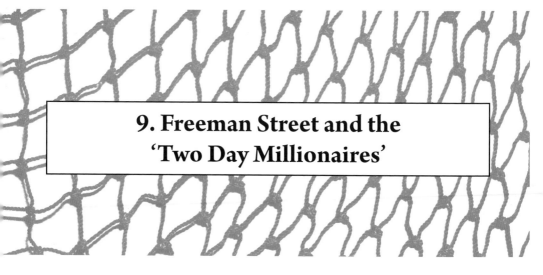

9. Freeman Street and the 'Two Day Millionaires'

'Who's he to come home and start bossing me about?'

An active and regularly employed fisherman spent the majority of his life at sea, with time in dock limited to three days or less before setting sail. Fishermen tried to make the most of their shore-time, spending their settlings, lavishing their family and loved ones with gifts, and frequenting pubs, clubs and theatres. As Ray Powell remembers, the temptation was that if you attempted to do everything, you'd end up doing nothing.

> 'You tried to be with your family and take them here, there and everywhere. I bought myself a car, went all over the country in it, then it was stuck outside the house for three weeks. You did try and cram as much into your life as you possibly could. I went out shopping, treating me wife and kids and that, especially on payday.'

Working away for weeks at a time put a strain on relationships, particularly with wives or partners and children. For Tom Smith, the fishing lifestyle contributed to the end of his first marriage.

> 'The life itself... you made the most of it. I married fairly youngish, got divorced in the 1970s, but was still fishing. Even when I was married we had a good life for those three days. We rigged the kids out, the house out, went out a couple of nights and that was it. When we got married, my wife would have been eighteen. I was nineteen. It was a long time for a young girl to be alone, especially when she had a baby as well. They realise what they're missing out on. So we divorced and that was it. I married again but I'd just finished fishing then so it was a lot easier with my second wife.'

Children saw even less of their fathers as they were usually at school during the day and too young to accompany them in the evening. David and Peter Coates remember their father, Sam, being absent for most of their childhood. They saw little of him even when he was at home, mainly because he wasn't home long enough. As David recalls, they were known as '36 hour wonders'.

'He used to come home, get up first thing in the morning to see the fish at the dockside, come home and have his breakfast, then go back down and settle up. Then at lunch time mam's gone out to meet him to make sure he doesn't spend it all. He'd be out all day, then he'd come in and be fast asleep on the floor when you got in from school. Then he'd wake up, have a quick bite and out he'd go again. Being kids we never saw him at night time, we'd have babysitters. We saw very little of him except when the ship was refitting.'

After many years fishing and missing out on special occasions, Bill Dillon made a promise to his wife to stay home for a Christmas, a decision he wishes he had made sooner.

'I never had a Christmas at home till about the last ten years of my sea career. It never bothered me having Christmas at home, but I missed the kids growing up - I was always at sea. It was them times when you either had to go to sea or struggle to make ends meet. It was the last ten years and my missus said, "Isn't it about time you had a Christmas at home?" I had one Christmas at home and I thought, *What have I missed?* And I never went anymore at Christmas. I wouldn't have that. I really missed out. I missed the kids growing up and everything.'

Women were invariably left to run households single-handedly. If they were lucky they had the support of neighbours, extended family or friends. With no men to support them, they dealt with tough times, brought up children and managed family affairs, often on strictly limited finances. Some fishermen, like Graham Howard, realised too late how much they had missed while at sea.

'I met my wife on a blind date. We used to meet up at the 'mucky duck' because the girls knew we were in dock. As a fisherman's daughter she knew the score. To someone who didn't know the fishing industry it did seem strange.

'You went to sea for your family, that's what it was all about. But what do the kids think when mam's the one in charge? Mam had to do everything, fixing a fuse, doing this or that, she had to do it. No one else was around. If you was a little kid, I always wondered to myself, you didn't see your dad for three weeks, but when he came home he was in charge and it was all dad for those three days. Like my lad, he would have been at school from nine o'clock until four, so by the time I come home it would be nearly time for him to go to bed. So all the time in them three days I was in dock I'd see my kid twelve hours and that would be it. What must he think? *Who's he to come home and start bossing me about?* When I don't see him for three weeks it's a hard thing like. I often wondered myself, even though I was a fisherman's son, but it just never entered my mind that people did anything else.

'It's not till much later in life that you do regret. I have loads of regrets because we was a little bit unfortunate me and the wife, we lost two babies and I was never there. I was never home. She had it all to do. I felt guilty for years afterwards, because it's not till later in life it starts to tell on yer and you start to think about what you have missed, like the kids playing football at school, or the girls dancing, things like that. You don't see that and that's what you gave up.

'We sent wires like for birthdays, anniversaries, but I didn't want to know if anything was wrong, nor did anyone else on the ship. It would distract from what you were doing, but what could you do about it? You'd be worrying about something you could do nothing about.'

Fishermen's wives built a strong fishing community whilst their husbands were away at sea, particularly among the small Victorian terraces clustered near the docks between Freeman Street, Park Street and Isaacs Hill. Before the 20th century, most of these houses had earth closet toilets which had to be emptied by night-soil men who carried waste through the house. Poor sanitation was reflected in a higher than average infant mortality rate compared to the rest of the Grimsby area. By the 1930s, the situation had barely changed. Around 300 two-room houses had survived, built back-to-back and accessed by a narrow alley. The industry was interspersed around the houses. A number of them had a one-man fish curing factory either built into the house, or very nearby.

In the 1940s and 1950s, close to 1,000 men were landing in the docks each day. A vast amount of their time and money was spent in Freeman Street – known as the 'Fisherman's High Street'. Built in the 1860s, Freeman Street was originally lined with houses, but its position as a direct thoroughfare to the docks led to many of these being converted into shops. Bill Dillon remembers the street's bustling atmosphere.

'It was busy, a gold mine, absolutely packed. You can't believe it now. You went in the pub and that, and it was full all the time, different blokes, fishermen with their wives and everybody mixing together. My wife used to meet me at half

Freeman Street circa 1950

past two and we'd go do a bit of shopping in Marks and Spencer's or wherever she wanted. Then we would go for a meal, maybe to Cox's Pea Bung. Or we'd go to a restaurant.

'It was a sailor town from one end to the other. Woollies and Marks and Spencer's were full. Every day was a pay day really. You'd get seven or eight ships, seventy or eighty blokes with their wives going down Freeman Street. If you were to go back thirty or forty years now you would never believe it. There was everything down there, and they was all profitable. It's unbelievable how much it has changed.

Freeman Street and the surrounding area was heavily populated by fishing families and their support networks. As Graham Hobson recalls, there were also the friendships which fishermen made within their own companies and ships.

'You was like a family within a family when you was at sea. Three weeks with twenty-two or twenty-three men it was like another family. You all had to get on, or else you never know what could happen when you was out there. You get on with your work and do what you were told to do. On the night time when you was steaming to Iceland, you used to play cards and dominoes in the mess room.'

But if maintaining relationships with people ashore was hard enough for fishermen, it was almost impossible to synchronise time in dock with friends and family in the fishing industry. Graham Howard's chance meeting with another fisherman turned into a lifelong friendship, but one that was difficult to maintain.

'Standing outside the Consol's office I met a guy and we become life-long friends. It was just a coincidence that we stood there yarning and we both clicked sorta thing. When we landed together we'd go out all the time. But I might go months and months without seeing him, then we would just click and other times we would be clicking every trip, it's just one of those things. 'After many many years we did work together. He was skipper and I was chief engineer on the *Ross Kelvin*. The skipper had been there and hadn't been doing too good and got the sack. And Tom'd just got his ticket. He had taken away her sister ship *The Northern Reward* and made a reasonable trip so he was offered the *Ross Kelvin* which was one of the lower end ships. The better the skipper, the better the ship but you had to work your way up. The only time we sailed together and basically we argued all the time.'

Socialising with crew members continued ashore in the pubs of Freeman Street. With approximately one pub for every 182 residents in the dock-area, drinking became heavily associated with the area and the industry. Fishermen were often depicted as heavy drinkers but as Robert Atmore explains, it wasn't always the case.

'They always said that fishermen was drinkers. But you only had forty-eight hours, because you was in, you landed that day, you had the spare day, and then you were away the next. The amount of beer that fishermen drunk was a lot less than a shore worker who used to drink regularly. I mean you used to get beer at sea, and rum - one in the morning and one at night but that was only 'cos of the cold weather. I was in one ship and I went for the bond and the skipper said, "I'll gi' you two cans now and I'll gi' you two…" I said, "It doesn't make much difference to me, because I don't drink." The mate, he got onto the skipper as the other crew used to get half a case or a case straight away but I didn't drink anyway, not while I was at sea.'

Stanley Johnson was another fisherman who chose to make his life at home with his wife and children the first priority.

'The living standard was good 'cos you had the money to do things. The kids was well shod, and I thought, *this is it.* As long as I was earning money to look after the wife and money to build a home, then I wasn't bothered about anything else. There's no point in going on the tipple and being skint like lots of 'em did. It was their way of life. I had a brother, it was his way of life. He never got married. He was a good lad, but he'd give his money to anyone when he landed, used to chuck it away like, 'soft Mick', but he only used to go to the old pubs. He used to come home, have a dinner, "'ello Mam," and off to the Clee Park. That was his favourite, near Ramsdens. But I wasn't like that, wife and family to look after.'

With time at home tight, as Charlie Briggs remembers, if the ship had missed the tide and had to drop anchor in the river, there was a chance for some of the crew to get themselves ashore.

'They'd say, "Right, half of you can go ashore in a tub, the other half will stay aboard and fetch her in." So half of us used to go ashore and we always used to have two or three bottles of rum. So we used to taxi into the basin, walk down Fish Dock Road and the customs officers' place used to be there. It'd be two or three o'clock in the morning and we'd put all these bottles of rum on the window ledge, go knock on the door and he used to come to the door and he'd have a mug with him. He'd say, "Now lads, how we doing, which one?" We used to tell him which ship. He'd go, "Alright, got 'owt' to declare?" And we'd say, "Just a drop. Then we used to fill his mug up and wish him g'night.'

For crew members who did socialise ashore, different companies and ships tended to have a preferred pub, with many split between ranks. David Rimmer understood all too well what happened if you found yourself in the wrong pub, even when fishing as far away as Lowestoft.

'The firm I was in, Consol's, we always used to use the engineers' back room of The Kent [Arms]. But a lot of the engineers from the Northern company, they used to use The Smokers. The deckies, they used to go in The Hitching Rail while the skipper and some mates, they were in The White Knight. You went in the back room of The White Knight and all the skippers and mates got served before you. Well they wouldn't even let us in the back room. You had to be 'suited and booted'. You were alright in the front room, that's where all the deckies went. It was the same in The Kent. It was our little room the back room where all the engineers went.

'When I went down to Lowestoft, I walked in a pub and he wouldn't serve me, just stood there. Served four or five other people. I said, "What's up with us?" He said, "It's because you're from Grimsby. He doesn't like Grimmies." He must have heard me. We were stood there talking and he *just would not* serve us. It's all to do with the fishing.'

One of Grimsby's most loved fisherman's pubs was the Grimsby Exchange Hotel, better known as 'The Barrel,' because of the barrel hanging over the entrance. Built in the 1830s and finally demolished in 1966 to make way for the Cleethorpe Road flyover, the pub saw many of the fishing industry's characters pass through its doors. In its earlier days The Barrel was the haunt of smugglers and the drinking den of innumerable skippers. Mr Charles Killan took over in 1889 and the bar stayed in the Killan family until its demolition. Charles Killan was admired by fisherman for his support during the fisherman strikes of 1901. When the strikers began to go short of food Killan provided bread and soup, and when the fishermen went on a rampage along Cleethorpe Road, breaking windows in frustration, The Barrel was left untouched.

The original Honest Lawyer in Kent Street was another much-loved fisherman's pub that was demolished in the 1960s, having served the East Marsh area for over 100 years. Alfred Freshney took over the pub in the 1920s, after sailing on fishing smacks to escape life in a Caistor orphanage. Traditional blue and white half gallon jugs lined the bar and ice from the fish docks was used in the summer to keep the beer cool. The pub also had a 'fisherman's corner' occupied by out-of-ship fishermen. Those who had returned from a successful trip would go in and send half-gallon jugs of beer 'round the corner' for their less fortunate mates.

The Sheffield Arms became so notorious for their clientele that, for many years, it was better known as the 'Rats Nest'. Located on Cleethorpe Road, the pub was associated with what local police described in the 1940s as 'an astonishing atmosphere'. Music from was accompanied by cries of fishermen singing different songs, whilst the barmaids touted for orders. Sailors would dance together, and it was even reported that one drunken fisherman began a striptease. The walls were lined with visitors selling anything from shellfish to cartoons of Hitler. The town magistrates refused to renew the landlord's licence in 1941.

Freeman Street's Corporation Arms is only one of two listed buildings in Freeman Street. The renowned 'smoke room' at the rear of the pub, contains some of the best historic interiors of the region including original wood panelled seating, and several large mirrors, one bearing the triangle logo of Bass Brewers. During a refurbishment in 1989, builders discovered graffiti on a wooden beam that referenced the notorious Grimsby murderer, Richard Insole, a fisherman who killed his wife after a domestic dispute and rumoured infidelity. The graffiti, now hanging in the pub amid photographs and newspaper clippings, reads. *'Insole Murderer, Hanging on the Gallows, Today, February 21, 1887.'* The pub has switched hands numerous times but is still open for business.

The Lincoln Arms had the pride of place in Riby Square and was one of the best known pubs in Grimsby in the 1950s and 60s. Many children remember waiting outside 'The Lincoln' whilst their fathers had a pint after collecting their settlings. Other children remember making a penny or two from fishermen heading to the Lincoln after landing in dock – fishermen would pay the children to run and let their wives know they were in the pub and would be home later. In some cases, this was the signal for a 'part time uncle' to depart the family home. The pub uniquely had entrances from three streets; drinkers could enter from Cleethorpe Road, Freeman Street or Strand Street. The beer was dropped off in Cleethorpe Road and the cellars ran all the way through to the back of the building at Strand Street. The location on Riby Square made the pub especially popular with foreign fishermen, seamen and sailors who landed in Grimsby, and as a result, it also attracted many of the town's prostitutes.

Arty Lea recalls that more colour could be seen in a couple of nights in Freeman Street than most people would see in a lifetime.

'You'd see the fights, the ladies, the drunks, it was fantastic. In the 50s there was one copper on there, one policemen, he was a big Scotchman, a sergeant. And he could run Freeman Street on his own. The Red Lion was the big pub on the corner, which was the main pub for the ladies of the night and that. The sergeant, we used to call him Jock, he didn't mess around with you if you was drunk. "I don't wanna see you again, get off." If he come along, they'd say, "Look out Jock's coming!" And then at The Red Lion there was big Jock at it. They had

The Lincoln Arms, Riby Square

the Lincoln as well. The rest of the pubs in between was the fisherman's pubs, like The White Bear, Cottees, then there was the Dogger Bank. But the ladies kept to The Red Lion and The Lincoln. If anybody wanted a 'one night', you'd want to be in the The Lincoln or The Red Lion.'

Grimsby's prostitutes kept an eye on which ships and fishermen were coming in dock on the next tide. It was their business to know who was a 'two day millionaire' and which men were out of a ship. They frequented the same pubs surrounding Freeman Street and the docks, and were often seen as 'one of the family' by fishermen. No strangers to the ups and downs of the industry, they could be relied on for drinks and money by fishermen down on their luck or out of a ship who would return the favour when a bumper catch came in. Robert Atmore recalls some of the female characters.

'Goodtime Betty, Fag-Ash Lil, Chandelier Queen. They went in the Red Lion, well most of the pubs down there. If you think of a good western saloon when they started fighting, that's how the Red Lion back room used to get. With 'women of the night' and the regulars like us. If we was out of a ship they'd give you your entrance fee – you'd get half a crown or five shillings to go in – and they'd always buy you a drink. They was good hearted like that.'

This same generosity was present in prosperous fishermen who 'looked after their own'. As Ken Morrison explains, they understood all too well that they could find themselves in the same situation next trip.

'You used to get in with lads that had landed in The White Bear or owt like that and if they had a good trip they used to treat yer. If you got nowt when you landed you got it from yer mate. He'd say, "Get yerself a drink." And he'd give you what money he had left from the trip. That's how it worked. You were never skint when you were at sea, as somebody would always help yer. We used to keep one another. If he was hard up and we got money we would drop 'em a few quid when we come in.

'If you were out of work, you'd be known as a 'Wesley' and someone'd drop you summat. I don't know where it come from I just heard it when I come to Grimsby. It weren't a national thing'.

For those fisherman lucky enough like Arty Lea, the feeling of being a two day millionaire was one they never forgot.

'A single bloke with money was fantastic, there on the market. You'd go to The Winter Gardens, The Bags Ball and the one across the road, the Cafe Dansant. And you was millionaires for two days. If there was plenty of fish to land, you used to call the lumpers 'midnight millionaires'. A pint was ninepence or a shilling. With three pound you could take yourself out for a good night and have money in your pocket for taxis.'

Taxis formed part of a fisherman's routine ashore and drivers formed an interesting relationship with fishermen and their families. As Richard Wright remembers, you had your own driver.

'They used to stay with 'em all the time, used to have a day out with 'em, cos there was no drink driving an' all this business. They did get drunk obviously, but if you got a taxi driver who was a nice bloke, you was paying him and buying him his dinner, he's with you all day. And if you

got hard up he'd lend you some money and square you when you come home, that's how it used to be.'

As well as many pubs, fishermen could find entertainment in Freeman Street in its busy market, specialist shops and many theatres and cinemas. The Prince of Wales Theatre opened in 1884, with its auditorium capable of seating an audience of 2,500. The theatre put on colourful musicals, and attracted some famous music hall performers. The thriving market place could attract 1,500 shoppers during its busiest times. Small businesses included fishmongers, fruit shops, sweet shops, tobacconists, bakers, florists, drapers and jewellers as well as numerous restaurants.

Richard Wright like a large number of fishermen used to spend most of his settlings in Freeman Street.

'You used to walk down there in your twenty-eight inch bottoms looking in the window thinking, *Some lucky swine's gonna get me*. All my money used to go on records and clothes, I used to drink but I didn't used to get legless. When I got married I had twenty-five suits and eighteen pair o' shoes I did, bloody did yeah. See when you came in from sea you didn't need money, not if you was in a ship. I used to go in a store called Gerald Baileys and I used to get my suits and socks and shirts. I'd get everything from there, just used to walk in, "Alright mate." They'd make you a cup of coffee. "I'll have a new suit, two shirts, a pair of socks." You didn't pay a penny. They took so much outta your settlings. So if you came in from sea and you had money or not it didn't mean a thing –

you could go in there in one suit and come out in another. And it was great. The same with records; you could go in these stores and get what you wanted. So you had money in your pocket and looked like a million dollars – these women have got it made an't they!'

Freeman Street circa 1960

For men whose lives at sea were largely spent in muck and blood and fish guts, looking just

136

right when they came ashore was important. It was a matter of self-respect and an opportunity to play the part – the successful fisherman.

In the 1920s and 30s Freeman Street's shops catered for fishermen's peacock tendencies. Among them were numerous tailors who supplied the fishermen with their particular 'fishermen's suits'. Fisherman would be measured at the end of a trip, return to sea and collect the finished suit their next time ashore. The suits usually had 22 inch bottoms with straight legs, a wide waist-band and turn-ups, so that shoes could only just be seen. The jackets were pleated in the back, often three pleats each side, with half-moon pockets and lapels and cuffs in black velvet to contrast the bright colour of the suit. These were worn with a white shirt, a thin tie and smart shoes.

By the 1960s, the seeds of Freeman Street's decline had already been sown. The numbers of shoppers were beginning to dwindle due the clearance of housing, the decline of the fishing industry, changes in the level of car ownership and the gradual migration of customers to the purpose built shopping centres at 'top town'.

As part of a post-war re-development, the fishermen's Victorian terraces which had been so closely linked with the Grimsby fish docks and the businesses surrounding it, were declared 'slums' and demolished. The area was described as 'one of the worst parts of Grimsby' with 85% of the houses declared unfit for human habitation. People were crammed into rooms seven to nine feet square and most of the area was affected by war damage. With the exclusion of a small area, including the Standard Cold Stores in Victor Street, the entire Bath Street district, covering just short of 24 acres, was handed over to the Grimsby Corporation for extensive redevelopment.

In 1978, the town mayor, Councillor Madge Elliot, spoke about the root cause of the decline of Freeman Street. 'It has been hit hard over the years by the redevelopment of the many adjacent side streets. Hundreds of people were moved out of the area, years of friendships and neighbourhood ties were broken, and so the decline set in.'

When the fishing families moved away from friends and neighbours who had supported them, the sense of a unified 'community' went with them. The redevelopment and relocation scheme was necessary, but it ended years of tradition. Once the industry no longer poured its cash from the docks directly into the businesses of Freeman Street, the street itself entered into terminal decline.

Since the 1980s several attempts at regeneration of the Freeman Street area have taken place. So far it has absorbed many millions of pounds of regeneration funding with little lasting effect. Periodically new schemes try to tackle the issues of crime, poor housing, deprivation and lack of opportunity. However, the main problem remains one of economics: Freeman Street's success grew out of the need to service an industry that no longer exists.

10. McKenzie/Grant photo collection

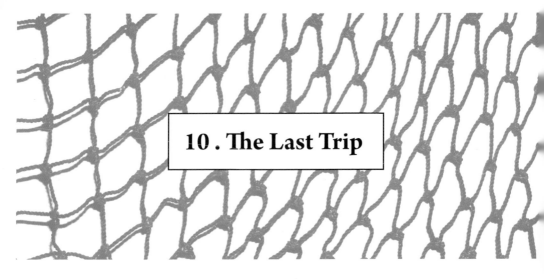

10 . The Last Trip

"Go shift your gear lads, that's it - she's going for scrap."

As early as June 1958, local newspapers were reporting that a 'single black line on the North Atlantic charts' would ruin Grimsby. The 'black line' was effectively drawn on 1 September 1958 when the Icelandic government extended their fishing limit from four to 12 miles, imposing a ban on all foreign fishing within the restricted area. In doing so, Iceland had fired the opening salvo in what became known as the 'cod wars' – the dispute which effectively signalled the end of Grimsby's fishing industry.

When the initial declaration of the 12 mile limit took place, catches within the contested area contributed £4m of the £11m net worth of fish landed in Grimsby each year. Of the town's 57,000 population, 25,000 were dependant on a thriving fishing industry. British distant-water trawlers had little choice other than to ignore the ban and continue fishing.

For the next three years as hostility increased, Britain came under pressure to accept the fishing limit. The cod war took place against a backdrop of international suspicion and unease provoked by Cold War fears. As a strategically important partner, NATO was committed to avoiding Icelandic withdrawal and maintaining their co-operation. Inflammatory statements by Icelandic ministers that they would withdraw from NATO, scrap their defence agreement with the United States of America, throw out American troops, and bring an immediate charge of 'aggression' against Britain at the United Nations heightened the pressure.

In 1961, the British government finally accepted the 12 mile fishing zone around Iceland on the condition that, for a three year transitional period, Iceland would allow British vessels to fish in specific 'zones' between six and 12 miles off the Icelandic coast in certain seasons of the year. Iceland also undertook to give six months' notice of any proposal to extend their fishery jurisdiction further. They further promised that any dispute arising from such a proposal should be referred to the International Court of Justice. During the three year fade-out period Britain's distant water fleet would be given government assistance to build new factory trawlers, enabling them to seek fishing grounds further afield – by the mid-50s many countries had turned over a major part of their fishing industry to long-range factory ships, which caught, gutted, filleted and froze the fish whilst at sea. Despite these reassurances, the settlement was viewed by fishermen as a complete surrender.

They were also incensed that under the agreement Icelandic ships were to continue to sell their fish on the British market. In a letter outlining his position to the Transport and General Workers Union, Captain DW Welsh, President of the Grimsby Trawler Officers Guild, said his 'members are more concerned, or at least equally concerned, over foreign landings as they are over the 12 mile limit'.

At a time when vision, modernisation and diversification on a wholesale level might have given the industry a fighting chance, there was clear evidence that for

Icelandic gunboat *Aegir* dodges the bows of *HMS Andromeda*

some companies, outmoded systems meant they were clinging on to past glories. Working for the most progressive Grimsby company, Jeff Beedham remembers a trip to see the first computer installed in Ross House in 1967. It was in stark contrast to his own workplace at Ross engineers on the docks.

'This computer occupied a full floor of Ross House. You can imagine glass windows and sealed doors. It was all kept at a certain temperature, only one person was allowed in at a time. And we was all looking through this window. There was this bank that was about six foot high, with these tapes going round, one of those massive tape spools. We thought, *brilliant, you know, that's the future*. I think it did the wages or something. We went back round the corner about a hundred yards to the workshop on the corner of Robinson lane. It was like going back a hundred years in time. Machinery hadn't changed for about sixty years and working behind the bench was fitters who had actually worked during the First World War on trawlers, and the Second World War, fitted 'em out as minesweepers and that.'

At the conclusion of the first cod war, Grimsby's skippers, mates and engineers who'd brought about mass industrial action in protest at the 1961 settlement declared their view that the first action of any new Icelandic government, 'would be to abrogate the proposed new agreement and again attempt to extend unilaterally her fishing limits to the Continental Shelf'.

Iceland continued to enforce its 12 mile limit and to land fish in Grimsby docks much to the consternation of local fishermen. As predicted, Iceland further extended its fishing limits to 50 miles in 1972 then to 200 miles in 1975 resulting in the second and third cod wars. By 1975 Ray Harries was a skipper and, like many, fought to maintain his livelihood at sea.

'We used to fish on the continental shelf, that's where the fish were. When we were out at two-hundred mile limits, we couldn't fish there. Their gunboats seemed to run rings around us. If they caught you, they had this big towing wire with a chopper on the end – if you imagine a Christmas tree towed backwards, it was all steel cutter blades, and you'd just feel a tug and all your gear's gone. We had some close calls. I used to scramble me gear aboard as quickly as possible. I did fish on the south side of Iceland. The *Odin* gunboat came on and said I was fishing in Icelandic territorial waters and he said he was coming to get me. He was about four mile off and he come charging at us. We heaved the warps up as quick as the winch would go, got the trawl doors up, heaved on the bridles, and the net's come up and there was a bag of fish at the end, just as the *Odin* come straight down me starboard side and he had his cutter out, and we had a rope around the sleeve of the trawl, and I said, "Heave on that rope!" We had the fish right at the side of the ship and he just missed us, passed us about twenty or thirty feet away. I got on the radio and said. "You missed us, *Odin*." He was fuming.

'I was about the last ship to fish at Iceland – I think it was the *Boston Boeing* – that was on the south side. We were catching fish, fifty or sixty baskets and we only had a couple of days to go. We put what you call a liner in the net – it was illegal – it had a narrower mesh and we ended up with a hundred and twenty or thirty baskets. And we'd just shot away when the *Odin* come up and said they had a BBC crew with them who wanted to come aboard and do an interview. I told them I'd only just shot my nets and would be some time. They said they'd bring this BBC crew across, anyway they come along the port side and the weather was bad and the sea was knocking them into the boat and they couldn't board me; they couldn't come on the trawl side and they left it – I was giving them the weather side. He went away, then twenty-minutes later he came back and asked if I'd go onto the verandah of the bridge and talk to them from there. Then he cleared off. I don't know what I'd have done if they'd come aboard.'

Graham Howard had been working on board the *Kelvin* in July 1974. The trawler had been under protection from the Royal Navy, but a call for help brought a brief respite from the hostilities.

Moment of impact as Icelandic gunboat *Odin* rams *HMS Andromeda*

'There was a volcanic eruption on the Westman Islands on the south side of Iceland. The Icelandic gunboats *Thor* and *Odin* asked for our help, all the trawlers in this fishing area, because we were restricted to fishing in what you called boxes. We all went to sea to go help get these people off the island. After about three hours the *Thor* came over and said, "Thank you very much for your assistance, it is no longer required because we've got plenty there." Our frigates had gone, they'd left us so we resumed fishing. Within an hour of us putting our gear on the bottom of the sea, the *Thor* come and chopped our gear. That finished me, that was it. Me best friend, he died at thirty-three, not at sea, he just died. It gets you thinking what you're missing.

'It didn't help matters Crosland turning down a deal that Iceland offered the British government. But it wasn't until fifteen or twenty years after we joined the EEC that we found out that pressure was put on and one of the reasons for Britain to join the EEC was to let Iceland have the two-hundred mile limit and restrict it to EEC ships. So who was the loser in that? We were, because when all the others came in we stood by the rules. Britain always does. Others are not quite like us and they don't and that's what screwed the job up basically.

'Billy Hardy carried on, bought his own ship. As the industry started to go they found oil in the North Sea and they needed ships to go and look after the rigs. Which was a Godsend for the trawler owners because they got compensation from the government, then flogged the ships and got more money as well. But they needed crew for these ships, so a lot of the deck hands on board and crew members went on these ships.'

For many fishermen the best years of the industry had all but disappeared by the mid-1970s. Hindsight suggests the traditional values and hierarchies of skipper and crew were starting to break down. Arty Lea had seen the writing on the wall.

'Everybody knew the fishing was finishing. There were too many youngsters on the top, skippers and that, and they wasn't like the old ones ruling the roost. When I first started in the fifties and sixties, if you were in a good ship, you stopped in it because you earned money. You respected the guy whether you liked him or not, played by his rules. At times you felt like killing him, but you were still earning. Too many youngsters come in who never had a clue about fishing.'

A sense of inevitability spread throughout the town's fishing community, that after the first two cod wars had seen the British government give way to international pressure, the third would only end one way. Stanley Johnson had a fair idea when his time was up.

'Sometimes you didn't know until you come in dock, went into the office and they'd say, "Go shift your gear lads, that's it - she's going for scrap." So when you was at sea and you heard things like that, you knew for a fact you were going. Next trip you went in, you were lucky to be going again, but you knew some time or another you were going to come in dock and that was going to be your last trip. Sometimes the crafty buggers, the trawler owners, they knew, so they'd send the skipper a message saying, "Will you get the lads to clear the fore-hold out?" You knew that when he got that message it was your last trip, but it saved the gaffer from getting a heavy gang out to go down there and dig it out, they got you to do it. The lads said no, let them do it ashore. They tried to get us to empty everything out on the deck. All they had to do then was get the heavy gang to ship it out onto the lorries. We knew then that the ship was on its last trip.

'I saw Mr Thompson the employment officer. You could either use your ticket and go fishing on the Spanish trawlers, or go on the stand-by boats out of Lowestoft and look after the gas rigs. I went to Lowestoft and I went on the safety vessel. On the labour you was just a registered fisherman. It didn't matter what capacity you was in, he was offering you a ship. And if you refused it they stopped your money. You had to take what you was offered in the end. When there was no redundancy in the ships; a lot of blokes went and worked in the factories and things like that. The younger blokes, even my lad, he went fishing out of Spain using his tickets on the Spanish trawlers but I didn't fancy it.'

Derek Grant had been a successful skipper for many years when he stopped fishing in 1972. He'd seen a decline in the calibre of those going to sea and sensed the time was right when his father invited him to join the family business.

'The trawler owners couldn't believe me when I said, "That's it, I'm finished." They said, "You can't do that." And I thought, *well I am, that's it.* And the outside manager, I saw him on the pontoon. He came up to me and said, "Look, you keep striking the iron whilst it's hot, you get yourself down there to a ship called the *Wolverhampton Wanderers.*" I said. "I'm sorry, but no." He said, "You'll be on your knees begging to me. You'll come crying to me." He could have done the better thing, but I was determined then that I wasn't going to go back. I had a week off and started with my father. I went in with a tie on and all that, and he said, "Get that off for a start. Get round to the store, start emptying tins out of there and take them back to the exchange." I'd gone from being a skipper to the lowest in our company. He made me start right at the bottom and work my way up, I had to do everything, every job. And eventually I ended up running the place. We was the main suppliers to Pedigree pet foods, with all the fish products. My father was doing it for fifty years but then things changed and a lot of it went abroad. So I made the decision that we'd change our operation, which we did, and now we've come out of fish all together, we're still on the fish docks but now we do recycling, all the polystyrene and cardboard all that sort of thing. My sons run it now I just pop in and see what's happening.'

Having made the move ashore, Derek saw many men who were drawn back to the sea.

'I've seen people come ashore and gone into a factory and they couldn't stand it so they've drifted back again. But I was fortunate in that I still kept in contact with the people in that industry. On the pontoon in the morning I'd see some of the mates and the owners and I knew them all and I'd go and have a look at their trips. So I kept amongst it the whole time, which you know just helped me. I never give it a thought. Once I make a decision that's it. I'm pleased I did because since I came ashore I've done things a younger person would do y'know in life. I've done it the other way around. I missed out on everything, but I wasn't too old when I'd finished, and I carried on with all different things.'

As the ships went for scrap, some to Belgium, some at Draper's scrap yard in Hull's Victoria Dock, they joined other ships making their final journeys. Jeff Beedham did some work on de-commissioning Grimsby ships in the Royal Dock.

'Firstly everything of value like compasses, the brass binnacles, telegraphs and ships' wheels, everything like that was stripped off, sold off or nicked you know. A lot of it was nicked, you know ships' bells and that. They did actually scrap a few trawlers down at the ship yard that used to be on the west side of the Royal Dock, the big slipway there. I was back working down the docks I think in about '76 –'77 and if you wanted to earn a few bob in your hand sort of, after tea you went on to the slip way there and helped them out scrapping a trawler. It was all cash in hand, even though it was an established firm. They had a lucrative little number going with all the slipways there and all the gear to sort of take everything apart, a lot of them ended their days there. Shame really because some was barely run in, some of these steam trawlers, the German built ones.'

Michael Sparkes found life ashore a tough adjustment. The monotony of working in one of Grimsby's many fish processing factories was deadening for men used to a life at sea.

'Like everybody else I went to work in the factories. I went to Birdseye for a while. They wanted fishermen on the night shift there, 'cos they made ideal night workers 'cos they was used to it you see. I had a few years there driving the forklifts, doing this and that in the cold store. It was like being back at Iceland. I got fed up with that. Then I did some work on the dock. Then I went on the Pyewipe and worked on the fish meal, doing bits down there. I didn't like that. So I thought I need to get away from Grimsby so I went to the steelworks at Scunthorpe. I had three years there at Appleby-Frodingham. The money was alright, I just couldn't settle on the job, being ruled by the clock, 'cos time didn't matter at sea. You worked round the clock and you didn't look at the clock, hardly, you know, not 'til it's time to come home… Maybe look at when it was tide time. But ashore it was always, get up at eight o'clock, work while half six. I couldn't get used to all that. It was a struggle really.

'I tried all sorts of little jobs. For the last thirteen years before I retired I worked for Danbrit Ship Management. They had trawlers and ships, I used to go down cleaning ships. I used to do all sorts of things on them, maintenance and stuff like that. I enjoyed it, I stayed thirteen years, right until I was sixty-four and then they moved to Filey. So they says, "What you doing Mick, do you wanna come?" I didn't want to uproot, so that was it, I retired. All I've got now is me memories. Life's a lot better now.'

There were men unable to adapt to life ashore; some became dependant on alcohol. This, in turn had an adverse impact on family life and placed an unbearable strain on marriages. Graham Hobson is just one former fisherman who has mixed feelings about the industry's passing. He kept working where others, toughened by a life at sea simply couldn't cope.

'I enjoyed it in one way and in another way I wish I'd never gone on a trawler. As the trawlers packed up – the North Sea ships first, then the older Faroe ships – I got a job ashore. A lot of fishermen, their wives left them, they got on the drink. Well I never did that, I looked for a job ashore. My brother had his own business so he gave me a job down the dock as a plumber's mate and then I went to work for another couple of companies when I got made redundant from there. I wish I'd have known about this shore life, instead of going to sea. There was one bloke, Benny, he struggled – he'd been at sea in the merchant navy and then sea fishing. He more or less drunk himself to death. Boredom. I get bored now I'm not working, I try to occupy my mind. It was just the way of life being at sea.'

As the industry declined, Ray Walker found a way to stay at sea for a short while, even managing to fish.

'I was excited on my first trip, my first going. Lovely it was. When I left fishing and I went in the merchant navy for a number of years, I always wanted to go back but fishing had gone. So I bought a small boat and I fished the river a bit. I used to get enough fish to last me throughout the summer and start again in the winter fishing for a bit of cod. But that's stopped now. They've stopped you fishing from the small boats there.'

Tom Smith began fishing in 1962 and stayed until 1981 when he went onto standby vessels for North Sea oil rigs. It's a living that suits him. Tom is due to retire in 2011 in what will be his 49th year at sea.

'You stand by and supply the platforms, water, fuel, cargo, and cover 'em for safety work and all that as well. It's a good job – which finishes next year for me because I retire or I will be doing. The skipper is 65 this year so… The rumours are that they are going to approach us, see if we wanna carry on. I said I might do, depends on how I feel at the time. I'd like to be able to do another couple of years to round it off, but…

'I tried seine netting, but that was a waste of space. It was just hard work for nothing. I only did the two trips and the ship broke down twice so I just gave up on that. I was lucky because as the decline went, the writing was on the wall before everything disappeared. And I just happened to go down dock one day, was on one of the Ross boats, I'd changed over from the *Jackal* after three years, and they said so and so wanted his pal to go as mate on this ship and someone would have to come out. So I said, "Sign me off then, I don't wanna go back there." They said, "What are you gonna do then?" I said, "Oh I'll find something else." And I walked up the dock and there was three Boston ships being converted for the oil rigs, the *Kestrel*, *Phantom* and the *Prince Phillip*. And my father was watchmen on them so he says, "They're getting converted for standby work, why don't you nip into Boston's?" There was a chap called Percy, the head watchman, I just managed to catch him as I was coming off the dock. "Percy is there any jobs going?" So that's how it kicked off.'

Ray Harries stayed at sea, going into partnership with another skipper, Derek Brown. The two of them went pair fishing with limited success. Ray's skills kept him in work and took him as far as the Falkland Islands taking part in a government survey following the 1982 conflict.

'After Iceland, they tied the big ships up. Some went on as safety ships, some got scrapped. Me and another skipper – Derek Brown – we was approached to go into pair fishing in the North Sea. A Danish skipper, Jens, he'd made a fortune out of it. It's like seine net size ships, so they don't need trawl doors and they don't take much fuel to tow and they're a quarter of a mile apart. He

148

must have made himself a millionaire and we had a go at that.

'The North Sea is a dangerous place to tow nets around the bottom unless you know where the wrecks are. Not only that, the big fishing was done on a very small patch of ground. The people who converted best were the seine net people who knew the nature of the bottom. But seine nets could only fish on fine ground.

'Jens had what he called his 'hotspots'. Me and Derek Brown went to sea with him, but he never told us any of these hotspots. He would have one of his men ready with a buoy and they would drop that and start fishing. They'd only tow for twenty minutes, but it wasn't a success for me. I went on the standby boats for the oil rigs. Then I did a two year inshore fishery survey down at the Falklands for the government.'

Peter Harrison's life in fishing has taken him through the most productive and profitable periods in the industry's history, through change, merger, cod war confrontation and increasingly damaging European policy. He has seen the gradual shrinking of the fleet from its heyday.

'It's sad that it got this way. The common market and the extension of the fishing limits in the seventies drove all the ships away. In 1970 I think we had around forty or fifty distant-water trawlers. By 1978 I think we were down to half a dozen. Ultimately they couldn't find anywhere to fish so they disappeared as well. And then we were left with about eight middle-water trawlers and that was the only trawlers left in the port other than the seine net fleet. From the 1960s the seine net fleet was about one-hundred and forty manned ships and that too then with the common market and restrictions and fishing quotas and all the rest of it that sort of died away. At the moment we have about ten or eleven ships registered with the association, but they don't always fish out of the port. I mean in the fifties and sixties vessels landed here, nowhere else unless it was an emergency. But from the seventies, certainly with the seine net vessels, they would land wherever the market was good. They would land in Holland rather than Grimsby because they would get a better price. Basically it was Holland, Denmark and occasionally Germany, wherever it was convenient and appropriate for that specific type of fish. I mean in the olden days if a skipper landed in any other port it would be, "What the hell are you doing?"

'The trawler owners always retained their individuality. The only mergers that took place were between Ross Group, they bought out companies. There were the Letten Brothers, they went into Northern Trawlers. There was Jack Croft-

Baker, Derwent Trawlers, they went into Ross Trawlers. But then they merged into British United Trawlers Ltd. But British United Trawlers also had a big say in Hull. A lot of the bigger people there combined to form into British United Trawlers Ltd. Crampin's went into Ross Trawlers as well. Northern Trawlers took over Letten Brothers then Ross Trawlers took over Jack Croft-Baker's. In the main, the big family firms stayed where they were, it was only the big limited companies that went together with some of the bigger ships. Most of the smaller North Sea people, the Taylors, Bannisters, Robinsons. They all stayed as family businesses leading up to when they ceased to trade, you know sold the vessels for ever.'

Speaking to former fishermen, there is an understandable sense of nostalgia for the industry, but always tempered with healthy dose of realism. When he was at home from sea, Ray Powell would take a walk down to the North Wall. In spite of his mixed feelings about the fishing industry, it's a trip he can no longer make.

'I don't go down there any more, I just can't because I've seen that dock when the ships were three deep. Now, what's down there? Nothing. And it's a lifetime that should still be running.

'I did [make the right decision] financially, because when I was fishing we was all making money. But then it got to fewer of us making money and there were fewer ships and they don't get rid of 'em when they're making money. I enjoyed the life I was in at that time. I enjoyed going to sea, I enjoyed coming home. Sometimes it was the bit in the middle I didn't like but when you stopped and looked out, with about two-foot of ice on everything you'd think, *What am I doing here?*'

It's a sentiment Arty Lea acknowledges. For him, quite simply, fishing was the life he chose.

'If it was still on the go I'd have never packed it in, deep water. 'Cos once you're brought up to it from the age of seventeen or eighteen it was a way of life. You just couldn't get away from. You think, *well I know I could go do anything.* You're that independent to say, "Well I'm not tied down to this job, but I like it that much I'm not gonna leave until I've got to." And I know a lot of people who said they hated it. But they'd come back to sea. It got in your blood. It was like a drug.'

Harry Drinkell remembers the docks as they were and as they are now.

'I think of all the thousands of fishermen I sailed with, said hello to and was friendly with, and all the dock workers. You go on there now and it's like a prison – they've got all them railings all the way round, and on the North Wall it used to be alive with people, and ships ready for sea. You'd see some of the crew and especially at dinnertime tide they used to come straight out of the pub, get the last few drinks in. And I see them trying to climb up the ladder to get on the ship and they'd fall. The ship's husband would be making sure they were all aboard. "Where's so and so and so and so?" Jumps in the taxi and goes into the Red Lion and drags 'em out. "C'mon, c'mon we're gonna sail."'

For Mike Debnam, the sea still has an unshakeable power.

'Like a lot of people I still live in the past. I still have got pictures of trawlers. My intention was that I go to art college. I want to paint ships and I can't. I paint churches. 'Cos I can't get my head around it. It's queer ain't it? I just love the trawling industry.'

Pete Woods first and last passion was always the trawlers themselves.

'There's no vessel ever been built that man can have a love affair with like a trawler. Most navy ships are big floating boxes. Royal Navy ships are just grey hulks. There's nothing loveable about them. The Merchant Navy they chip and scrape, put the gear in the hold, whatever it is they're carrying, that's it. That's as much as they do. They don't do what we did which was actually work the ship.'

Michael Sparkes is one of many whose view of trawler owners and the subsequent treatment of fishermen still infuriates.

'I thought the trawler owners came out of it smelling of roses really, because they got it all ways. They got compensation from the government to lay the ships up, they got paid for laying the ships up, but then after that they went and sold the ships as well, to other people. They didn't scrap them. They went and sold them abroad, America, Australia, places like that. What did they give the fishermen? Nothing. They was all left on the dole.

'And it was a skilled job, fishing was a skilled job there's no two ways about that. To be a deep-water deck hand, just a deck hand, you had to know your compass, you had to know how to splice, you had to know how to net mend, you had to know all the weaving, the bobbins, you had to know everything on deck. If you didn't, you just didn't get a ship. They wouldn't have you. You had to be an experienced person. We'd trained for it from being young. I can still do it; I've got it all up 'ere. I could still do it but it's no good to me.'

Derek Grant has a clear perspective on the industry's eventual decline. In his view, an ill-considered negotiating strategy by the British government was instrumental in undermining the industry's chances.

'I think now that I was one of those people with blinkers on. Iceland, they've got nothing else, they can't farm, they can't go down pits, they've got no industry as such manufacturing things so fish was their only livelihood. I can understand it now wanting to control fish around their coast. It would have been ok if our government hadn't sent Anthony Crosland out there without a brief to try and negotiate. We was taking about one hundred and sixty-five thousand ton out of Iceland a year, not just Grimsby, you know the whole fleet, and what they wanted to cut it down to was sixty-eight thousand tons, that's not a lot, so they said fine you get nothing. Get out. So they'd chase you cutting your warps away and everything. But if we'd accepted that with the sixty-eight thousand tons and your supplement from others areas, it would still be a strong industry.

'But once Iceland had said, "Out." And Russia said we're having it now, they all put two-hundred mile limits on and that was the end of business. So I came out of it at the right time. The heart-breaking thing about it was with this payment for the redundant fishermen, 'cos they'd done nothing but fleeced them. I mean Dolly Hardie, she was a wonderful woman you know she worked hard at it. And the payoff, it was pittance and the excuse was that they weren't employed, they were part-time casual workers, part-time workers working twenty hours a day! And the other thing they said 'cos they had to sign the log book every trip, and that was a total lie, I don't know why that never came out 'cos I never signed a log book every trip. Once I signed on, I was on that log book until I came out of the ship, so I never resigned at all. And they're still struggling to get reasonable payouts. You got the miners with a big payout, all the textile industries, everything else you could think of. But let's face it, we're the backbone of this country, we're a seafaring nation and they turned their backs on us.'

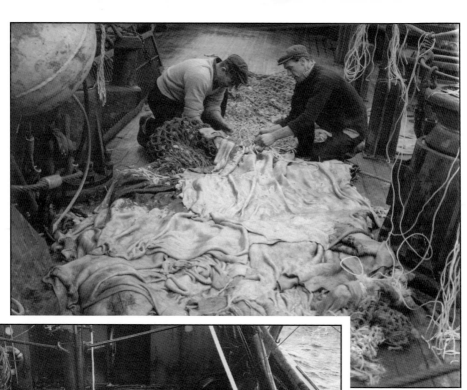

11. McKenzie/Grant photo collection

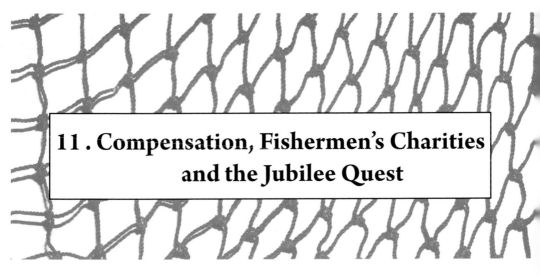

11 . Compensation, Fishermen's Charities and the Jubilee Quest

'Bloody freezing, even the penguins left the toilet.'

Since the collapse of the fishing industry in Grimsby, the main stumbling block for ex-fishermen has been the battle for recognition. The fishing industry functioned by means of a clear-cut hierarchy. Value and self-worth came from the work men undertook, the rank they attained and how they were paid for their labour. There were many who felt they had been shunted aside, that their exploits at sea, away from the public gaze, had been underappreciated. With successive governments failing to adequately address the issue, in spite of campaigns and lobbying of fishermen's groups, led in Grimsby by the estimable Dolly Hardie who sadly died in 2008, there are still those who feel that fishermen were given a raw deal. Over the years there have been schemes, ex-gratia payments, conditions and pre-conditions, information and mis-information. As ever, the deadlock is caused by the amount of time each fishermen spent at sea and their status as 'casual labour', a term Arty lea still refuses to accept.

> 'Tony Crosland, all he was talking about was that casual labour. I said, "For your casual labour, what did we have to go to school for? For a decky's ticket, third hand's ticket, a mate's ticket, a skipper's ticket?" I said, "Get them all together, all them tickets put them in a black bag, take them to London and say: there's your casual labour."'

Tom Smith has issues with the way successive schemes would give with one hand and take away with the other. There was also the issue of the amount of time fishermen needed to have at sea before qualifying for compensation.

> 'The first scheme was when the old conservative Government decided to give

us an ex-gratia payment. Which is a gift. They worded it on our payments as redundancy – it wasn't. We got a few quid out of it. Well they thought they'd done the deed, but they hadn't fully compensated. When Tony Blair was in, to make him look good they were like, *Yeah, we'll sort the fishermen out.* But it was a shambles. They did it from Watford. Nobody knew what they were doing, what fisherman's records were all about. They never spoke to any fishermen, asked their advice or whatever, just went ahead, got their record, said, *you're allowed that, you're entitled to that, you're not.* And the payment we got then they deducted the ex-gratia back out! Different government altogether, a different scheme, but they took it back.

'Most fishermen couldn't get that two years in, because during the cod wars the trawler owners were laying up trawlers. So you might even sign on, go down to sail and they would be laying it up, scrapping the ship. They was watching the quotas as well, thinking Iceland was gonna put a quota on, which they did. Crews were put out of work then. Every ship that come along was fighting for a job. But trying to get this two year, seven-hundred and thirty days in that gap 1973 to 1976, a lot of fishermen didn't qualify and that was the qualifying test.'

For Michael Sparkes, the knock on effects of the cod wars and the industry's decline to middle and near water fleets was not given due consideration in compensation schemes.

'When they stopped the fishing in Iceland, the big ships tried to come to Faroe, middle water. The middle water ships had to come North Sea. In the end it just wasn't paying. So that's why I think all fishermen should have got compensation, whether you fished at Iceland, Faroe, or near water. Some lost their compensation 'cos they went to the White Sea and Bear Island. Which was ridiculous 'cos we was all fishermen. If you look at the miners, they didn't say, you was a miner who went underground and you was a miner on the top. They all got paid. It's the same with the lumpers and the dockers, they was just classed as all dockers an' they all got paid no matter what the job they did. But because some fishermen didn't fish actually in Iceland and in this certain time, they never got compensation. We was all fishermen; we should all have got it.'

Richard Wright's experience gives an insight to the fisherman's relationship with his port record book.

'I paid for it and paid for the photograph that got put in it. When you came ashore you handed it into the trawler owners. Now they had my book, I gave up my first book from 1957 up to 1963, then they give me a new book. Now I got three-thousand pound about a year ago from Norwich Union I didn't even know about it. Someone saw my name and that in the library, honestly, and I phoned up the Norwich Union and they said I had to send my birth certificate off to 'em, and they paid me from 1961 up to 1974. I said, "What about the other four or five years?" They said, "Oh, we want nothing to do with it."

Peter Harrison has worked extensively supporting Grimsby fishermen with compensation claims. The major obstacle in evidencing each trip was the port record book.* *(see appendix)* Peter has a unique insight to the various schemes and difficulties in making claims – a difficult situation made worse following an arson attack in 2000. As a result of water damage, all the surviving port record books had to be professionally salvaged, dried and re-sorted.

Eddie Whyte's port record book from 1961

'The port record book says that it *"… remains the property of the Grimsby fishing owners and may be withdrawn at any time."* The basis of that was that they did not want people to use the books for matters outside of the industry, passing books on, or altering the contents. It was a security matter. But the Association maintained records, and we still have records. And over the years they've been used by numerous fishermen. In 1993 there was the *ex gratia* scheme, in 2000 there was a compensation scheme. Then in 2009, there was this other scheme again. The records are still available to some extent. We lost around twelve per-cent with the fire out on the North Wall. They were all stored in a separate room with cupboards, in envelopes all nicely laid out. One Saturday afternoon some little horrors decided to set fire to it, so it was arson. Just vandalism and when the firemen came they put it out and it was smouldering. So they just took all the things out and damped it down. I went down on Sunday, looked at them and I thought, *what we need is a big skip*. But we were persuaded by the Borough archivist, John Wilson, that they were saveable by sending them away for freeze drying. The only problem was that when they came back not only were they mixed up when they came out of the cupboards, they were mixed up even further. So it took us six months to go through seventeen thousand records or what was left of them. Then start to put them together again in an order that we could sort of fathom. Fortunately the master card system was not in the room where the fire took place, it was in my office. By hook or by crook, we were able to match up numbers either by dates of birth, registration numbers, pension numbers, and fire numbers on the system and try and get them put back together again. So records are available, about eighty per-cent of them.

'I think from this compensation scheme that has been going on, there are fourteen or fifteen people who have no records whatsoever. And of course they had to go to the NHIP pension people. The involvement I have is on the records, not involved the actual principle of it. I will be looking a bit more at the records of people that are not complete, or have no records. They want me to be involved in that sort of thing, from the information I have here and the information they get provided and try and make an honest assessment. Some people will get some satisfaction. But the main quibble is always the method of calculation.'

As Peter acknowledges, there is the feeling that the owners were compensated for the loss of their ships, but the men were never fully recompensed for their loss of livelihood.

'They would just sign on the dole and that was it. And the fight over the years is that they should have got compensation. And quite rightly so, they should do. They were redundant, there is no doubt about it. But how could the trawler owner calculate a redundancy? I could do three weeks on board this ship, then three weeks with another company then three weeks with another. How do you calculate it? The only way it could have been calculated was by some sort of government body. In my opinion, that is only my personal opinion, the calculation is quite easy.'

With life at sea effectively at an end many fishermen found themselves struggling to adjust to shore work. As it became clear that compensation would be a struggle to obtain and with an ageing fishing population, the support offered by local and national maritime charities has been invaluable for those who have come up against hard times. Of course, the fishermen's mission hostel 'Hotel de Mish' always offered working fishermen a bed and hot meals. As former galley-boy Michael Surr remembers, accommodation was basic.

'I got woke up a five in the morning 'cos they were unloading the trawlers and you could hear all these metal crates banging about. You had five to a room and you never knew who you were gonna end up sharing with. Some of them weren't actually fishermen, they'd just been released from prison, in those days they didn't ask for any proof. Just up the road, there was a seamen's hostel I think it was Scandinavian and it was completely different. I had a few nights there. Your meals were in a restaurant with a proper menu, it was cleaner, a lot more modern. That fishermen's mission was an old building even in them days. It always had that smell of disinfectant.'

As the focus for mission activity moved towards supporting retired families and those in need, there were many who benefited from a helping hand. For Richard Wright this meant he was able to have new carpets installed at a time when without help, it would have been impossible.

'When we moved in here me and my missus, we was getting seventy pound a week, and we was bloody hard up. I've never been outta work in my life, and I thought, *why're they not helping me?* Turns out, I went self-employed. And when my missus got cancer I nursed her whilst she died, I didn't get no stamps and tax so it's the last two years of your working life that count so you don't get owt, just the bare necessities. And that's what we was getting, when we was married, that's what we was getting for seven years, seventy odd pound a week. It was only when Labour came in and started looking after us and giving us those cold weather payments and what have you, 'cos last year we spent three-hundred odd pounds on coal. Bloody freezing, even the penguins left the toilet.'

Graham Dolby in front of the fisherman's memorial statue July 2007

The heart and soul of efforts to support the fishing community has always been the Grimsby Mission. Graham Hobson remembers a visit from the Graham Dolby a much-missed and highly-respected former Port Missioner.

'Graham Dolby, he was a smashing bloke. I first got to meet him about seven or eight years ago, just after I had my accident. Someone put me on to him, my washer had broke down and he come round and saw me and I got a new washer from him. And I needed new carpets, they were all worn so I had new carpets put in. And he used to come round to see me once a month, every month.'

Graham Dolby was one in a long line of men and women who dedicated their lives to improving the standard of living for fishermen and their relatives. A graduate of Grimsby's Nautical School and a former merchant seaman, he was instrumental in ensuring the town had a permanent memorial to its fishermen. The memorial statue, sculpted by Trevor Harries, nephew of former skipper Ray Harries, was unveiled in 2005 and stands proudly in the shadow of Grimsby Minster. The statue is the focal point for the town's annual memorial service to fishermen lost at sea.

Throughout the history of the fishing industry the Royal National Mission for Deep Sea Fishermen has been an organisation to which fishermen and their families turned in times of need. Launched as a Christian charity in 1881, the mission continues to provide pastoral and practical care to fishermen across the country. Grimsby's current Port Missioner is Tony Jewitt. He follows in some illustrious footsteps. None more so than Captain William Smedley who became Port Missioner for Grimsby in 1895. Smedley served in the post for 37 years.

After his retirement in 1933 at the age of 70, Captain Smedley took on the task of building retirement homes for aged fishermen and their families. He hoped to build 50 cottages, purchasing three acres of land at Waltham. He was keen to see that the retirement cottages were 'real homes,' a far cry from the cramped terraces surrounding the dock area that housed the majority of Grimsby's fishing community. All the cottages were to have proper drainage, electric light, and be surrounded by trees. Smedley wanted to offer comfort and security to fishermen in their retirement, and to provide them with a weekly allowance.

Funds were raised from numerous sources including generous contributions from trawler owners. Sadly, Captain Smedley did not live to see the fruition of his work. He died in 1935 aged 72 following an illness. Smedley's successors continued his work and six cottages dedicated to Captain Smedley were opened on 23 July 1938.

Smedley Homes, the charity bearing his name, continued its work until 2006, when along with Diamond Jubilee Provident Homes, Harbour of Wreckage and the Grimsby Fisherman's Dependents Fund it merged to become the Grimsby Sailors and Fishing Charity. The charity is managed by Duncan Watt who has been able to oversee much needed renovation to fishermen's properties. Duncan is conscious of the charity's heritage.

'The Fisherman's Dependents Fund was funded by fishermen and trawler owners as far back as the 1930s. They paid in weekly sums for the dependants of families of those who were lost at sea. It was recognised that there was declining need for the fund because there were less and less fisherman. And the homes weren't being maintained properly 'cos they hadn't got any money. So they put the four charities together and it's now properly funded and we're able to upgrade the properties.

'There are one-hundred and forty-two properties in Grimsby and the criteria for entry into these properties is that the one of the residents has to be a fisherman or a retired fisherman, usually sixty-plus years old, although there are one or two exceptions.

'The charity has been very successful in the past few years in that we have been able to refurbish nearly all of the properties, for instance in the last three years we've put in something like eighty bathroom conversions; we've put in almost sixty kitchens and it's an on-going process. We monitor it all the time, but the properties now are of a very high standard.

The benefits to residents are many with the charity paying water rates and telephone line rental. Residents pay a weekly maintenance contribution with the cheapest one-bedroom properties costing £53.00 per week and the most expensive two-bedroom bungalows with garages and gardens costing £79.00 per week.

'We also have care link in every house, and on top of that we also give weekly and quarterly benefits to about thirty families in the form of a grant, basically for widows of fisherman lost at sea particularly those who left children behind them. We also give quite a substantial grant to the Royal National Mission for Deep Sea Fishermen to support their work in Grimsby, and the total of those benefits together are about thirty-five thousand pounds a year.'

Those currently on the waiting list find themselves in a variety of circumstances. None more so than one recent client who came to the charity for help.

'We were able to give a property to a guy at the back end of last year, who was actually living on a boat, he was a fisherman. The owner of the boat sold the fishing quota and the boat, and he suddenly had nowhere to live. He literally had nothing, no furniture, basically only the clothes he stood up in. He was still working, he wasn't quite sixty but there was a need there. The mission were able to provide various bits of furniture to get him going, he's now a very happy man.'

The Square in Grimsby's Castle Street is home to a number of retired fishermen and dependants of fishermen, the majority of whom receive benefits and would otherwise struggle to pay commercial rents.

'In a few cases they get a little bit extra on top of that because of their circumstances. I know two or three people down there who get slightly reduced housing benefits because of a merchant navy pension for instance. But we get other people who are getting extra to help them.'

Duncan Watt is clear that the charity will continue to support fishermen for as long as there are fishermen in need.

'In the last three years we've had grants from the Merchant Navy Welfare Board for four major projects. The first was for electrical inspections to comply with legislation. That was all done, then the last two years it was towards the bathroom project, putting wet rooms in. This is partly because of a huge need gap; some of these bathrooms are a hundred years old and little baths that you sit in with your knees under your chin. We've got rid of all those now we were able to fund those projects. And it's also looking to the future when we know people are going to get older obviously and will find it difficult to get in their baths, so we put in wet rooms. Same with the kitchens, they are always built along the lines that they are easy to operate.'

The Grimsby trawling industry that began with the railways' intervention in the 1850s, effectively came to an end when the last trawlers were laid up and British United Trawlers sold up in 1986. Since then there have been developments, though for the most part, the docks infrastructure has degenerated to a point where the amount of investment required to update and invigorate tired buildings, pitted roads and Dickensian architecture is beyond any but a major public and private sector partnership. Unlikely, given current economic conditions.

There are success stories, driven largely by the entrepreneurial spirit of local business people. Grimsby Fish Market is recognised as being one of the most important fish markets in Europe. It is renowned for the quality and diversity of its fish, together with its long established buying strength. It attracts fish supplies from local, UK and foreign vessels, regular overland fish deliveries arrive from Scotland, Ireland and other British Ports.

Owned by Grimsby Fish Dock Enterprises Ltd., and opened in 1996, the market is one of the most advanced facilities in the UK.

With ever tighter margins and restrictive quotas as well as renewed environmental concerns of over-fishing and depleted stocks, you would be forgiven for thinking the days of Grimsby as a fishing port were over. Peter Harrison retains his links with the Grimsby Fishing Vessel Owners Association. These days its members include merchants on Grimsby fish market.

'The membership now has only two vessel-owners – Jubilee Fishing Company and Omar Management. There are then another four members who are basically involved in fish selling. They bring fish into the port, sell it on the market and they are under the umbrella of the Vessel Owners Association. But there are still two vessel owners who are operating. Mainly it's Jubilee in Grimsby. The other vessel owner used to operate from Grimsby but now he's part Icelandic owned, so the vessels are free to trawl out of any operating port. They fish in Russian waters, Norwegian waters and they will land wherever the demand is for the fish. But they are still a member of the association.'

Andrew Allard

Andrew Allard is the owner of Jubilee Fishing Company. He started the company in 1977 following generations of fishermen in his family, starting with his great grandfather, Harry Allard, a skipper in 1907. In November 2009, the company launched the *Jubilee Quest* a state of the art 22 metre trawler with capacity for 1,200 boxes of fish. The ship fishes the North Sea from the Norwegian coast to the Thames Estuary, crewed by Grimsby fishermen, some of whom have up to 35 years' experience.

'We've been successful; the vessel's performed well. Going forward we would like to build more, but there are rules and regulations and licences and quotas. Before you even get a licence you need to have the quota sorted out. Taking the licenses and quotas into account, the *Jubilee Quest* is a two-million pound investment and there were no grants, no public money.

'We're restricted by the number of "days at sea". We've got a basic 135 day rate annually So sometimes we land at Scotland and have the fish transported to Grimsby by road, but I'd say seventy-five per-cent of our fish is landed in Grimsby.'

After 150 years, the men who fished, the families who waited for their return, the industries that supported them and profited from them, have their place in history assured. The success of the *Jubilee Quest* is a positive sign for the town and the industry with which it has been identified for generations. Yet there is a need to move on. Andrew Allard is realistic.

> 'We can retain a catching industry in Grimsby, but only on a much smaller scale than it was in the 1970s and 80s. We can't expand as much as we might want to because of the licences and quotas, but we're leaner and fitter and we are a viable business.'

*

12. McKenzie/Grant photo collection

Appendix I

'Notes relating to the Terms and Conditions of Employment of Trawler Fishermen sailing on board trawlers registered with the Grimsby Fishing Vessel Owners Association from the port of Grimsby (excluding share fishermen).'

The Grimsby Fishing Vessel Owners Association produced regulations which applied to all trawler owners. The document, *'Terms and Conditions of Employment of Trawler Fishermen sailing on board trawlers registered with the Grimsby Fishing Vessel Owners Association'* aimed to standardise and control practices on the dock. The document is, in effect, a contract, a 'final registration' form for fishermen to accept when signing on and collecting a port record book for Grimsby dock. It outlines the terms and conditions adhered to by all trawler owners who were part of the Grimsby Fishing Vessel Owners Association, and details of what was expected from their employees.

An earlier draft of the registration scheme in the Association's records includes a set of detailed *'Notes relating to the Terms and Conditions'*, and a number of appendices that cover salaries and holiday pay, issuing of bedding and protective clothing, and regulations for breaks and rest periods.

The final registration document, *'Grimsby Fishing Vessel Owners Association Registration Scheme for trawl fishermen'* states that the scheme began on 1 January 1967. It was approved by the Grimsby Port Committee of the National Joint Council for the Trawler Fishing Industry. The scheme does not apply to skippers, mates or radio operators, nor is it relevant for share fishermen. The scheme applies to regular deck hands who receive a standardised weekly wage, as well as a poundage contribution – a significant majority of employees within the industry. Fishermen already employed within this capacity and in possession of a port record book are already deemed registered by the terms and conditions, with no further actions necessary. For new fishermen joining the industry after 1967, it was necessary to fill in a duplicate form of registration, one copy of which was sent to Lowndes Associated Pensions Ltd, and the other retained by the Association. Each new entrant was allocated a number, which became their registration, pension and holiday-with-pay number, making each employee easily identifiable. The registration number was printed in their port record book along with all personal information and qualifications.

A number of significant changes exist between the draft edition of the registration scheme and the final document. In the draft, a list of scheme objectives are listed. The originally proposed objects of the scheme were to:

1. Create the conditions in which trawl fishermen may enjoy regular employment.
2. Provide and efficient means for the effective utilisation of the fishing labour force.
3. Raise the general efficiency of persons employed in trawl fishing.
4. Encourage the entry of young persons into the fishing industry.
5. Introduce a system by means of which skill and expertise may be attained and tested.
6. Encourage trawl fishermen to remain in continuous employment.

These objectives were removed from the final registration document. The repeated use of the terms 'regular employment' and 'continuous employment' suggest a concern for, and desire to rectify, the 'casual' employment status of most fishermen. For owners, the benefits include a more 'efficient' labour force and a more attractive and organised industry, whereby skill and expertise is rewarded and young people can join with the prospect of a secure and prosperous career.

Signing a register of 'terms and conditions,' and keeping an employment record in the form of a port record book, shows that most fishermen regarded themselves as permanently employed. Furthermore, included in the draft is the clause, 'All trawl fishermen who complete less than 200 days on articles during a calendar year may be removed from the register.' Therefore, a commitment of less than 200 days at sea meant that a fisherman's contract, in the form of registration, was effectively ended. It does not restrict fishermen to a single owner and acknowledges the breaks in employment that were an inevitable result of Grimsby port's 'pool system'.

Included alongside the final registration document and draft is the extensive 'Notes relating to the Terms and Conditions of Employment of Trawler Fishermen,' which accompanies and expands on the original clauses. The notes stress that 'all trawl fishermen,' with the exception of skippers, mates, share fishermen and seine net fishermen, are 'to be registered with the Grimsby Fishing Vessel Owners Association in accordance with the registration scheme'.

The notes discuss the procedure for paying fishermen who were left abroad through injury or illness, an area not covered in the draft or final registration document. It is stated that, when men are left abroad through injury or illness, the Grimsby trawler owner on whose vessel the injured or ill man was signed will continue to pay the basic rate of wage to that trawl fisherman. This will continue from the time he is left abroad, due to injury or illness through no fault of his own, up until either the time his trawler lands in Grimsby, or the time he is declared fit by a member of the medical office in Fish Dock Road, Grimsby.

The owner's commitment was to pay up until whichever occurrence came first. Therefore, even if a fisherman was left abroad in hospital for an extended period, if his ship landed back in Grimsby his wage would be stopped. He did not receive any compensation for injury whilst on board the owner's vessel, or any sick pay to cover his inability to work. Furthermore, ill fishermen only received poundage according to the time he actually sailed on the vessel, and no payments were made to other members of the crew as shorthand money.

Further appendices to the document include the policy of deductions to fishermen's wage for various unions and charities. Deductions for trade union contributions were permitted to be taken from a fisherman's settlings for the Transport and General Workers Union, only if the union were able to provide the necessary documents, indicating the man's full name and official registration number. It was the responsibility of the union concerned to collect the money that was deducted by the cashiers from the owner's office.

The document makes it clear that from 1967 there existed a set of 'Terms and Conditions of Employment' for trawl fishermen sailing out of Grimsby, on vessels whose owners were members of the Grimsby Fishing Vessel Owners Association. The existence of official registration 'terms' disputes the commonly held notion that all fishermen were casual labour who were not bound by a contract, or that the conditions adhered to when sailing out of Grimsby dock were simply assumptions or traditions without supporting documentation. The majority of trawl fishermen were registered workers, and, providing they sailed over 200 days per year, their registration remained valid for their entire fishing careers.

The registration document is an indication of the extent of control trawler owners could exercise over the workforce. The original set of objectives contained in the draft version, which worked to satisfy the interests of both fishermen and trawler owners, were completely removed, to the detriment of subsequent compensation claims. The objectives made the intention of regular and continuous employment clear. Yet through the registration scheme, members of the Grimsby Fishing Vessel Owners Association ensured their labour force were tied by the terms and conditions of permanent workers, but that in return the owners assumed the legitimacy to regard the fishermen as flexible 'casual labour'.

*

Acknowledgements

The authors would like to thank: Heritage Lottery Fund, for their support and understanding of the importance of the project; CPO Media – Stephen Ryder and staff; Grimsby Fishermen's Mission and the Port Missioner, Tony Jewitt; The Grimsby Telegraph, particularly Michelle Lalor, Editor and Linda Roberts for help sourcing images and for allowing us to use archive images; Austin Mitchell MP, Mirror Group/Mirrorpix for their permission to publish Derek Grant's collection of photographs; Channel 7/TV4Change; Wintringham Oasis Academy – Principal Jane Bowman, Learning Director of English, Rachel Revell; pupils of Wintringham Oasis Academy -Sharna Ramsden, Charmaine Riggall, Nathan Williamson, Kieran Yeoman, Harry Dixon, Georgia Clark; Jenny Mooney, Local Studies Librarian at Grimsby Central Library; North East Lincolnshire Archives – John Wilson Archivist and Phil Melladay Archivist Assistant.

Special thanks also to Grimsby Artist, Dale Mackie for painting 'Distant Water' and Gill Gibbon and Elaine Munson at Abbey Walk Gallery for support.

We are grateful to the following CPO Media volunteers who gave their time to the project: Joshua Dennis; Peter Johnson; Daniel Khan; Eleanor Morley; Karen Richardson; Gareth Roberts; Rich Tipple; Stevie Thornton; David Whittingham; members of CPO Media's Community Task Force.

Most importantly, we would like to thank those who came forward and patiently gave us their time, their reminiscences and trusted us to tell their story.

The Interviewees

Andrew Allard
Robert Atmore
Jeff Beedham
Charlie Briggs
Jim Clark
Peter Coates
David Coates
Norman Crampin
Sheila Crampin
Mike Debnam
Bill Dillon
Harry Drinkell
Derek Grant

Thomas 'Chukka' Green
Jack Greenwood
Ray Harries
Peter Harrison
Graham Hobson
Ina Howden
Stanley Johnson
Arty Lea
Ina Howden
Michael Mason
Ken Morrison
George Nicholson
Ray Powell
Graham Pullen
David Rimmer
Tom Smith
Valerie Smith
Michael Sparkes
Michael Surr
Geoffrey Todd
Doreen Tyson
Raymond Walker
Duncan Watt
Sid West
Edward Whyte
Valerie Whyte
Pete Woods
Richard Wright

Bibliography

Primary Sources

Board of Trade Registers – Grimsby Fishing Apprentice Registers 1880 -1937
Merchant Shipping (Fishing Boats) Bill, 1883
The Grimsby Directory 1893
The Official Souvenir of a Grand County Bazaar, Town Hall, Grimsby, February 6, 7,8th 1907
Port Instructions to Masters of Grimsby Steam Fishing Vessels - Issued 1908
Port Instructions to Masters of Grimsby Steam Fishing Vessels - Issued 1931
The Grimsby Chamber of Commerce and Shipping Booklet, August 1939

Ross Group
- Schedules and Accounts 1948-9
- Provisional Three Year Plan, 5th June 1967
- Trawling Division – Summary of Results for 6 Months to 31st March 1968
- Annual Report 1965-7
- Some Facts About The Ross Group c./1965-6
- The Opening of Ross House by Sir Keith Joseph, 25th Oct. 1965

Grimsby Fishing Vessel Owners Association (GFVOA) Documents
- Official Minutes
- The Grimsby Exchange Official Credit List, 2nd July 1951
- 'Silver Cod Trophy,' memorandum concerning operation and proposed reforms of – 1963
- Icelandic Press Reports, translations 1963 – 70
- Notes relating to the terms and conditions of employment of trawler fishermen sailing on board trawlers registered with the Grimsby Fishing Vessel Owners Association from the port of Grimsby (excluding share fishermen)

Lincolnshire Steam Trawlers Mutual Insurance and Protecting Co. Ltd. Directors Minutes 1954-61
The Fishing Industry: Its economic significance in the Yorkshire and Humberside Ports A report prepared by the Research Group of the Yorkshire and Humberside Economic Planning Board, Revised May 1977
Reynolds Memoirs, 1979
Consolidated Fisheries – Reports and Accounts, 31st Dec, 1980
Grimsby Sailors and Fishing Charity – Scheme, 16th December 2005

Secondary Sources

i) Books

Anson, Peter F., *Fishermen and Fishing Ways* (London: 1932)

Boswell, David, *Sea Fishing Apprentices of Grimsby* (Louth: 1974)

Daunton, M. J., *Progress and Poverty: An Economic and Social History of Britain 1700-1850* (Oxford: 1995)

Dennis, E.T.W., *Olsens Fisherman's Nautical Almanac,* (1928)

Dowling, Alan, *Grimsby: Making the Town 1800-1914* (London: 2007)

Drury, Edward, *The Great Grimsby Story: Book 2 1870 to 1940* (The author circa 1980s)

Drury, Edward, *The Great Grimsby Story: Book 4: Fishing, Our Heritage* (The author: 1993)

Ekberg, Charles, *Grimsby Fish* (Buckingham: 1984)

Gerrish, Margaret, *Streets, Shops and Shopping in 'between wars' Grimsby* (Grimsby: 1998)

Gillett, Edward, *A History of Grimsby* (Hull: 1970)

Goddard, John and Spalding, Roger, *Fish and Ships: The Rise and Fall of Grimsby, the Worlds Premier Fishing Port* (Lancaster: 1987)

Hodson, A., *Introduction to Trawling* (Grimsby: 1949)

Holroyd, John, *The Great Grimsby Lockout of 1901* (1986)

King, Paul and Pulfrey, Steve, *Grimsby Trawlers: The Final Years of the Side Trawler* (Beverley: 1991)

Roberts, R. F., *Trawlers of Humberside* (Gloucestershire: 2005)

Robinson, Robb, *Trawling: The Rise and Fall of the British Trawl Fishery* (Exeter: 1996)

Russell, Stuart, *Memory Lane, Grimsby* (Derby: 1999)

Sherard, Robert Harborough, *The Child Slaves of Britain* (London: 1905)

Tunstall, Jeremy, *The Fishermen* (London: 1962)

Wright, Neil R., *Lincolnshire Towns and Industry 1700 – 1914* (Lincoln: 1982)

ii) Newspapers and Magazines

Ashore and Afloat

Bygones

Daily Express

The Daily Mirror

Fishing News

Fish Trades Gazette

Grimsby Evening Telegraph

The Grimsby News

Grimsby Observer

The Helmsman

The Hull Packet and East Riding Times
The Leeds Mercury
The Times
Toilers of the Deep

iii) Journals

Moore, S. R. W., 'The Occupation of Trawl Fishing and the Medical Aid Available to the Grimsby Deep Sea Fisherman,' *British Journal of Industrial Medicine,* Vol. 26, No. 1 (Jan., 1969) pp. 1-24

Mumby-Croft, Roger, 'The Living Conditions On Board UK Distant Water Trawlers, 1945-1970,' *The Northern Mariner* IX No. 4, (Oct., 1999) pp. 25-33

iv) Websites

www.fishermensmission.org.uk/
www.grimsbycleecivic.co.uk/Pubs.html
Hansard – House of Commons Debate (6 March 1873)
www.nationalarchives.gov.uk/cabinetpapers/themes/cod-wars.htm
www.shorelinehp.com
Sidewinder – www.homepage.ntlworld.com/grimsby.trawlers/

About the Authors

Nick Triplow

Nick is a freelance writer, editor and teacher. Born in London, he graduated with an honours degree in Writing, Publishing and English from Middlesex University in 1995 and was awarded a distinction on Sheffield Hallam University's MA Writing course in 2007.

The author of *The Women They Left Behind – Stories from Grimsby's Fishing Families, Family Ties – Stories from Hall's Barton Ropery,* Nick has also written the script for *Ted's Return Home,* a short film about Ted Lewis, author of *Get Carter.* The film premiered at the 2009 Humber Mouth Festival.

He is currently writing a biography of Lewis, and his recently completed novel, *Frank's Wild Years,* a crime story based in Nick's native south London will be published by independent publisher Caffeine Nights in autumn 2011. For information: *www.nicktriplow.blogspot.com*

Tina Bramhill

Grimsby born and bred, Tina has been involved in community media projects in North East Lincolnshire since 2006, when she started as a volunteer on the editorial team of *Clee View* magazine.

In 2008 she gained a first class degree in professional writing and went on to work on the CPO Heritage Lottery project *The Women They Left Behind,* where she gained a greater understanding about Grimsby's growth and decline as a fishing port and the effects of the industry loss on its community.

In addition to both oral history projects, Tina has worked on the content and design of various publications, including *Insight* and *VOXX* magazines well as recruiting and training volunteers and managing CPO projects.

Her highlight to date was being interviewed by Jenni Murray on BBC Radio 4's Woman's Hour about *The Women They Left Behind.*

Sophie James

Born in Grimsby, Sophie graduated from the University of York in 2010 with a Joint Honours in History and English Literature. Her academic interests include 18th Century British and French history, feminist studies and Romantic literature. Distant Water is her first published work.

'Working on *Distant Water* has been a wonderfully insightful experience. As my research progressed, I began to understand more about my hometown, and see that Grimsby as it exists today is a product of a rich and vibrant past.'

'Every fisherman's story helps to foster an unique appreciation of this rapidly vanishing way of life. Grimsby has a history, and a community, of which we should all be proud.'

Sophie would like to dedicate her work to her Great Grandfather, Skipper Herbert Wilkinson.

CPO Media

CPO Media is delighted to have managed a second Heritage Lottery Project and to have assisted in the publishing of another excellent book.

Distant Water may seem like distant times to many, but they are not forgotten. However, for younger readers these are times they never knew, even if they aware of Grimsby's heritage, its association with the sea and the bounty it gave up. I hope all readers of *Distant Water* will agree the authors and those interviewed have brought an industry's heritage to life. The cost of the gifts the waters gave up was at times painful and too often tragic; no apology is made for an honest account of the trawlermen's sacrifice, that would be a disservice. *Distant Water* reflects a bygone era when Grimsby was the busiest fishing port in the world and the men who sailed from these shores did indeed make the town great.

History must report the past but it also plays an important role in understanding the present. As a company founded under the banner of regeneration, CPO Media is more than aware of where we are in Grimsby and where we have come from – the two are inextricably linked. I hope that the reader will be as proud of our heritage as I am of this project. It is my wish also that, as we pause for a moment to look back, we are also ready to embrace the future and the riches and uncertainty that it too will offer.

Stephen Ryder Managing Director, CPO Media

LIVERPOOL
SAILING SHIPS

LIVERPOOL
SAILING SHIPS

MICHAEL STAMMERS

Cover image: Furling the sails on the German training vessel *Gorch Fock* before she enters the Mersey, July 1984.

Frontispiece: A Rivers Class yacht sets off from Rock Ferry with the old warship training schools in the background about 1910.

First published 2008

The History Press
The Mill, Brimscombe Port,
Stroud, Gloucestershire, GL5 2QG
www.thehistorypress.co.uk

Reprinted 2010, 2011

© Michael Stammers, 2011

British Library Cataloguing in Publication Data.
A catalogue record for this book is available from the British Library.

ISBN 978 0 7524 4243 3

Typesetting and origination by The History Press
Printed and bound in Great Britain by
Marston Book Services Limited, Didcot

CONTENTS

INTRODUCTION

No one knows when the first sail was raised to propel a boat on the River Mersey. Log boats carved out of single tree trunks have been found on the upper parts of the river around Warrington from Victoria's reign up to the 1960s. It was originally thought that they were made in the Bronze Age, but the last one recovered was radiocarbon dated to the Middle Ages. Such shallow draft, narrow-beamed craft were not suitable for sailing. We know that British tribes used boats with sails around the time of Julius Caesar's invasion. We also know that the Irish Sea was not a barrier, but a highway for sailors 2,000 years ago. We can also infer from the finds found at the Roman industrial complex at Wilderspool, Warrington, that the occasional Roman cargo ship must have called there.

The Scandinavian settlers who occupied the lower shores of the Mersey must have had boats. Their presence is detected by place names such as Formby, Crosby, Irby or West Kirby. Toxteth and Croxteth are the most interesting because their names are formed of a personal name and the word 'staithe' which means a landing place. That of course argues for the presence of boats and also suggests that the River Alt was once navigable well inland. There is also the huge collection of finds which range from coins to brooches that have been found at Meols on the Wirral. Archaeologists are not quite sure what they represent. It is possible that there was some kind of maritime trading place or mart there in Viking and medieval times – and here again sailing ships would have been involved. Boat finds all over Scandinavia from the seventh century onwards have provided specific evidence of sailing ships. They were wooden clinker-built vessels that could be rowed and sailed. The familiar Viking warships for raiding were long and narrow while the cargo-carrying knars were broader for a good cargo capacity. One of the ships excavated at Roskilde in Denmark has been shown by tree-ring evidence to have been built at Dublin and that is about as close as you can get for Viking ships in the Mersey.

As for Liverpool itself, it seems to have been no more than one of a number of fishing villages along the Mersey. In 1207, King John's charter gave it the enhanced status of a town with trading rights and a royal castle for protection. This put it in direct competition with Chester for the Irish Sea trade and it could be that John also saw it as a possible military supply base for campaigning in Ireland. By the thirteenth century, larger-decked sailing ships were in common use, usually with a single mast and square sail. The Benedictine priory of St James, Birkenhead, was granted the right to ferry travellers and goods across the Mersey to Liverpool in 1330. This was the first water route that linked Liverpool to its hinterland. Links with other places on the Mersey's south bank such as Seacombe, Eastham and Runcorn were gradually extended during the Middle Ages.

The real expansion took place in the eighteenth century. The first phase was the building of locks on the Mersey, Irwell and Weaver to provide barge access to Manchester and the salt towns of Cheshire. The second involved the digging of artificial waterways to link Liverpool with the coalmines around St Helens and provide through-routes to Lancashire, Yorkshire, the Potteries and the Black Country.

Liverpool seems to have beaten Chester in the Irish trade by the beginning of the sixteenth century because the Mersey was a better haven than the shallow Dee, and the taxes on ships were much less than those at Chester. John Leland, one of the first travel writers, visited Liverpool in Henry VIII's reign and noted that many Irish merchants resorted to Liverpool to sell their goods. In 1565, we have the first list of Liverpool ships. There were twelve, ranging from the barque *Eagle* of 40 tons to the boat *Good Luck* of 6 tons with an average size of around 20 tons. Barques seem to have been two-masted vessels with large square mainsail and a triangular mizzen and not the more familiar nineteenth-century three- and four-masted barques. There were no ships and 'ship' meant a larger three-masted vessel. There were also barques owned in outlying settlements such as Wallasey, Hilbre and Formby. These barques may well have been forerunners of the flat, the distinctive Mersey sailing barge.

It is possible that by the 1630s, Liverpool ships had become involved in the trade to the pioneer English colonies of Virginia and Barbadoes for tobacco, sugar and rum, and these would have required ships and not barques for the ocean passage. Such transatlantic ventures were stopped by the outbreak of the English Civil War in 1641, and Liverpool was in the firing line on several occasions. Liverpool's proper take-off into deep sea shipping began after 1660 with the restoration of Charles II to the throne. By 1680, the port was busy in the estuary, coastal, Irish and Atlantic trades. This was the year of the very first topographical view of Liverpool. It reflected the bustle of the port which was still basically an anchorage off the town.

The port facilities were transformed by the opening of the port's first dock in 1715. The Liverpool anchorage was vulnerable to the fast current, the high tidal range of the river and gales sweeping in from the north-west. The three-and-a-half acre dock gave the bigger ships a safe place to load and unload. It was the starting point for over two centuries of building new docks, and these developments spread from Liverpool across the river to Birkenhead and up to Garston, Widnes and Runcorn. Before the first steamer dock – the Clarence Dock of 1830 – all the docks were designed for sailing ships. Some docks came to specialise in specific trades. Queen's Dock of 1796 was the dock for timber ships and whaling vessels, and Princes Dock of 1816 was the terminal for the New York to Liverpool sailing packets.

The eighteenth-century port of Liverpool prospered overall and the fleet of locally-owned ships increased in number and size. Even so, around 1800, the biggest ship built and owned in the port was the *Watt* of 1797 which was all of 500 tons. By about 1750 the slave trade had become one of the major trades of the port and remained so until its abolition in 1807. Liverpool ships loaded cloth, guns, alcohol and other barter goods, would sail to West Africa and exchange the cargo for a ship-load of Africans who were then carried in horrific squalor across the Atlantic for slave work in plantations. The frequent naval wars, mainly with the French, disrupted ordinary commerce and some Liverpool vessels were armed and licensed as private warships (privateers) to attack enemy shipping.

The number of ships owned (and mostly built) in Liverpool increased during the eighteenth century. The first surviving list of deep sea ships dated from 1739 listed 221 vessels. The Liverpool Shipping Registers which were begun in 1786 show that by 1790 there were 479 ships totalling 76,251 tons. By 1805, the total had doubled to 970 ships, totalling 164,563 tons. Most were square-rigged three-masted ships or two-masted brigs.

The Liverpool shipbuilders had a reputation for good workmanship to the extent that they gained orders for warships from the Admiralty. This was in spite of the fact that the shipwrights were a turbulent set of employees. But by 1850, the local industry faced a problem of competition from overseas: from Canadian shipyards. By that year, Canadian-built vessels made up half the Liverpool sailing ships. Local shipbuilders could not compete with the Canadians' lower wages and material costs. They also suffered from not having long-term leases on their shipyards. So, if their yards obstructed the building of a commercial dock they were forced to move. This happened when the Albert Dock was built in the early 1840s. The more progressive turned to iron and steam technology and followed the lead set by John Laird's yard at Birkenhead. Some such as R.&J. Evans and William Potter came to specialise in building large iron or steel bulk-carrying sailing ships, and this kind of work carried them through to the middle of the 1890s when they were all forced to close to make way for the reconstruction and extension of Queens and Brunswick Docks.

The arrival of steamers (the first was a ferry of 1812) initially had a positive result for sailing ships. Steam tugs could provide a safer and faster arrival and departure for sailing ships at Liverpool. They were no longer dependent on the wind to get them up to the dock entrances. Ocean-going steamers first competed with sailing ships on the lucrative Atlantic route from 1838. This had been dominated from the 1820s by large American-owned packet ships that ran a regular service for passengers and premium cargoes. Packets continued to thrive up until the outbreak of the American Civil War in 1861. The pioneer oceanic steamers were hampered by high fuel consumption which meant that much of the hull was taken up by coal bunkers instead of paying cargo. Most of the long-distance steamer services depended on subsidies for carrying mail to pay their way. Technical developments from the late 1850s with higher pressure boilers and compound engines made the steamer gradually more competitive. The opening of the Suez Canal between the Mediterranean and the Red Sea also assisted them because it cut out the long route around the Cape of Good Hope, which sailing ships had to take to get to India, the Far East and Australia.

In 1850, steamers made up just over 2 per cent of the total Liverpool fleet. Twenty years later steamers accounted for nearly 20 per cent and by 1880 it was 36 per cent. Nevertheless, there were 1,079,014 tons of sailing ships owned by the members of the Liverpool Sailing Ship Owners' Mutual Indemnity Association, and that only covered the ocean-going ships and barques and not the coasters and the flats. The members' vessels were mainly iron - or steel-hulled bulk carriers which could carry up to 5,000 tons of cargo. They were tramps that worked from one voyage to the next, not on regular routes and carried commodities such as coal, grain, metal ores and nitrates (used as fertilizer and in explosives). Between 1900 and 1914 almost all these deep-sea ships were sold from Liverpool – mainly to Scandinavian owners. Further vessels were sunk by enemy action in the First World War and by 1923 the *Liverpool Who's Who in Shipping* listed only two: the *Birkdale* of 1,483 tons and the *Terpisichore* of 1,935 tons. This was not the end of sailing cargo ships arriving at Liverpool. Sailing ships under the Swedish and Finnish flags could still make a living by transporting grain from Australia to Europe and some of those shipments were bound for mills at Liverpool and Birkenhead.

The mid-nineteenth century has often been seen as the Golden Age of the Sailing Ship because of the building of very fast sailing clippers. The Americans started the trend with the design of packets for running fast regular services across the Atlantic, and were spurred to extreme designs to cope with the demands for passenger berths and cargo space out to the Californian gold fields which were discovered in 1849. Liverpool had its share of notable ships, but they were employed in supplying a service out to New South Wales where gold had been found in 1851. The clippers of the Black Ball and White Star lines were especially famous for their size and record-breaking voyages. The China tea trade was the other traffic for which large numbers of clippers were built. This was because there was a high premium on the first of the new tea crop. Most clippers were owned in London but there were a few Liverpool examples such as the *Scawfell* of 1858 which was owned by Rathbones, a firm that is still going as a financial services company.

The ships used for the Irish and coastal trades were generally much smaller than those in longer distance trades, and many of the vessels involved were owned at smaller ports rather than Liverpool. In the nineteenth century both Runcorn, on the upper Mersey and estuary and Connah's Quay, on the Dee were centres for building and owning coasting vessels. Many of the Runcorn ships were involved in carrying coal to Cornwall and returning with china clay for the Staffordshire Potteries. Another fleet was owned in the Irish port of Arklow and these specialised in bringing pit props to Garston and returning with cargoes of coal. A few of these coastal schooners lasted as auxiliary vessels with engines until the 1950s.

The Mersey flat was a local sailing barge that was capable of sailing on the inland waterways linked to the Mersey and undertaking coastal voyages. This distinctive design seems to have emerged around 1700 possibly as a sailing lighter for collecting goods from ships at anchor in the Mersey or at the outer of anchorage off the Wirral – the Hoyle Lake. They were usually stoutly built with flat bottoms to allow them to sit on the mud at low tide. They were first rigged with a single square sail, but after about 1750 they were rigged as sloops with a triangular foresail and a large gaff mainsail. There were several hundred at work by the mid-nineteenth century; but the introduction of steam tugs meant that many flats were converted into dumb barges without sails. The last sailing flat lost her sails sometime during the Second World War.

Other types of Mersey working sailing boat included the pilot cutters and their successors from 1852, the pilot schooners. There were only twelve of these at any given time and they had to be fast and seaworthy to stay on station off the Mersey entrance in all kinds of weather. They were reluctantly replaced by four steamers in the late 1890s. The Mersey ferries disappeared much earlier. They were mainly open boats on the shorter routes while the longer ones to Eastham and further up the estuary were decked cutters with cabins and deck space for carriages and horses. The first steamers on the Mersey were ferries and they had displaced the sailing/rowing ferry boats by 1850. The Mersey gig boats that were used to assist ships into dock lasted longer and a few were retained for racing up until the 1930s. Their hull shape was also used as a model for the design of the open racing yachts built for the New Brighton Sailing Club from the 1880s.

Yachts are another component of the Mersey sailing vessel heritage. The Royal Mersey Yacht Club was established in 1844 and still races Mylne-class yachts which are a seventy-year-old design. There are even older designs going back to the 1890s raced at other clubs such as the Half-Raters at Wallasey and the Stars and Operas at West Kirby and Hoylake.

The nobby is a local design of fishing trawler specialising in trawling for shrimps that was perfected in the 1890s and widely built from Conway up to Morecambe Bay. They had the fine lines of a yacht to allow them to race their perishable catches to market. About thirty survived as fishing boats to the time when they were recognised as historic and bought for conversion into yachts. An annual Mersey Nobby Race was established in the 1980s and usually attracts a double-figure entry.

Training young people in sailing ships has grown from a part of naval training to a widely accepted way of broadening experience and building confidence, and even as a reform programme for the wayward. The first manifestation on the Mersey was the berthing of obsolete wooden warships of Nelson's era as school ships. The boys were trained for a sea career and very soon became expert boatmen because rowing/sailing boats were the only links with the shore. The sail-training movement started in the 1950s and brought together youth training ships from many countries to take part in long distance races. This Tall Ships fleet has visited Liverpool in 1984 and again in 1992 and they will make another visit in 2008. There are also regular visits by other sailing ships. The larger square riggers recall the days when Liverpool docks were filled with masts and they are a hugely popular spectacle especially when they all leave the Mersey in line astern. So while the old commercial sailing ship is extinct, sail still lives on in the Mersey in yachting and in the sail-training ships. The old days are recalled in the models, paintings and relics held in local museums and in a handful of surviving Mersey-built or Mersey-owned sailing ships. The pictures in this book have been gathered from a number of different people and institutions and these are acknowledged after each caption.

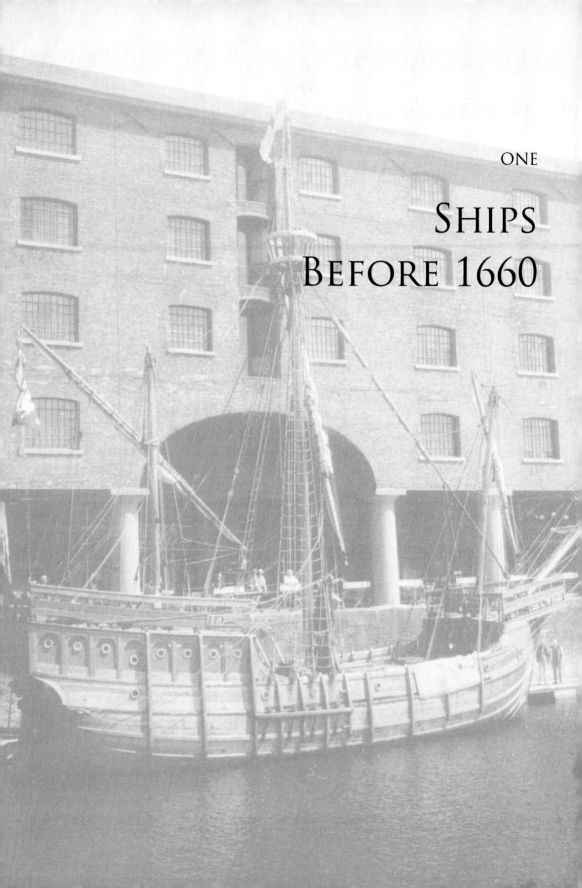

ONE

SHIPS
BEFORE 1660

To be honest, there is no evidence for sailing ships on the Mersey before the Middle Ages. We can infer their existence from land-based archaeological finds and the origins of some coastal place names. In Roman times, the site of a riverside Roman settlement at Wilderspool, near Warrington, has yielded finds such as an imported lead ingot. This almost certainly had been transported by water. That, along with other goods, may have been transported in the type of small Romano-British barge that has been found on the Thames and at Barlands Farm, near Newport, on the banks of the Bristol Channel. The chances are that the first sail was a simple rectangular piece of canvas lifted aloft on a spar.

These Romano-British barges were built with heavy internal frames and smooth (carvel) planking. The later Scandinavian ships, on the other hand, were built with overlapping (clinker planks with lighter internal frames which were inserted after the planks had been fastened together). Once again we lack any surviving remnants of Viking boats, but the coastal settlements with a 'by' ending, and especially Toxteth which means Toca's staithe or landing place, points to the use of boats. Their clinker-boat-building technique was carried on into the Middle Ages. Carvel building continued to be used around the Mediterranean and was reintroduced to England around the fifteenth century.

The first Liverpool vessels for which we have names were the twelve listed as part of a national census of shipping in 1565. The average tonnage of these and for later vessels up to 1660 was between 20 and 30 tons. The commonly-used proportions for a vessel of the period was a length of keel to width of 3 to 1, and width to depth of 2 to 1. This meant that a 20-ton barque would measure 33ft on her keel (with overhangs at her bow and stern), 11ft wide (beam) and 5.5ft depth. Contemporary pictures from other ports suggest that these barques had one or two masts: a tall mainmast with two square sails and a smaller mizzen with a triangular lateen sail. The latter had been introduced from the Mediterranean in the fifteenth century.

By 1626, when the Earl of Derby compiled another return of local ships, the number of Liverpool ships had surpassed those belonging to Chester, its main rival in the North West. Liverpool had twenty-four vessels totalling 462 tons and Chester had fifteen totalling 383 tons. Liverpool's biggest, the *Swan* was only 40 tons and the only one capable of carrying guns. The *Bennett* of Formby which was then a haven at the mouth of the River Alt measured 60 tons and may have been rigged as a three-masted full-rigged ship with a bowsprit projecting over the bow with a square sail and two square sails on the fore and main masts and a lateen on the mizzen. By then the 'ship' had become the standard rig for deep sea vessels. The replica of Sir Francis Drake's late sixteenth-century ship, the *Golden Hind*, has visited Liverpool and Birkenhead several times, and gave a good idea of the appearance of these sixteenth-century vessels.

We can only guess that a Roman barge on the Mersey would have been similar in size and construction to the late third-century Romano-British Barlands Farm boat which was discovered in 1993. It measured just over 37ft long by 10ft wide and carried about 6.5 tons of cargo. It might have been a square sailor or possibly a lug sail and was seaworthy enough to ply the Bristol Channel.

Above: The Scandinavian people who settled in Kirby, Crosby, Formby and on the Wirral would have probably used boats like this replica of an eleventh-century Viking ship under construction at the Viking Museum at Roskilde, Denmark. (Viking Ship Museum, Roskilde)

Above right: Ships increased in size and were fitted with decks and superstructures in the Middle Ages. The cog which originated in North Germany was one of the most common types. It was built with carvel bottom planks and clinker sides and a large single square sail. Cogs were known to trade in the Irish Sea. This one is a replica of the 1389 cog discovered at Bremen in 1962.

Right: The carrack was a three-masted vessel developed in the later Middle Ages. It carried what was to become the standard deep-sea rig for centuries afterwards. A bowsprit projecting over the bow carried a square sail (the spritsail), the foremast a single square sail and the main two square sails (the mainsail and a topsail) and the mizzen carried a lateen sail. Bristol was a major port and Liverpool a minor coastal port when John Cabot's carrack *The Matthew* set out to explore North America in 1497. Five hundred years later a replica carrack based on the best available evidence was built at Bristol and made a trip to Liverpool's Albert Dock in 2003.

Carrickfergus was one the ports that traded with Liverpool in the late sixteenth century. It was a military base to which troops, horses and military supplies were delivered from Liverpool. This view of 1560 shows two kinds of Irish Sea trader: a three-masted ship to the left, and in the centre a double-end single-masted barque. There is also a large unrigged hull above that and three double-ended clinker-built open boats which were doubtless

descendants of Viking boats. The Liverpool ships of this era were probably similar to the barque. Detailed pictures of ships other than naval vessels are rare at this time. (British Library)

The replica of the *Golden Hind* fires a salute on arrival at Liverpool on one of her several visits in the 1980s and 1990s. The original ship circumnavigated the globe under the command of Sir Francis Drake between 1577 and 1580. This 100-ton vessel was larger than the biggest Liverpool ships of around 40 tons.

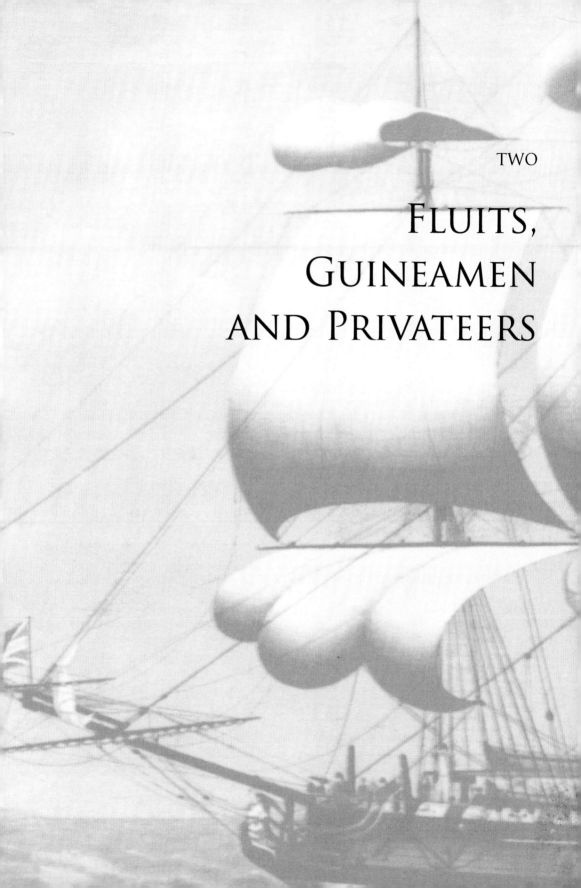

TWO

FLUITS,
GUINEAMEN
AND PRIVATEERS

The restoration of the English monarchy in 1660 marks the start of Liverpool's rapid rise as a port and shipowning centre. The Town had suffered from the successive occupation by the Royalists and the Parliamentarians during the Civil War. It is unclear what happened to its ships because the records have not survived. While the Irish trade remained important with its small barques, larger full-rigged ships of 100 tons or more were built to ply the Atlantic to freight tobacco from Virginia and the Carolinas, and sugar from the British West Indian possessions. The pictorial evidence is contained within the portrait of Liverpool of 1680.

In the late seventeenth century England contested the mercantile dominance of the Dutch Republic. One of the latter's advantages was their development of a new type of cargo carrier – the fluit – which could carry more cargo with a smaller crew. Many of the fluits were captured in the three naval wars and passed into English ownership. The *Mulberry* which was owned by Brian Blundell of Liverpool in the early 1700s may have been a prize taken from the Dutch, or English-built along Dutch lines. She had the distinction of being the first vessel to enter the new dock in 1715.

The demand for labour in colonial plantations had led to the development of the slave trade, where West Africans were bartered for European goods and shipped across the Atlantic in horrifically packed conditions to work as slaves cultivating sugar, tobacco and other tropical crops. London and Bristol were the leading slave-ship ports up to 1730. After that Liverpool gradually overhauled them and by 1780 was the dominant European slaving port. Of the 11,000 recorded slaving voyages from England to Africa in the eighteenth century, 5,300 (48 per cent) sailed from the Mersey. The slave ships or 'Guineamen' were on average larger with finer lines than the average merchant ship. Some were described as 'frigate-built' with a raised forecastle and quarter deck. This not only enlarged their accommodation, it also gave the crew defensible positions if the Africans on the Middle Passage broke out from the stuffy hell of the ship's hold.

In the eighteenth century, Britain fought a series of naval wars with France, its principal European rival. These culminated in the American War of Independence (1775-83) and the Revolutionary and Napoleonic Wars lasting, with two pauses, from 1793 to 1815. Liverpool's ships were vulnerable to capture and many were armed for their own protection. There were also privateering ventures where armed Liverpool ships were licensed to capture enemy ships. There were ninety-nine involved at various times in the American War of Independence when the American trade had been cut off. Most were ships and carried an average of between sixteen and twenty cannon.

Liverpool had some involvement in other trades. For example, there were a few local whalers that sailed to the Arctic and the Baltic timber trade, and the Irish trade was also important. Most of the town's deep-sea ships were full-rigged ships with some two-masted brigs and snows as well. The latter were a variant on the brig with a separate little mast behind the mainmast to carry the spanker. This was the fore and aft sail which was supported by a spar (gaff) at the top and a spar (boom) at the bottom which replaced the lateen sail in the late eighteenth century. Eighteenth-century vessels also carried triangular jibs and stay sails. These were fastened to the stays that supported the masts from along the length of the ship. These all helped to make the ships more manoeuvrable when tacking and more weatherly overall. The introduction of steering wheels instead of tillers at the beginning of the eighteenth century was an important innovation. Another one introduced in the eighteenth century was the use of copper sheathing to prevent marine-boring creatures from attacking the planking.

This painting of Liverpool in 1680 is the first known view of the port and its ships. It was an anchorage port where the deep-sea ships anchor off the shore and had their cargoes delivered by barges. The vessel in the left foreground is typical of the late seventeenth century English deep-sea cargo ship. Her stern was highly decorated, and her bow (a beak head) was quite low. Guns were carried as a matter of course as a defence against national enemies and pirates. (The Trustees National Museums Liverpool)

The *Mulberrry* was a Liverpool ship which was clearly a fluit design. It is not known whether she was a prize taken from the Dutch or built locally. Her owner Bryan Blundell drew pictures of his ships in a journal of his voyages. The horizontal dotted lines across the sails represent reef points. These were short lengths of rope which could be used to reduce the sail area in blowy weather. (Lancashire Record Office)

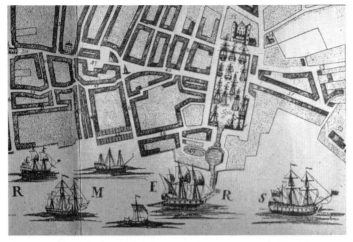

Perry's Plan of Liverpool of 1725 shows the first dock opened in 1715. The dock was built at the mouth of the Pool and provided 3 acres of enclosed water space. Perry shows the dock crowded with shipping and several ships lying at anchor in the river. A ship is approaching the entrance is sailing off the entrance under topsails.

The head of the dock in the mid-eighteenth century. Many merchant ships imitated the decorative fashion of warships and had a leaping lion as a figurehead. The beak head was an open structure behind the lion and served as the crew's 'necessary house' hence the term heads for a maritime lavatory.

The Guineamen, as the slave ships were known, were among the largest and fastest Liverpool sailing ships after 1750. This painting by William Jackson (active about 1770 to about 1803) shows just such a vessel. He painted this slave ship about 1780. Her name is unknown, but she carries a figurehead in classical dress and was equipped with sixteen guns. She has two jibs on her bowsprit as well two spritsails below the spar. She is also rigged with a spanker on the mizzen.

Above: This close-up of her hull shows why she can be identified as a slave ship. Just above the black band on the hull and to the right of the anchor and to the left of the rigging of the foremast there are square ventilation ports which could be opened when there were slaves packed in the hold for the Middle Passage from West Africa to the West Indies. The large ship's boats were also essential for operations in West Africa. The ship would anchor off one of the slave forts and the unfortunate Africans, many of whom were prisoners of war of African kings, would be ferried to the ship. (The Trustees of National Museums Liverpool)

Right: The list of slave ships and their voyages as listed in 1771 shows the full extent of Liverpool's involvement in this shocking trade. The smallest could carry 100 slaves and the biggest such as the *Prince of Wales* could load 600. These people were chained prone in the hold and only allowed on deck for short periods. There were many deaths from disease and suffocation on voyages that could last months. Some of the ships' names seem singularly inappropriate – family names such as *Agnes, Nancy* or *Jenny* and abstract ones such as *Industry, Friendship* or *Liberty*.

68   STATE OF COMMERCE.   CHAP. VI.

A LIST of AFRICAN SHIPS

for the Year 1771.

When cleared	Ships.	Where bound.	No. of Slaves.	When cleared	Ships.	Where bound.	No. of Slaves.
January 17.	Agnes,	Windward Coast,	200.	July 4.	Ellis,	Bonny,	500.
10.	Nancy,	Gold Coast,	500		Charlotte,	Gold Coast,	100.
22.	Corsican Hero,	Do.	500		John,	Old Callabar,	400.
23.	John,	Windward Coast,	300.	6.	Flumper,	Bonny,	450.
25.	Violet,	Do.	300.	8.	Harriet,	Windward Coast,	250.
February 6.	Lord Cassills,	Old Callabar,	400.	9.	Croker,	Do.	300.
9.	Industry,	Windward Coast,	200.	11.	Carrick,	Do.	250.
15.	Friendship,	Gambia,	100.		Ann,	Bonny,	350.
	Lively,	Do.	200.	13.	Little Ben,	Windward Coast,	160.
	Jellicoat,	Do.	400.	19.	Kelfy,	Do.	300.
28.	Lark,	Windward Coast,	100.	23.	Jack,	Gold Coast,	200.
March 6.	Providence,	Bonny,	350.	24.	Nancy,	Bonny,	400.
7.	Juno,	Senegal,	100.	August 3.	Peggy,	Do.	100.
	Dorey,	Windward Coast,	100.	7.	Sisters,	Do.	100.
9.	Warren,	Do.	150.	13.	Society,	Do.	300.
20.	Hare,	Benin,	400.		Unity,	Do.	300.
21.	Sam,	Senegal,	100.	12.	Liberty,	Bonny,	400.
26.	Peggy,	Windward Coast,	250.	15.	Lord North,	Do.	400.
	Benin,	Benin,	450.		Barbadoes Packet,	Windward Coast,	200.
28.	Hector,	Old Callabar,	400.	16.	Mentor,	Gold Coast,	300.
April 6.	Hawke,	Windward Coast,	300.		Townshend,	Windward Coast,	300.
9.	Ferret,	Do.	250.	20.	Union,	Gold Coast,	200.
15.	May,	Old Callabar,	200.	25.	Captain,	Windward Coast,	300.
18.	Tom,	Bonny,	450.	26.	Bell,	Gold Coast,	250.
20.	Mary,	Sierraleone,	300.	27.	Pearle,	Windward Coast,	200.
26.	Polly,	New Callabar,	350.	28.	Swift,	Old Callabar,	200.
29.	Greyhound,	Bonny,	500.	30.	President,	Do.	200.
May 3.	Edgar,	Do.	400.	September 4.	Marcia,	Cammeroons,	300.
	Elizabeth,	New Callabar,	350.	5.	Prince of Wales,	Bonny,	600.
7.	King of Prussia,	Cammeroons,	250		Patty,	Windward Coast,	250.
23.	St. John,	Gambia,	300.	13.	Renown,	Do.	200.
25.	Betty,	Bonny,	450.	17.	Nancy,	Do.	300.
26.	Whitee,	Cammeroons,	200.	18.	Myrtle,	Do.	300.
	John,	Windward Coast,	250.	23.	Molly,	Gambia,	300.
22.	Effer,	Do.	200.	27.	Meredith,	Sierraleone,	250.
24.	Mercury,	Gold Coast,	200.		Portland,	Windward Coast,	200.
	Jenny,	Windward Coast,	100.	28.	Marcia,	Old Callabar,	300.
June 1.	Dalrymple,	Old Callabar,	400.		John,	Gold Coast,	350.
6.	Rumbold,	Bonny,	450.	October 1.	William,	Windward Coast,	150.
8.	Tom,	Windward Coast,	250.	17.	Marty,	Do.	250.
13.	Lancashire Witch,	Do.	300.	30.	Integrity,	Old Callabar,	250.
15.	Prince George,	Do.	300.	November 2.	Austin,	Bonny,	350.
17.	Little Will,	Do.	300.	8.	Saville,	Windward Coast,	250.
	Andromache,	Old Callabar,	400.		Cammeroons,	Do.	250.
18.	Hazard,	Windward Coast,	200.	20.	Dispatch,	Gold Coast,	300.
	Nancy,	Bonny,	350.	21.	Forrest,	Windward Coast,	150.
20.	Molly,	Old Callabar,	400.	25.	Solly,	Do.	200.
20.	Sportsman,	Old Callabar,	200.	December 9.	Lilly,	Do.	200.
21.	Afton,	Gambia,	300.	9.	Mars,	Do.	250.
23.	Apollo,	Windward Coast,	200.	19.	Bella,	Cammeroons,	250.
26.	Jenny,	New Callabar,	150.				
July 2.	Nancy,	Bonny,	450.				

Total of Ships 105   Total of Slaves 28200

THE

This punchbowl is decorated with a portrait of the brig *King George* of about 1770. These ship bowls were produced by the Liverpool potteries and were probably commissioned by the shipowners to celebrate the launch of a new ship or to mark a new venture. The *King George* was capable of sailing on deep-sea voyages and was particularly suited to shorter distance trades such as the timber and ship materials trade from the Baltic.

Privateering was an alternative to commercial carrying. It could bring rich prizes but it was always a gamble because of the heavy costs of fitting out and the large crew required. John Jenkinson, a marine artist active between 1800 and 1821, depicted a large twenty-four-gun vessel which is probably a local privateer and not a naval vessel. Note she carries more sails on each mast. Above the lowest sails are topsails, topgallants and royals. (The Trustees of National Museums Liverpool)

THREE

Wooden Hulls and Iron Knees: Liverpool's Early Nineteenth-Century Square Riggers

The fleet of ships owned in Liverpool carried on growing in the nineteenth century. The official figures show that 173,782 tons of shipping was locally owned in 1820. By 1850, the total had risen to 503,224 tons of sailing ships plus another 11,411 tons of steamers. The majority of these ships were wooden sailing ships. This made Liverpool the second biggest shipowning centre after London. The reasons for this rapid growth included the general expansion of the British economy and its global industrial dominance, a rising urban population which needed imported food, Liverpool's proximity to the main centres of industrial production and the extension of her trading connections. The abolition of the slave trade did not have the dire effects on Liverpool shipping that had been predicted. Other trades opened up including traffic to the new republics of South America, to India and China with the end of the East India Company's monopolies and to the growing colonies especially in Australia.

The size and construction of ships changed as well. The average size of a local vessel was below 200 tons before 1815. Between 1829 and 1835 it had risen to 235 tons and by 1854 it had almost doubled to 444 tons.

Ships built from wood are made up of hundreds of individual components. So for example, the frames which delineate the shape and provide support for the inner and outer planking were not single pieces of timber. They were made of smaller sections jointed together, and these and other similar parts could work loose as the ship ploughed its way through the sea, and especially as it grew older and the wooden, iron or copper fastenings loosened or corroded. The problem was more acute for a larger ship. As their length increased, they needed greater structural strength. The introduction of iron components greatly helped with the problem. Iron was especially used for the big brackets known as 'knees' that reinforced the sides of the ship. Iron was also used for the pillars that were fixed under the centre of each beam. Wrought-iron anchor-cable came into general use to replace hemp cable. The former was both lighter and stronger than its organic predecessor. More labour saving devices such as capstans and geared windlasses (for raising the anchors) were also fitted to cope with the heavier sails and spars on the bigger vessels.

The profile (sheer) of ships had changed from those of the early eighteenth century. As the hull became longer, the raised quarterdeck at the stern had gradually become far less prominent, and by the early 1800s, many ships had a virtually flat profile with very little curvature between stem and stern. The low beak head also disappeared and was replaced by a higher bow. This might have a bust or a full length figurehead standing on a pedestal rather than a figurehead with his or her legs straddling the stem.

The three-masted barque rig also became increasingly popular. It did away with square sails on the mizzen mast with little detraction on the performance of an average cargo carrier. It offered instead savings in spars and canvas and the number of crew needed.

In the eighteenth century, Liverpool's own shipbuilders had supplied most local needs. By the 1830s, they were on the point of being supplanted by shipbuilders in Canada – especially at Quebec and the New Brunswick ports. The Canadians had access to unlimited supplies of cheap timber and paid lower wages than the British. Their ships were mainly built for export to Great Britain and Liverpool became the centre for their sale. By 1854 nearly 50 per cent of the Liverpool fleet had been built in Canada.

SCENE IN THE MERSEY ON THE TERMINATION OF THE LATE GALE.—VESSELS OUTWARD-BOUND.

The increasing volume of trade at Liverpool after 1815 was reflected in the number of ships using the port. As ships were dependent on the wind, a spell of gales could cause delays in sailing. This meant massive fleets of up to fifty ships leaving the port on one tide. This impressive spectacle was captured in this 1850s woodcut.

The storms from the North West blew directly up the Mersey and horrendous seas could build up when the wind was against the direction of the tide. This gale-lashed scene in the Mersey in 1836 may look exaggerated but is not far from the fact. (The Trustees of National Museums Liverpool)

23

Above: The increasing number of ships and cargoes caused congestion problems in the docks and between 1840 and 1860 the water space in the docks was more than doubled. The problem of large numbers of small wooden sailing ships crowding the Georges and Princes Docks in the early 1860s. This stereographic print is one of the first photographic views of the port.

Left: The lower profile of the stern of an early nineteenth-century merchant ship compared with its predecessors can be seen in this photograph of a wooden three-masted barque in Georges Dock. The stern was also built in a more rounded 'counter' than the earlier square transom stern. In the background to the right was the tower of the Liverpool to Holyhead chain of semaphore stations. These gave early warning of ships approaching Liverpool.

A snow sails from the Mersey in the early 1800s. A snow, unlike a brig, had a small mast aft of the mainmast that carried the spanker. She is well-armed with fourteen guns and has a full-length female figurehead. It is possible that she was among the last of the slave ships out of Liverpool before the abolition of the trade in 1807. (The Trustees of National Museums Liverpool)

The two decades after the end of the Napoleonic war in 1815 saw the opening up of new trades for Liverpool ships. The *Perseverance* was owned by Thomas and John Brocklebank. They built this 513-ton ship in their own shipyard at Whitehaven in 1819 specifically for trade to British India. This was also the year they moved their ship management office to Liverpool. As was the marine artistic convention she was shown in two different positions. (The Trustees of National Museums Liverpool)

The full-rigged ship *Helen* shows how much had changed since the *Perseverance*'s launch in 1819. The *Helen* was built in 1840 in Quebec, Canada. She is painted with a similar broad band with black gun ports picked out as the older ship. But on the *Helen* they were only decorative. At 861 tons she had a considerably larger cargo capacity than the *Perseverance* and much of this was in a deep draught hull of over 22ft. (The Trustees of National Museums Liverpool)

The three-masted barque *Lahore* was one of an increasing number of vessels with this economical rig. She was built at Liverpool in 1845 and had a tonnage of 535 tons. W.J. Lockett, her owner, used her for trading to the west coast of South America. She was shown off the Liverpool Pier Head in three positions. The cutter to the left was a Liverpool pilot boat.

The only wooden deep-sea sailing ship built at Liverpool to survive is the *Jhelum*. She was a full-rigged ship of 428 tons and was built in 1849 by Joseph Steel and Son at Queens Dock. Her builders also traded with her mainly to Chile and Peru. They sold her in 1863. In August 1870, she arrived in distress at Port Stanley in the Falkland Islands. In a storm in October 2009, the *Jhelum's* bow section collapsed

In 1871 she was condemned as unseaworthy, and beached to act as a store and workshop for the firm of Packe Brothers. Her masts and spars were removed (probably for re-use on other damaged ships calling at Stanley) and her stern area was clad in corrugated iron. A large loading hatch was cut in her sides and this has caused her hull to become distorted.

Above: Her deterioration in the bow has been speeded up by the loss of many planks along the wind and water line. This allows the full power of the waves to attack the frames which will eventually collapse. The diagonal component in the top-right corner is one of the iron knees that helped to make the *Jhelum* a very strong ship.

Left: The inside of the *Jhelum*'s hull is in fine condition under the roofed area but not so good in the bows. The port-side frames which are of English oak are intact but two of the horizontal deck beams which were fashioned from an equally tough tropical hardwood have rotted away. They can be seen in the centre and to the right. The iron knees which supported them from below are clearly visible.

Wooden sailing ships needed constant repair and this accident befell the *Baboo* when she was in Canning Number One dry dock. The wooden props (shores) that held her hull upright collapsed and her ballast shifted as she was being refloated in 1841. The picture recorded her salvage.

Collisions and stranding were common accidents for wooden sailing ships. Explosions were not. In 1863, the 300-ton barque *Lottie Sleigh* had taken a shipment of gunpowder while at anchor in the Mersey. There was a huge explosion which all but destroyed the ship and caused a lot of broken windows in Liverpool.

This seascape of about 1850 shows a full rigged ship ashore at low tide with a Mersey flat and a topsail schooner alongside receiving her cargo to lighten her. To the right a paddle tug is standing by and will attempt to tow her off at high tide. Such strandings were common events on the approaches to Liverpool.

Canning Dock and its neighbour Georges Dock were the two main docks where wooden sailing ships could still be seen towards the end of the nineteenth century. They were too shallow and small for large iron steamers. Georges Dock was a noted place for fruit schooners from the Azores and the Mediterranean.

Opposite below: The approaches to Liverpool were fraught with danger for a sailing ship. The prevailing westerly wind could drive ships ashore on the north bank of the estuary. This brig or barque which may have been the *Star of Hope* was blown ashore at Ainsdale some twenty miles north of Liverpool, probably in the 1880s. One hundred years later, a gale scoured her remains from the sand.

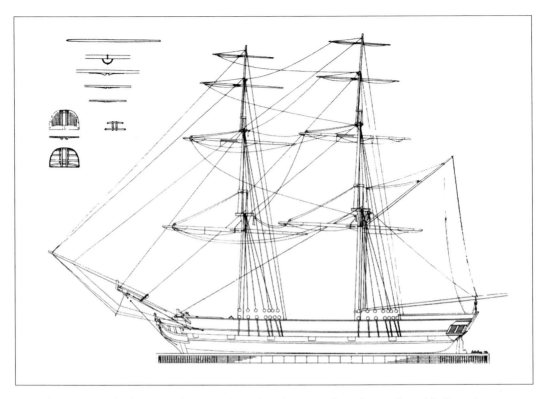

One of the sources of information about wooden sailing ships apart from shipwrecks and hulks such as the *Jhelum* are the surviving scale models of specific vessels. This plan was drawn by the late A.B. Salisbury from a contemporary model of the snow *Black Prince* of Liverpool of 1838. (The Trustees of National Museums Liverpool)

FOUR

Packet Ships and Clippers

In the early nineteenth century the average British sailing ship had a bluff hull designed to carry the maximum amount of cargo rather than to sail fast. There were a few exceptions such as the mail packet ships across the Atlantic and to southern Europe from Falmouth. Most ships sailing from Liverpool would depart only when their holds were full rather than sail according to an advertised timetable. This changed in 1818. The firms of Marshall and Thompson in New York and Cropper, Benson & Co. at Liverpool agreed to set up a shipping line which ran on a fixed route, with or without cargo, and sailing from each port on a fixed day of each month. Their Black Ball Line was an immediate success. The staple cargoes were raw cotton from New York and passengers and finished cloth back from Liverpool. The Line attracted imitators sailing from New York and other US east coast ports, and running services not only to Liverpool, but to France, Belgium, New Orleans and California.

The ships employed were all American-built and-owned. Shipbuilders like Donald McKay in Boston and William Webb, New York, built ships of increasing size and with finer lines that could travel the Atlantic in the fastest possible time. They increased the length of the hull in proportion to its width. Speed under sail is partly a function of length.

The term 'clipper' has been used loosely to describe any fast sailing ship. It was probably first applied to American fast schooners built around Baltimore in the first two decades of the nineteenth century. The first square-rigged clipper was launched at Baltimore in 1833. But it was the discovery of gold in California in 1848 and in Australia in 1850, and the repeal of the British Navigation Acts in 1849 which restricted foreign-built ships on the British flag, that gave a stimulus to the building of large fast clippers. Donald McKay was their leading builder and in 1854 received orders from James Baines & Co. of Liverpool for four huge clippers of over 2,000 tons. These were intended to make the fastest passage out to the goldfields of New South Wales. Baines' Liverpool-Australia Black Ball Line and its competitors, such as the White Star and Golden Lines, gave Liverpool owners a dominant role in the Gold Rush business. However, the boom began to evaporate by 1855.

The American shipbuilders' innovations were imitated by British shipbuilders who sought orders for clippers. These were mainly for the growing premium tea trade from China to London. The outbreak of the American Civil War in 1861 and the increasing efficiency of steamships together fatally damaged the American dominance of the Atlantic packet trades and clipper-building. John Jordan, a Liverpool shipbuilder, patented composite hull construction with iron frames and wooden planking in 1853. His system was adopted by British clipper shipbuilders and the *Cutty Sark* of 1869, the only clipper to survive, has this type of build. Liverpool shipbuilders were less involved in clipper-building than in producing iron-hulled sailing ships, cargo steamers and warships.

There were a few outright tea clippers built for Liverpool owners. The tea trade under sail gradually petered out in the 1870s thanks to the opening of the Suez Canal in 1869. This gave steamers a short route out to the Far East and enabled them to compete with sailing ships for this premium trade.

The Black Ball Line was the first of the packet ship lines. Their ships carried a distinctive black ball (what we call a 'logo' today) on their fore topsails. Rival lines carried other symbols such as a red star or a black 'T' for Train & Co.'s line. The latter ran to Boston from 1844 and eventually owned thirty ships which ran a sailing every week to and from Liverpool.

Two American packet ships pass each other in the River Mersey off New Brighton. Robert Salmon (1775–c.1845) has captured the power and beauty of the biggest ships using the port in the 1820s. The packet with long pennant is outward bound for New York and her decks are lined with passengers. (The Trustees of National Museums Liverpool)

The *Roger Stewart* was a later packet ship built in Maine by the Skolfield family in 1852. She measured 1,052 tons and carried as many as 600 passengers, most of whom would be accommodated in temporary bunks rigged in her upper hold. She sailed various routes and for a time served in the Black Star Line. Her last voyage was from Mobile to Liverpool with a cargo of cotton in 1860. She sank in a gale mid-ocean. (The Pejopscot Historical Society)

The American *Alliance* was painted in the Mersey by John Desilva who combined in mid-nineteenth-century Liverpool the trades of plumber and glazier while taking commissions for painting ship portraits. An American family of shipowners and masters were one of his patrons and this painting remains in the family home. (Private Collection)

Canadian shipbuilders would build very large ships on speculation and dispatch them to Liverpool for sale. James Smith, a shipbuilder of St John, New Brunswick, launched a 1,625-ton three-decked ship called the *Marco Polo* in April 1851. She was sent to Liverpool with a cargo of timber but failed to find a buyer. Captain Amos Crosby, her first master had her painted in full sail. (Yarmouth County Museum, Nova Scotia)

In 1852, the *Marco Polo* was bought by James Baines & Co. for their fast packet service out to Melbourne and the Australian goldfields in 1852. They packed her with over 900 passengers. Her new master James ('Bully') Forbes sailed to Melbourne and back in six months. The *Marco Polo* was lauded as the fastest ship in the world and the reputation of the new line was made. (Oscar and Peter Johnson Ltd)

The *Marco Polo* continued to sail on the Liverpool to Melbourne route until 1866. Her hull was fairly worn out with sailing through some of the stormiest waters in the world, she was reduced to carrying timber across the Atlantic. After her wreck on Prince Edward Island in 1883, some of her stern carvings were salvaged including this attractive carving of an elephant.

In 1852, Gibbs, Bright & Co. of London, Liverpool and Bristol, who were merchants and shipowners, decided that the Australian gold rush was a new business opportunity. They started the Eagle Line from Liverpool with the *Eagle* and the *Albatross* which were both built at St John, New Brunswick, in 1852 and 1851 by different builders. They were smaller than the *Marco Polo* at just over 1,000 tons.

James Baines & Co., after the *Marco Polo's* record voyage, were convinced that bigger clipper ships would give them an advantage. In 1853, they chartered Donald McKay's *Sovereign of the Seas* of 1852 for one voyage. On the basis of this, they ordered four huge clippers all of over 2,000 tons from him. The second of the batch, the *Champion of the Seas* was credited with sailing a record 427 miles in twenty-four hours – a record which stood until the era of the round-the-world super yachts. (The late H. Friberg)

James Baines was a great publicist and egomaniac and the third clipper was named after him. Her figurehead was carved from life in Liverpool and sent across to Boston for fitting on the ship. This picture shows her with extra sails (sky sails) above the usual four and extra light-weather (studding) sails extending out on the right of the foresails. (The late Alex A. Hurst)

The *James Baines* caught fire while she lay unloading at Huskisson Dock, Liverpool on 22 April 1857. The fire took complete hold and her masts and rigging were cut away and she was left to burn in the centre of the dock. Her charred hull was only fit for use as a coal-storage hulk. (Private Collection)

The *Donald McKay*, the last of the four and the biggest measured 2,604 tons and her sails amounted to 15,000 yards of canvas. Her topsails were so big that it was decided to give her an upper and lower topsail to make these important sails more manageable. Her figurehead of a kilted highlander is preserved at the Mystic Seaport Museum on the east coast of the USA. (The late Alex A. Hurst)

Right: Clipper ships required large crews to man them. This able seaman was believed to have been carved as a Liverpool tobacconist's sign. He is very similar to the standing full-length figureheads that graced the bows of many of these 1850s clippers. (The Trustees of National Museums on Merseyside)

Below: The fortunes of the Black Ball Line and other Liverpool lines declined in the late 1850s. There was a brief revival for the Black Ball Line in the early 1860s when they were able to buy some fine American clippers cheaply and employ them on a new service from Liverpool and London to Queensland. Their *Light Brigade* was originally the *Ocean Telegraph* of 1854. She survived James Baines & Co.'s two bankruptcies in 1866 and 1871 and continued taking regular sailings to Australia and New Zealand until 1875.

Cope's Philadelphia-Liverpool Line was one of the lesser packet lines. Their finest vessel was the *Shackamaxon*, 1,369 tons, built in 1851. She was auctioned at Liverpool in 1854 for the very good price of £28,000, and this compared well with the new price of the *Lightning* which was £30,000. The shipping business went through a series of cycles of booms and slumps and the canny shipowner would try and buy at the bottom of the cycle and then sell on in a boom period.

New docks were built at Liverpool to cope with the demand for quay space. In 1848, a complex of five docks was opened to the north of the existing ones. These included the Standley Dock which was equipped with capacious quayside warehouses which could receive cargoes such as cotton bales, spirit casks and other valuable commodities directly into storage. It and two similar docks were often used by clipper ships.

Opposite above: The 1,346-ton *Bosphorus* was built at St John, New Brunswick, in 1855 and bought by Rathbones, one of the Liverpool merchant houses specialising in the India and China trades. This ship is shown at the entrance of the Mersey with her uppermost (royal) sails and her fore and mainsails about to be furled. It would be an imprudent master who sailed up the crowded Mersey under full-sail in a stiff breeze. (The Trustees of National Museums Liverpool)

Rathbones were also one of the few Liverpool operators of tea clippers. They had the 826-ton
Scaufell built at Workington in 1858. Under Captain Robert Thomson she made her fastest passage
in 1866. Shortly afterwards Thomson left to join a steamship. His surviving letters to his wife show
the job of commanding a crack clipper was anything but glamorous: actually rather stressful and
frustrating. He was nevertheless proud of his ship and commissioned this portrait of her from a
Chinese artist in Hong Kong. (The Trustees of National Museums Liverpool)

Above: The *Cutty Sark* of 1869 was among the last of the fine-lined tea clippers. London-owned, she spent the years up to 1883 in the tea trade. She was then transferred to the wool trade from Australia and then sold to Portuguese owners and renamed *Ferreira* in 1895. She was still sufficiently famous for the Dock Board's photographer to take her picture in the West Float, Birkenhead in 1914.

Left: Merseyside Maritime Museum has a fine collection of packet and clipper models including the *Marco Polo, Flying Cloud, Fiery Cross, Scaufell, Vision, Cutty Sark* and this huge model of a 'Blackwall frigate'. This was the nickname for the large fast passenger ships that were built on the Thames for trade with the Far East and Australia. Her identity is unknown. But the fine-lined hull and tall masts which were so essential to fast clippers are very obvious.

FIVE

IRON TRAMPS

Liverpool shipbuilders were among the first to employ wrought iron to build ships. John Laird was the pioneer from 1829. Initially, he built only barges and steamers. The first iron sailing ship was built at Liverpool in 1836 and she was a 77-ton coaster. The first deep-sea iron ship was the *Ironsides* launched in 1838 by Jackson, Gordon & Co. from their yard in the South Docks. However, iron sailing ships remained rare until the mid-1850s. They were costly to build and there was a great deal of prejudice against them. Lloyd's Register, whose rules on the building of ships were highly influential with shipbuilders, owners and insurers, was slow to adapt to iron vessels. So much so, that in 1862, a separate breakaway Liverpool Iron Ship Register was established which lasted until 1885.

The early 1850s had seen an unprecedented boom in building fast ships and this finished with the end of the Crimean War in April 1856. In the slump that followed cargo-carrying sailing ships reverted to full-bodied hulls. Rapidly improving iron shipbuilding techniques allowed for the construction of long boxy structures. These were ideal for moving large quantities of bulk cargo at low, but still profitable freight rates. Sailing ships had much lower running costs than steamers and owners could allow them to linger, loading in difficult anchorage ports such as those on the west coast of South America. They could also be easily laid up in slumps. Their long hulls could have only been built in iron, and from the 1880s up to 1905 steel sailing ships continued to be built in British yards. Liverpool builders stopped in 1894. From 1869, more steamers were being built than sailing ships.

There were many Liverpool sailing ship owners in the second half of the nineteenth century. They tended to be small family firms or partnerships while the big steamship lines such as Cunard tended to be limited companies. Nevertheless a good living could be made by the local sailing ship owners. For example, R.W. Leyland, who owned some of the biggest Liverpool sailing ships in the 1880s, owned a mansion – Upton Manor – on the Wirral and drove a carriage and four.

The size of these bulk carriers continued to increase. The biggest were under the German flag, but Liverpool had some very big ships such as R.W. Leyland's *Liverpool*. Built in 1889, she could carry over 3,000 tons of cargo. The odd thing was that Liverpool was not very welcoming for sailing ships. The steam cargo lines took precedence and sailing ships were confined to the smaller, less convenient docks. There were also not many cargoes that could be obtained for sailing ships from Liverpool. Cheshire salt in bulk was the main one. Many Liverpool-owned ships loaded at coal ports such as those of South Wales, and then returned with cargoes such as wheat from California or Australia. Voyages were on a tramping basis which took them to wherever cargo was offered and not to a regular timetable.

The size of these of these ships also affected their rig. They had metal masts and spars (except for the very topmost ones) which were supported and worked by wire ropes. The topsails were divided into two sails which made for easier handling and later the next sail up – the topgallant was also divided into an upper and lower sail. As hulls grew longer and bigger and extra or jigger mast was added at the stern. A few ships had square sails on this jigger mast, but the most successful arrangement in terms of economical running was the four-masted barque rig.

Liverpool sailing ship owners had no more new ships built after 1897 and rapidly disposed of their fleets in the slump of the first decade of the twentieth century. A number survived under foreign ownership and a few such as the *Wavertree* in New York, or the *Glen Lee* in Glasgow, survived to become museum ships.

Laird & Co.'s shipyard at Birkenhead was the biggest on the Mersey. Although it tended to specialise in iron steamers and warships, it also built sailing ships. This print shows the yard around 1859. There are three sailing ships and an auxiliary steamer in the dry docks. The Merseyside Maritime Museum has a half-model of the 1,077-ton full-rigged ships *John Cropper* and *Calcutta* launched by Lairds for A. Clint & Co. of Liverpool in 1863.

William Potter set up his shipyard at Queen's Dock, Liverpool, in 1858. He specialised in iron sailing ships. He launched his masterpiece in 1891: the steel 2,903-ton four-masted barque *Wanderer*. Merseyside Maritime Museum has a fine model. The crew accommodation was in the centre of the ship in what was known as a 'Liverpool house'. This contributed to the structural strength as well as the comfort and safety of the crew. Deeply loaded bulk sailing ships often had their decks underwater when on passage, and sailors were often swept over the side. (The Trustees of Merseyside Maritime Museum)

The *Bayard* was a three-masted 1,335-ton iron ship built by Thomas Vernon & Son at Liverpool in 1864. Her hull was 219ft long and the length to width ratio was 6 to 1. Such a long narrow structure could not have been economically built in wood. In 1911, she served as a coal hulk at Ocean Harbour whaling station, South Georgia. She lies there today aground on a pinnacle of rock – the oldest surviving Liverpool-built iron sailing ship.

The rusting hulk of the *Garland* lies off Goose Green in the Falkland Islands. She was a 600-ton three-masted barque built by R.&J. Evans at Liverpool in 1865. She arrived in the Falklands in distress in 1897. Among her cargo was a consignment of sulphuric acid in glass carboys. These got smashed and the acid bit through her iron bottom plates causing her to leak badly.

Above: In the late nineteenth century, sailing ships were confined to the older smaller docks at Liverpool. Canning, Salthouse and Wapping Docks were always crowded with sailing ships in the 1890s. They were frequently photographed and this view, from Salthouse Dock towards Wapping, King's and Queen's Docks, contains a forest of masts and spars. The ship in the foreground has a very slab-sided hull which was typical of the bulk carrying sailers.

Right: The *Garland's* headless figurehead has been preserved at the Falklands Museum in Stanley. This is a fine piece and her garland is particularly well-carved. (The Falkland Islands Trust)

Conditions aboard the later iron sailing ships were very hard. Their gear was much heavier than their predecessors and the crews often smaller in number. They were frequently very low in the water when loaded which made them wet and dangerous. The steering position was right aft at the stern and without shelter. (Yarmouth County Museum, Nova Scotia)

Above: David Hughes and his sons were the last figurehead carvers. Hughes set up his business in 1890 close to the local shipyards at Queen's Dock. As business was slow, he diversified into carving antique furniture and eventually emigrated to Utah. He used his wife and daughters as his female subjects and this one was modelled by his wife. (Mrs Aneesa Thomas)

Right: The figurehead of the *Allahabad* in Salthouse Dock. This 1,186-ton iron ship was built for London owners by William Potter in 1864. Her figurehead was almost certainly carved by one of the half dozen Liverpool firms that specialised in carving figureheads and other ships' ornaments. Her damaged paintwork and the rust stains on the bow suggest she had had a rough passage.

Opposite below: Liverpool retained its distinct 'sailortown' around the docks with a mixture of shipping offices, pubs and seamens' homes. This 1890s trio have a seafaring air about them as they sit outside the Customs House in Canning Place. I would love to know what their story was. Were they between ships? Were they sleeping off a good session in a nearby pub?

The four-masted barque *Benares* was berthed temporarily on the north quay of Canning Half-tide Dock about 1910. Her master was waiting for the lock gates to open. She was one of the many British-owned sailing ships which had been sold to Norwegian owners (who could operate these vessels cheaply). She was not carrying her uppermost yard (the royals). Whether this was a temporary measure or a matter of economy is unclear.

Leaving Canning Half-tide Dock: a three-masted barque is ready to cast off, and the funnel of the tug which will tow her out into the Irish Sea can be seen in the centre of the picture. Penniless seamen often hung around hoping there might be vacancies in the crew and they could make a last minute 'pier-head' jump back into employment.

Messrs Tho. & Jno. Brocklebank and a few other local firms were able to continue in liner trade to India with sailing ships until the late 1880s, but then they were old and distinctively conservative firms. Harland & Wolff of Belfast built them the *Majestic* in 1875. She really was an aptly named, beautiful ship, and was photographed at the shipyard's fitting-out quay, ready for sea.
(National Museums and Galleries of Northern Ireland, Ulster Folk and Transport Museum)

The huge size of the late nineteenth-century sailing ships is brought home with this deck scene of Tho. & Jno. Brocklebank's *Bolan* of 1883. Looking forward from the stern, the figures of the firm's principals are dwarfed by her tall masts. (The Trustees of National Museums Liverpool)

The four-masted ship *Liverpool*, built for R.W. Leyland as the flagship of his fleet by Russell & Co. at Port Glasgow in 1889 was, at 3,300 tons among the biggest ships owned at Liverpool. She only lasted thirteen years and became a total loss after going ashore on Alderney in the Channel Islands. (The Trustees of National Museums Liverpool)

The four-masted barque *Windermere* was launched by Oswald & Mordaunt of Southampton, who were one of the most prolific of the later sailing shipbuilders for Fisher & Sprott of Liverpool. She too was over 3,000 tons. She was built of steel, and her topgallant sails have been divided into upper and lower sails to make them easier to handle. (The Trustees of National Museums Liverpool)

Right: The White Star Line is normally associated with liners such as the *Titanic.* It started as a line of Australian clippers in 1852. When the original owners became bankrupt in 1867, their flag and goodwill were bought by Thomas Ismay. He and his partner Joseph Imrie rebuilt the White Star Line into one of the leading transatlantic passenger liner companies. The line continued to run sailing ships and their last sailing ship was the training ship *Mersey.*

Below: The *Elissa* was a small three-masted barque built in Aberdeen in 1877 for her master-owner, Henry Fowler-Watt. He was obliged to sell her in 1897. She then passed though a whole series of foreign owners and progressively lost her original rig. She ended up as a motor coaster at Piraeus, Greece. Her sailing ship lines are still in evidence even though she has lost her clipper bow and masts.

She was rescued by the Galveston Historical Society. Restoration started with hull repairs at Piraeus with about 70 per cent of her plating being renewed. Rigging and fitting-out took place at Galveston, and the final result was a magnificently restored historic ship that was capable of going to sea. (Galveston Historical Society)

Opposite: The thoroughness of her restoration and the capabilities of her volunteer crew were put to the test in long voyages for example to New York in the Tall Ships Race. This dramatic picture is one of the best of a sailing ship in a gale. (Galveston Historical Society)

Many sailing ships were sunk in the First World War. A few sailing ships continued to deliver grain cargoes to the mills to Liverpool and Birkenhead. The Finnish four-masted barque *Lawhill* sailed up the Mersey in 1926 when the tugmen were on strike. The *Lawhill* was once briefly owned by Winram & Co. of Liverpool.

Other later sailing arrivals included wooden American and Canadian schooners loaded with timber such as the *Helen Mather* waiting for a lock into Birkenhead about 1920.

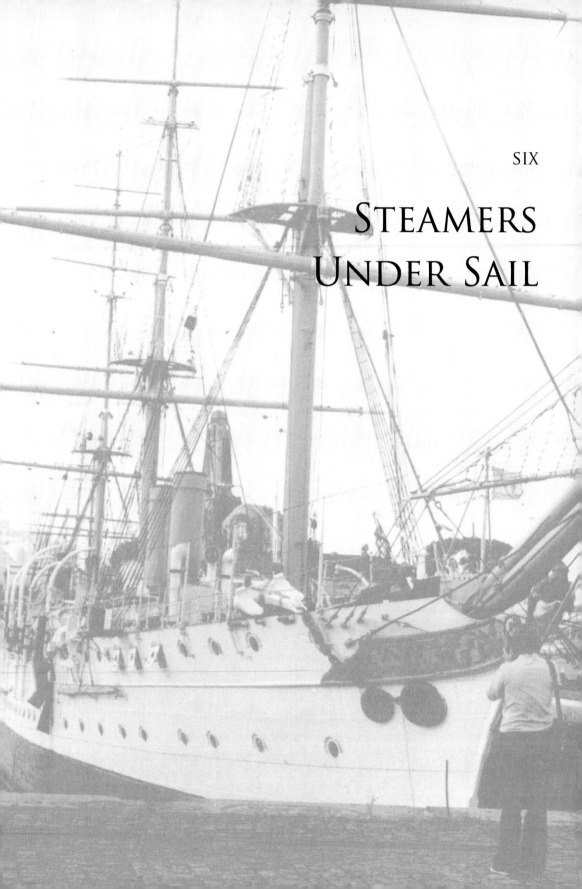

SIX

STEAMERS
UNDER SAIL

The previous chapters have probably given the impression that sailing ships and steamers were always in direct competition. That is true after about 1860 when the progress in boiler design and compound engines made it possible to build steamers that could not carry an economical quantity of cargo because of their large coal bunkers. Before that date steamers were really only viable on short distance routes or on long distance ones if they received a government subsidy for carrying mail, officials or soldiers. This left many plum trades such as the China tea trade to the sailing ship.

There was in fact a mutual dependence between the sailing ship and the steamer which started with the introduction of steam tugs in the 1820s and ran through to the end of the nineteenth century. The sailing ships came to depend on steam tugs to tow them in and out of harbour. Steam towage became important for the sailing packets that sought to run to a schedule and for the safety of the increasing size of ships – both in a regular 'pluck' into dock and in salvage situations when the ship had got ashore. Steamers on the long distance routes depended on regularly spaced coaling stations to refuel. Most of these stations had no local coal supplies and the most economical way of bringing them coal was to carry it in sailing ships. And even in old age, the sailing ship could be the servant of the steamer when she became a coal hulk swinging at a permanent mooring.

At the same time, all deep-sea steamers carried sails. They were needed in case of breakdown; there was no radio by which to summon help. A set of sails was 'a get you home' insurance policy and there were occasions when steamers with failed engines or broken propellers were forced to proceed under sail alone to the nearest port. Sails set in fair weather also helped ease the strain on the engines and contributed to the fuel economy. Incidentally, the idea of 'sail-assist' has been tried several times in the late twentieth century when oil fuel prices were rising rapidly. Perhaps they will be revived again if the present fuel price rises persist.

The fore and aft sails also contributed to the stability of a ship in heavy weather. They were often retained when the square sails were removed. Most of the passenger liners had the latter taken off around the 1890s as an economy measure. But the triangular staysails were often fitted to new vessels into the early twentieth century. Most of the masters of steamers and marine superintendents of shipping lines had done their apprenticeships in sailing ships and were happy to retain sails on their steamers.

The *Great Britain* was a pioneer steamer designed by the great Victorian engineer I.K. Brunel. She set all sorts of precedents in terms of screw propulsion and iron construction. What is perhaps not appreciated is that she was also an innovative sailing ship. She had iron masts with iron wire-rigging; her topmasts could be easily lowered to reduce rolling in bad weather and her gaff sails were permanently rigged aloft and could be set by only two men. After her salvage from running ashore at Dundrum Bay in 1846, she was re-rigged, first as a four-masted vessel and then as a standard three-masted full-rigged ship. In fact, she had been changed from a steamer into a sailing ship with an auxiliary steam engine, and she performed very satisfactorily on the Australian route in this guise from 1852 until 1876. Several other large steamers were converted into sailing ships when their engines and boilers wore out.

The early Liverpool paddle tugs were often dual purpose vessels used for both towage and as passenger tenders to ferry people out to ships anchored in the Mersey. About 1853, the *Lady Ebrington* had been chartered to take the 3rd Lancashire Militia to Gibraltar. This woodcut shows some of the soldiers being transferred from a tug to the ship. The same tug would have no doubt towed the ship out of the Mersey into the Irish Sea once she had her full complement.

Inward bound, a large full-rigged ship was in charge of two tugs waiting for the Canning Half-tide Dock gates to open. This entrance was difficult to enter because of the force of the current running past it. The second tug alongside the ship would have pushed sideways on her hull to keep her lined up with the entrance while the head tug towed her in.

Opposite: Most later sailing ships picked up their tugs off the Mersey approach Channel some 7 miles out from Liverpool. The three-masted barque *Kilmallie* has just picked her tow. She still has some sails up to steady her and the Liverpool pilot boat stationed at the Mersey Bar can be seen in the background.

Right: The four-masted barque *Moshulu* was inward bound with a cargo of grain for Birkenhead probably in the 1930s. Screw-propelled tugs gradually replaced paddle tugs from the 1860s. The *Moshulu* is still afloat as a restaurant in Philadelphia, USA. The tug belonged to the Alexandra Towing Co. of Liverpool.

Sailing ships carrying cargo even coastwise became less and less frequent in the Mersey after the Second World War. But sailing ships needing a tow never stopped altogether. Now, they were sail training ships and the Polish three-masted ship *Dar Pomorza* of 1909 was an early arrival in the 1950s.

Left: The topsail schooner *Emma & Esther* off Canning Half-tide Dock entrance in charge of a small tug owned by J.H. Lamey & Co. of Liverpool in 1927. She was inward bound from Bridgwater, Somerset. She was built in 1873 and was broken up in 1930 – fifty-three years of hard service in the coasting trade. (The late David Smith Collection, the Trustees of National Museums Liverpool)

Below: I.K. Brunel's *Great Britain* of 1843 was an innovative sailing ship as well as a pioneering iron screw-propelled steamer. Since her salvage from the Falkland Islands in 1971, she has been progressively restored back to her original appearance including the reinstatement of her six-masted rig.

Opposite above: The *Great Britain* in her second rebuild was given a full three-masted ship rig. Her new steam engine was an auxiliary unit and her propeller could be raised when not required. This shows her at the end of a voyage from Liverpool waiting for the pilot schooner before entering the port of Melbourne.

Centre: I.K. Brunel's *Great Eastern* was the last and biggest of his three ships. Launched on the Thames in 1858 it was about three times as big as any existing ship and was designed to sail out to Australia or the Far East. She was equipped with a screw propeller, paddles and no less than six masts. She was never sailed on her intended route: In 1861 she carried over 2,000 soldiers from Liverpool to Canada and then made several trips from Liverpool to New York over the next two years. In 1888, she was broken up on the Mersey after various roles as a cable ship and a fun fair. (The Trustees of National Museums Liverpool)

Below: Established in 1840, the Cunard Line was the first successful transatlantic passenger and mail service. It depended on a Government grant for carrying the mail and on its impeccable reputation for safe crossings. Early paddle steamers could steam faster than screw-propelled vessels. In 1856, the Cunard Line commissioned the *Persia* in order to capture the transatlantic speed record. She proved very successful and worked for the Line until 1868 after which she was converted into a pure sailing ship. (The Trustees of National Museums Liverpool)

Auxiliary steamers were a compromise between a sailing vessel and a steamer. The *Antelope* was a 600-ton auxiliary steamer designed by John Grantham, a pioneer Liverpool naval architect in 1846. She was intended for the Brazilian trade. She was lengthened and re-engined to sail for Miller & Thompson's Australian Golden Line. She made at least one trip to Melbourne, after which her career is unrecorded.

Thomas Ismay's White Star Line became a major force in the transatlantic liner trade in the 1870s. Their new steamers were noted for their spacious accommodation and their speed. They were also very long and narrow with a length to width ratio of 10 to 1. The *Britannic* of 1874-5 can be seen off the Liverpool Landing Stage in the 1880s and is rigged as a four-masted barque.

There was astonishing competition on the Atlantic after 1860 with more than half a dozen major steamer lines running from Liverpool. The Guion Line emerged from the old Black Star Line of packet ships when one of its partners – Stephen Guion – set up his own line in 1866. His *Arizona* of 1879 was notable for being the largest and fastest liner on the Atlantic. (The Trustees of National Museums Liverpool)

The Allan Line ran steamers from Liverpool to Canadian ports from 1854. When launched in 1881, their ship *Parisian* was the largest steel ship afloat. She is lying at anchor off Waterloo Dock, Liverpool. Like many liners she was four-masted, which was partly a matter of prestige and partly to support cargo derricks and sails. Her rig was much simpler than her predecessors with only square sails on the foremast.

Many cargo liners carried sails. The *Pindari* of 1891 was only Tho. & Jno. Brocklebank's third steamer and being a conservative-minded company, they equipped her with sails. But her rig is much simplified with only three square sails and triangular staysails instead of the large gaff sails. This saved on spars aloft and the number of crew needed on-board.

The *Lady Jocelyn* had been built as an auxiliary steamer in 1852 for running between Southampton and Australia. She was later converted into a sailing ship and finally became the Shipping Federation's base ship for breaking seamens' strikes such as that at Liverpool in 1911.

Most liners had straight bows, but the Inman Line's *City of Paris* of 1889 was an exception. A lean 10,000-ton vessel with a graceful clipper bow and figurehead, she is seen amidst a busy high tide on the Mersey with two sailing ships to her left, a ferry and two Mersey sailing flats to her right. This painting by Max Sinclair is dated 1889 which suggests it was painted to commemorate her maiden voyage to New York (The Trustees of National Museums Liverpool)

The *Navahoe* of 1907 was a 7,700-ton six-masted schooner-barge for carrying oil in bulk. She was towed by the oil tanker *Iroquois,* and seen here entering one of Cammell Laird's dry docks about 1910. Her sails were designed to assist the engines of the *Iroquois*. This novel outfit was not copied.

Cammell Laird built many naval vessels for foreign navies. The light cruiser *Capitan O'Brien* of 1901 was built for the Chilean Navy . Notice that she carries two steadying sails on her fore stays. These were probably rigged for the long delivery voyage which involved rounding Cape Horn because there was no Panama Canal until 1914.

Left: Two of Lairds' sailing warships (the Cammell was added in 1903) have been preserved at Buenos Aires. The *Uruguay* was built as a cruising gunboat for the Argentine Navy in 1874. She measured 550 tons and was capable of voyaging under sail alone on long-range patrols. She was famous for rescuing the members of the Nordensklold Expedition from the Antarctic Peninsula in 1903 after their own ship had been crushed.

Below left: The *Presidente Sarmiento* was built in 1897 as a training ship for the Argentine Naval Academy. She measured 2,750 tons and had a 1,000hp 3-cylinder compound steam engine and a ship rig. She made thirty-seven annual cruises including six circumnavigations of the world. She became a stationary training ship from 1938 to 1961. Today, both she and the *Uruguay* are on public display and are a great statement to the building quality of Laird Brothers.

Above right: Sails lasted into the era of diesel engines. The Dutch shipbuilders, who were among the pioneers of diesel for ships, produced a series of coastal motor schooners during the First World War. One of them, the *De Wadden*, was bought by Irish shipowners Hall & Tyrrell of Arklow in 1921. She was the last sailing vessel to trade into the Mersey and was bought by Merseyside Maritime Museum in 1984. This picture shows her undergoing restoration in the Museum's dry dock at Canning Dock.
(The Trustees of National Museums Liverpool)

SEVEN

SERVICE
UNDER SAIL

The first organised pilotage service on the Mersey started in 1766. The same service continues to this day because the need for expert advice to enter and leave the River Mersey safely remains. The first pilot boats were cutters about 50ft long and painted in distinctive stripes with large numbers painted on their sails. By the early 1800s, there were about a dozen of them carrying six or seven pilots and a crew of a master and three trainee pilots. There were usually two masters so that boats could be kept at sea as much as possible. They were normally stationed in a chain that started off the north coast of Anglesey to the Mersey Bar. This meant that ships seeking a pilot had several opportunities to pick one up.

It was a hazardous job because the cutters kept station in all but the worst storms. The most dangerous part was the transfer from the pilot boat to the ship in a small rowing boat. In 1852, larger two-masted schooners were introduced to replace the cutters. They continued to provide the service until 1896. The increasing volume of steamers had put them at risk, and half of the twelve in service had been sunk or badly damaged in collisions with steamers. Fog was a particular hazard in the days before radar.

Mersey gig boats were open rowing and sailing boats which were used as water taxis in the River and for assisting with passing ropes between the ships and the quays. They carried out passengers and their luggage to ships at anchor in the river. They would also convey ships' agents and crews and even prostitutes to inward bound ships. Competition between gigs was fierce and some were known to sail out as far as Holyhead seeking inward bound ships. Gig boatmen were a fairly lawless lot and the Dock Board insisted on issuing licences to them in the 1860s. In 1863, they also established a police gig to patrol the Mersey.

Gig boats were rigged with two or three spritsails. The third sail was usually rigged in the summer. Spritsails can be set and brought in very quickly which is a useful attribute in a small boat. They could also be rowed by two or more men. Gig owners liked to race their boats in summer and several sailing gigs were retained for racing after the introduction of motor boats in the 1930s. The New Brighton Sailing Club used gig boats and later a modified design of gig boat for their races.

Ferries to cross the Mersey were another important local service. Until steam ferries arrived in the early nineteenth century, passengers, goods and animals and horse-drawn carriages were all regularly transported in sailing and rowing boats. There were two sizes of sailing ferry. The larger ones were decked and carried on the longer distance services to Runcorn and to Eastham; the smaller ones were open. They were variously rigged. The late seventeenth-century ferries seem to have been rigged with a single square sail. But later ones could be lug-, sloop- or schooner-rigged. They died out around about 1850 because they could not offer the reliability of the steam ferries.

The local sailing and rowing lifeboats must also be mentioned. The first lifeboat station was set up at Formby on the approach to the Mersey in 1775. It was probably the first of its kind in the British Isles. The volume of ships entering the Mersey, with the consequent increase in casualties, grew to such an extent that the port authorities established a network of six stations from the Point of Air on the coast of Wales to the Liverpool Pier Head. In addition, there were RNLI stations at New Brighton and Southport.

The first Liverpool pilot boats were cutters which were fairly tubby in shape but thoroughly seaworthy. No.9, the *Liver*, the second of that number, was built in 1796 and entered the Service in 1799. She measured 42 tons and was 46ft long by 15ft 4in beam. (The Trustees of National Museums Liverpool)

Georges Dock and its entrance basin was the base of the pilot cutters and one of them can be seen hoisting its mainsail. The tower to the right was used for the semaphore signal station which gave early warning of ships approaching Liverpool.

Transferring or collecting pilots to ships was hazardous because they were ferried across in small rowing boats known as punts. The ship *Sandbach* has her mainsails backed to slow her to take on her pilot.

Bigger and faster schooners were introduced with No.6 *Pioneer* in 1852. No.1, the *Queen* was the fourth built. Launched in 1856, she measured 61 tons and was 79ft long by 17ft beam. She was built by Michael Ratsey, a noted Isle of Wight yacht-builder and was sold out of the Service in 1898. She had another thirty-five years working life, latterly as an Icelandic fishing boat. (The Trustees of National Museums Liverpool)

Georges Dock about 1870 with a pilot schooner in the foreground. The schooner's punt can be seen hoisted up amidships. To its left, there is a small canvas screen or dodger which gave the pilot waiting to board some shelter.

Pilot schooner No.9, the *Guide* of 1862, was built at Ramsey in the Isle of Man. At 90 tons she was bigger than her predecessors. She was sunk by the steamer *Mariner* in February 1882. Collisions with steamers became an increasing problem for these schooners.

The *Mersey*, No. 11 was built by William Thomas at Amlwch, a tiny port on the north coast of Anglesey in 1875. This drawing is taken from a faded photograph of her on the building berth. She was built entirely in the open and her timbers were fashioned with hand tools.

On-board the *George Holt*, the last pilot schooner built. The men with the caps on to the left and right appear to be the pilots, and the master appears to be the man in the tam o'shanter. The boy is a puzzle because he is too young to have been an apprentice pilot. Note the octagonal skylight in the foreground.

This was presumably a royal visit to the Mersey and may be the occasion of the extension of Birkenhead docks in 1866. The warship is firing a salute and in the foreground, four pilot schooners are anchored and dressed overall.

Pilot schooners managed to deliver their pilots on most occasions whatever the weather. It was unusual for them to have to signal waiting ships to follow them in over the Mersey Bar. This happened on 8 February 1881 when the *Leader* conducted a fleet of ships to safety. The incident was commemorated in several paintings by the local artist J. Witham.

No.7, *Lancashire Witch* was painted by J. Ogilvy off the outer pilot station at Point Lynas, Anglesey. Built by Michael Ratsey in 1863, she was withdrawn from the Service in 1896. Notice she carries a full rig with a topsail on the mainmast. There were no additional sails on the foremasts and the bowsprit could be slid inboard in rough weather or in dock. (The Trustees of National Museums Liverpool)

The *George Holt* was built in 1892 at Dartmouth by Philip & Son and started a long line of orders to this shipyard from the Mersey Docks & Harbour Board. She only lasted on the Mersey until 1904. In that year, she was sold for trading around the Falkland Islands and sank in Stanley harbour in 1933.

Gig boats seem to have originated in the eighteenth century. In this dramatic scene of 1796 a group was assisting a fire-stricken brig and the crew of the two-masted ferry schooner appeared to be salvaging something from the water.

Gig boats were always kept handy around Georges Dock Basin or the neighbouring tidal inlets. Two gigs can be seen afloat with a third on the quay. Their spritsails could be easily furled and can be seen lashed to their foremasts.

Gig boats normally carried two spritsails with one on the foremast and a smaller mizzen projecting over the stern. This made for a handy balanced rig with plenty of space amidships for rowing. In summer and for long seeking trips out into Liverpool Bay a third mainmast might be added as can be seen in Queens Dock about 1840. (Private Collection)

Gig boats were also raced extensively in local regattas over the summer and even after motor gigs had been introduced; some sailing gigs were retained for racing only. The New Brighton Sailing Club also adopted the gig design for their first yachts.

Above: This view of Liverpool from the Mersey in about 1831 shows a gig boat in the foreground with passengers on-board coming alongside a Mersey flat. Presumably, the gigs passengers are going to transfer to the flat, perhaps for a passage inland to Manchester.

Right: This ferry schooner was not the main subject of the painting and yet the artist, John Jenkinson, has captured her appearance very well. She has two tall masts unsupported by any rigging and no bowsprit. This was known as a shallop rig and could be found on boats used to ferry sugar casks to ships at anchor off the West Indian sugar-producing islands.

Opposite below: Gig boats could be used for providing pleasure trips from the beaches of local seaside resorts. The Bootle shore which is now lined with docks was an important local resort in the early nineteenth century and a number of gigs can be seen plying for hire with a group of bathing machines in the background.

This shows one of the smaller single-masted ferries caught in a squall off New Brighton lighthouse in the 1830s. Transporting a horse in such a small boat must have been difficult even in calm weather. Possibly this was artistic licence to make the foreground interesting.

The Southport lifeboat station was the most northerly of the stations set up around Liverpool Bay in the nineteenth century. The Southport lifeboat *Eliza Ferneley* went to the rescue of the crew of the German barque *Mexico* stranded at Ainsdale in 1886. Unfortunately, she overturned, drowning all but two of her crew.

The Liverpool boatbuilder Thomas Costain was responsible for developing the 'Liverpool' type of lifeboat from 1841. This was both light and seaworthy and could be launched from beaches. In 1851 his design was endorsed by the RNLI and influenced the hull-shape and lay-out of many later rowing/sailing lifeboats such as the *Dodo* stationed at Workington in 1886.

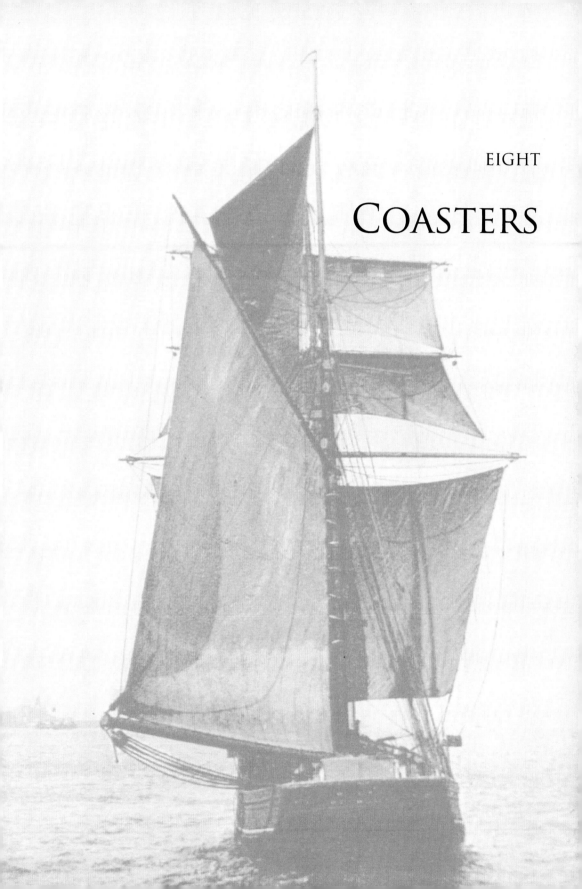

EIGHT

COASTERS

Coastal and Irish traffic grew along with the oceanic trades in the eighteenth and nineteenth centuries. In 1850, they accounted for about one-sixth of the total volume of shipping using the port. Coastal traffic was divided between the packet and the bulk trades. The former was conducted in small single-masted sloops and cutters. They carried on fairly regular services to Ireland, the Isle of Man, the Clyde, North Wales, Lancashire and Cumbria. The most important were the postal and passenger packets, many of which went from either Parkgate on the Dee or Holyhead rather than Liverpool. The main freights were small consignments of goods for local shopkeepers and for the country gentry. These could be anything from barrels of spirits to books, bales of paper and bales of cloth. They were vital links in the distribution of freight to and from Liverpool.

In the 1820s these packets were gradually displaced by steamships which could provide faster and more reliable sailings. The building of a national network of railways from the 1830s onwards also contributed to the decline of the sailing packets. The longest sailing service was to London and the main export was Cheshire cheese. Despite the distance, it was cheaper to send the cheese by water than by road. It was mainly loaded upriver at Frodsham.

Bulk cargoes included copper ore from Anglesey, all kinds of corn and agricultural produce from Ireland, lead from the Dee and timber from North Wales. Building materials, though a low-paying freight, were always being brought in for the expanding towns of Lancashire. They included bricks from the Dee, roofing slates from North Wales and granite setts from Annalong in Northern Ireland and from Scotland. Stone provided one of the last paying cargoes for sailing coasters. China clay loaded in South Devon and Cornwall was carried up the Mersey to Runcorn where it was trans-shipped into canal boats for onward transport to the Staffordshire potteries. Coal and Cheshire salt were staple return cargoes from the Mersey.

Late seventeenth-century coasters had changed rig from the old barque rig to a fore and aft sail. As can be seen in the 1680 painting of Liverpool, the coasters have been painted with four-sided mainsails with a gaff at the top and a boom at the bottom, and with triangular foresails. The bigger coasters tended to remain square-rigged until the end of the eighteenth century. These brigs and snows were gradually displaced by schooners, especially topsail schooners. These combined the manoeuvrability of the fore and aft rig with the driving power of square topsails on the foremast.

Runcorn was a major centre for building and running schooners in the nineteenth century. Many schooners survived with auxiliary engines until the Second World War. They carried china clay and pit props inward and took coal out to the West Country and Ireland. Their numbers were gradually reduced through old age and wreck, and the last cargoes were carried in 1960.

Regular Communication
BETWEEN
IVERPOOL AND MARYPORT.

THE FINE FAST-SAILING NEW SCHOONER

JOHN GLAISTER,
DAN GLAISTER, Master;

Sail punctually Once a Fortnight, with Goods and Passengers, Liverpool for MARYPORT, COCKERMOUTH, KESWICK, NBY, WIGTON, &c. and return from MARYPORT, after lying eek, with the same punctuality, weather permitting.
ppers are requested to be very particular in directing their s to be sent to the *John Glaister*, Canning Dock, Liverpool.
r further information apply to the AGENTS,

J. NELSON WOOD & CO.
24, CHAPEL-WALKS, LIVERPOOL.

Liverpool was the hub of coastal packet services around and across the Irish Sea and further afield as far as London. Maryport on the Cumbrian coast was a coal-exporting port which had a packet service provided by the *John Glaister* in 1825. The advert promises punctuality, weather permitting.

Canning Dock was the centre of much of this packet trade. Even after these regular services disappeared, it remained one of the docks that specialised in handling coastal ships. About 1890, a ketch can be seen about to berth on the south quay with a sloop (possibly of Welsh ownership) already tied up there.

The coasting ketch *Alfred* setting sail just outside Canning Half-tide Dock entrance. She has her anchor down and it looks as if she may be at risk of being swept into the river wall by the tide.

Salthouse Dock connects with Canning Dock and was another gathering place for coastal sailing ships at the end of the nineteenth century. To the left there are two topsail schooners with a Weaver steam barge (or packet) astern and on the right a ketch. Ketches had a smaller mast aft and no square sails.

A schooner and a steam barge alongside Canning Half-tide Dock north quay in the 1920s. This quay had a depot for receiving stone imported mainly from Ireland. Most of it was delivered in sailing schooners.

By the twentieth century most coastal sailing vessels were ketches or two- or three-masted schooners. There were occasional exceptions such as this Scandinavian four-masted schooner under repair in Canning dry dock No. 2 in the 1930s.

The *Henrietta* of Truro was photographed by the late David Smith at Canning Half-tide Dock north quay in 1928. He managed to photograph many of the last coastal sailing ships calling at Liverpool before the Second World War. (The late David Smith Collection, Trustees of National Museums Liverpool)

Opposite above: Many of the coastal schooners were the objects of great pride to their owners. Some were also owned by their skippers. In spite of their small size, many such as the *Old Hunter* carried figureheads. Notice also the flax canvas sail hauled up to dry before it rots.

Opposite below: Congestion was a feature of Runcorn docks around the 1900s. It specialised in china clay. Most of these schooners carried no more than 200 tons of cargo. They carried coal back to their home ports. The schooner on the right is the *Tregunnel* of Padstow.

The three-masted schooner *Fanny Crossfield* lies at anchor in the Mersey in the 1930s as the latest White Star liner the *Britannic* sails for New York. The former was built at Carrickfergus in 1880 by Paul Rodgers, one of the best of the schooner-builders. Today, her last remains lie buried in the mud of Strangford Lough.

The *Lochranza Castle* outward bound, probably with coal from Runcorn or Garston, makes a fine sight off Birkenhead. She was built in 1876 at Ardrossan and was only 76 gross tonnage. Nevertheless she continued to find employment until lost at sea in the early 1930s.

This topsail schooner was also photographed outward bound about 1900. Her name is unknown, but her small size and chunky lines suggest that she was a good age. Possibly she was built on the east coast of England where schooners tended to be smaller and a bluffer shape than those built in the West Country.

A steam tug has three schooners in tow in the 1920s. They are in the act of setting their sails and will cast off the tow very soon. Coastal sailing ships were entitled to a free tow up the Manchester Ship Canal to Runcorn after it opened in 1894. (The late David Smith Collection, the Trustees of National Museums Liverpool)

Above: Barquentines were three- or four-masted vessels with square sails on the foremast and fore and aft sails on the others. The *Waterwitch* was the last barquentine under the British flag. By the 1920s, she was no longer capable of deep-sea trading and worked in the china clay trade until laid up in 1935. (The late David Smith Collection, the Trustees of National Museums Liverpool)

Left: A second view of the *Waterwitch* in the Mersey carrying most of her sails with a Wallasey ferry in the background. (The late David Smith Collection, the Trustees of National Museums Liverpool)

Schooners built in the North West of England were generally a different shape to those from Wales and the West Country. They were flatter on the bottom and many could sail without ballast and they had a short rounded stern with the rudder hung abaft it. This is the *Nellie Bywater* tacking across the Mersey in a light condition. She was built at Millom, Cumbria in 1873. (The late David Smith Collection, the Trustees of National Museums Liverpool)

My Lady running before the wind in light weather. Her mainsail and its topsail are well over to port and there is a large light-weather square sail rigged below the two topsails on the foremast. She was built at Kingsbridge, Devon in 1889 and was deeper with finer lines than the *Nellie Bywater*. (The late David Smith Collection, the Trustees of National Museums Liverpool)

Above: The Albert Dock and the adjacent docks were closed to all traffic in 1971. A Government-funded development corporation restored them as amenities in 1984 and since then there have been a succession of visits by former coastal sailing vessels. This German-built iron topsail schooner *Trade Winds* lay at Canning Half-tide Dock north quay for sale in the mid-1990s.

Left: The West Country ketch *Bessie Ellen* was rescued from Denmark in the 1990s and now earns a living carrying passengers. She has made several visits to Liverpool for the Mersey River Festival and in 2004 was tied up at the same berth in Canning Dock as the ketch and sloop pictured at the start of this chapter.

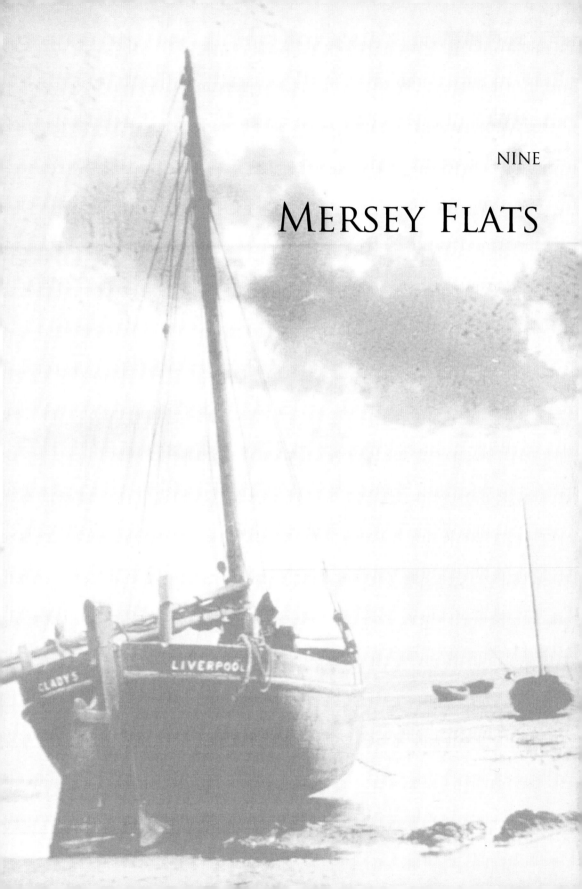

NINE

MERSEY FLATS

Just as the Severn had its Trow and the Humber its Keel, the Mersey had its own distinctive sailing barge: the Flat. Flats probably evolved from the coasters and sailing lighters that served Liverpool and its outer anchorage at Hoylake in the late seventeenth century. The original flats were square-rigged like the Humber keels and some of the inland trading ones seem to have retained that rig up until about 1750. Most flats were sloop-rigged with a large mainsail and a single foresail. Some of the coastal ones also carried bowsprits, and in the late nineteenth century a number of large two-masted ketch or jigger flats were built for coastal trading.

As the name suggests flats were flat-bottomed. They were very stoutly built with a round bow and either a square (transom) or a round stern. The hull shape was designed for cargo capacity and not speed, and their skippers were adept at working the strong tides on the Mersey. They also had very large hatches for ease of cargo handling which also meant that the rest of the hull had to be as stiff as possible to resist bending and flexing especially when lying aground.

Internally, they were framed in a way that suggested they originated from an older type of vessel, and the little rail around the stern also hinted at an older coaster origin. The earlier pictures of flats show them with a raised stern. This was eliminated by about 1770 and they became virtually flat in profile. They were often loaded right down until their decks were awash. Some of the coastal flats either had guard ropes or built-up rails to protect the crew. The latter seem to have been sometimes called sloops. All the same they had a flat-shaped hull. A few were even converted to topsail schooners in the mid-nineteenth century. Their wide hatches made them vulnerable in heavy seas.

'Inside' flats, which traded inland up the navigable rivers Weaver, Mersey, Irwell and Douglas and artificial waterways including the Sankey and the Bridgewater Canals, were built with lowering masts to negotiate fixed bridges. Where the wind could not assist them, they were towed by gangs of men or horses. In 1836, the Mersey & Irwell Navigation was the first to use steam tugs to tow flats. From 1863, self-propelled steam flats which were nicknamed 'packets' were successfully introduced on the Weaver and they too were used to tow flats. The result was that the sailing flats which had once numbered hundreds began to lose their sails and new dumb flats were built which retained the old hull design but without the sails. The last trades for sailing flats were the delivery of coal to steamers anchored in the Mersey and the dredging of sand for the Lancashire glass industry. The last flat to sail was the *Keskadale* of Widnes which carried sails until about 1945.

Perhaps the Mersey Flat should be called the North West of England Flat because flats were built from Conway on the coast of North Wales right up to Whitehaven on the Cumbrian coast. This shows what a versatile design of sailing barge it was. The last sailing flats to be built were launched at Sankey Bridges on the Sankey Canal in 1905-6. But dumb flats continued to be built in small numbers right up to 1954.

Right: Flats probably developed in the early eighteenth century from the small coasters that traded out of Liverpool. They were probably square-rigged like the sixteenth-century Carrickfergus ship (1) and square-rigged flats were used on the Mersey inland as shown in prints of 1728 and 1742 (2 and 4). At the same time, a coastal flat with fore and aft sails was in existence as shown in the 1728 print. (4)

Below: Sailing flats at anchor off Liverpool waiting for the tide to change in 1877. The strong Mersey tides governed the flats' movements. Sailing flats were still numerous in this decade.

Above: Flats were literally flat-bottomed and their hulls were strongly built to allow them to sit on the bottom at low tide. Here a two-masted flat (known as a jigger flat) and a sloop-rigged flat are lying on the shore near Widnes in about 1900.

Right: Widnes West Bank Dock around 1900 was a major centre for flats. This photograph showed five flats and a topsail schooner. The flat in the foreground has rails around her deck which indicated that she was a coastal trader. She also carried a second staysail. Her wind vane showed that she was the *Liverpool* of 1877. (The Trustees of National Museums Liverpool)

Opposite above: Two flats under sail off Salisbury Dock, Liverpool in 1882. This showed their simple rig of gaff mainsail and foresail. The mainsail had a distinctive sharply angled gaff. Both were well loaded and towing their cock boats astern.

Opposite below: A more romantic vision of a flat seen from astern off Birkenhead on a sunny day.

Flats came in a wide range of sizes. The tiny *Gladys* was probably no more than 15 tons and was probably used for carrying sand from local sand banks.

At the other end of the range, there were some ketch-rigged or jigger flats. *Santa Rosa* was the last sailing flat built. Launched broadside at Sankey Bridges in 1906 she measured 94 gross tons.

The hulls of flats were built up with heavy frames and thick planking, and many lasted with regular repairs for more than half a century. The *Chester* was launched in 1827 and was still delivering heavy cargoes of stone for the Dock Board in 1906. (The Trustees of National Museums Liverpool)

The *Keskadale* was the last flat to trade under sail. She was used to collect sand dredged up from the Mersey estuary and deliver it to Widnes West Bank Dock. She would use her sails when the wind served; otherwise she would accept a tow. In this case, she was under tow from the owner's motor yacht.

Above The fate of most flats was either abandonment or burning. Their strong hulls made them difficult to break up. These flats were dumped in the bottom basin of the flight of locks from the Mersey to the Bridgewater Canal at Runcorn. Note that the flat on the left has a square stern which was as common as the round stern. These flats remain buried to this day. (The late Jack Parkinson)

Left: The *Oakdale*, built in 1953 is one of two surviving flats, Her latter owner rigged her with a small mast. Today, she is based at Millom, Cumbria.

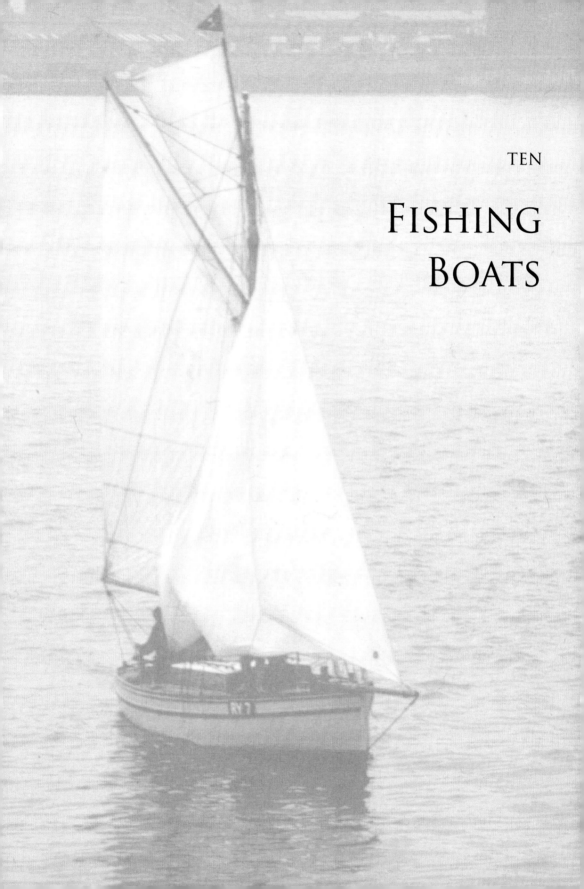

TEN

FISHING
BOATS

Liverpool never developed as a major fishing port. But it had a long history as a place to sell fish. Many fishing boats from other parts delivered their catches to the fish market. In the past, Liverpool Bay was also noted for its seasonal shoals of herring. Above Liverpool there were once fixed fish traps stretching out from the banks of the river. Some of these must have been quite long because in 1694 they had to be demolished to make the river navigable up to Warrington.

Medieval and Tudor fishing boats based in Liverpool were almost certainly dual-purpose vessels that could carry cargo or catch fish according to the season. Late eighteenth and early nineteenth-century prints and paintings suggest that local fishing boats at that period were two-masted luggers. There is also a late eighteenth-century ship bowl which depicts a two-masted schooner trawling. It may be that this was exceptional, on the other hand, small two-masted schooners were employed as ferries and were certainly in use for fishing around the Irish Sea.

By the late nineteenth century Hoylake was the local centre for owning fishing trawlers. Large ketch-rigged trawlers based there would go out into the Irish Sea and trawl for up to a week and then deliver their catch to Liverpool. Many called at the Albert Dock from the early 1900s because a new refrigerated store in one of the warehouses could supply them with ice to preserve their catches. The last one, the *Robert and Ellen* seems to have been fishing under sail and motor into the 1940s.

A smaller inshore boat, known as a 'nobby', was also found on the Mersey. They were single-masted cutters, 32ft long on average. They specialised in trawling for shrimps or prawns. They had to have little draught to work the best grounds and fast to deliver their perishable catch. Many carried small boilers to prepare their catches before they were landed. There was a large fleet based at Southport up the coast from Liverpool where they supplied the holiday trade. There were also smaller fleets based at the Cockle Hole in the Liverpool South Docks, at New Brighton, Rock Ferry and Runcorn. Nobbies have survived in fair numbers and have been converted into yachts and still race every year under their traditional rig.

Opposite above: The rising population of Liverpool in the early nineteenth century provided a ready market for fish. The docks and industry of the town form a background to this print which depicts the Mersey shore to the north. The fishing boats in the foreground appear to be luggers.

Opposite middle: The tidal basin which formed the entrance to the first dock had a slipway where a group of fishing smacks landed their catch in 1826. There were several trawlers and a smaller lugger in front of them. She probably fished with drift nets or long lines as luggers were unable to generate the power to drag a trawl net.

Opposite below: Trawling became a common method of fishing in the early nineteenth century. This decorated late eighteenth-century Liverpool punch bowl celebrated the schooner *Isabella*. The artist has depicted her with trawl-net ropes streaming aft which is an unusual detail and therefore probably accurate.

A Hoylake trawler had set all her sails to tack out of the Mersey for her Irish Sea fishing grounds. A typical ketch was between 38 and 40 tons and 48ft long on the keel. The other sails were those of a Mersey flat.

Left: A Hoylake trawler was anchored at Canning Half-tide Dock entrance waiting for the gates to open. The end of the beam trawl was lashed on the starboard side and was almost as long as the boat.

Opposite above: The five-man crew of the Hoylake trawler *Emblematic* consisted of the skipper in the centre (in a waistcoat and cap), the mate to the left (beard and clay pipe), two hands and a boy wearing heavy leather sea boots. The chimney in the foreground was for the small steam engine that hauled up the trawl.

Opposite below: The *Emblematic* was driven ashore off the moorings at Hoylake and on to the sea wall at Meols in January 1883. She could not be salvaged and was buried where she lay. In 1976, she was rediscovered when the sea defences were being rebuilt.

The Liverpool Museum staff tried to salvage this unique survivor. Having refloated her from the sea wall, she was wrecked a second time while waiting for transport to Liverpool. She rapidly became known as *Problematic* and apart from a few sample timbers, she had to be broken where she lay.

This dramatic photograph of the nobby *Alice Allan* trawling emphasises the risks and harsh life of local fishermen. The chimney behind the crew was boiling the catch. The helmsman's head was just visible above the wave. (Keith Willacy)

By the 1890s, Lancashire boatbuilders had developed the nobby along the lines of contemporary yachts. One of these vessels lay on the shore at New Brighton alongside an early motor launch, around 1910.

Right: This restored nobby has an engine but retained the typical layout with a low cabin forward and a narrow open cockpit with broad side decks for the trawl and handling the catch.

Below: Some survived as motor fishing boats and were rebuilt as sailing craft. Two were being worked on at Sid Higgins' boatyard at West Kirby in 1970. The one on the left is the *Daystar* which had just been bought by Liverpool Museum.

Above: An annual Mersey nobby race was established in the late 1980s and up to twenty boats compete. The local yacht clubs also include a nobby class in their annual regattas.

Left: The beauty of the rig of these working fishing boats is exemplified in this picture of a nobby from the Isle of Man which regularly came to compete in the Mersey race. Such a rig was designed not only to provide power to drag the trawl but also to speed the catch to market.

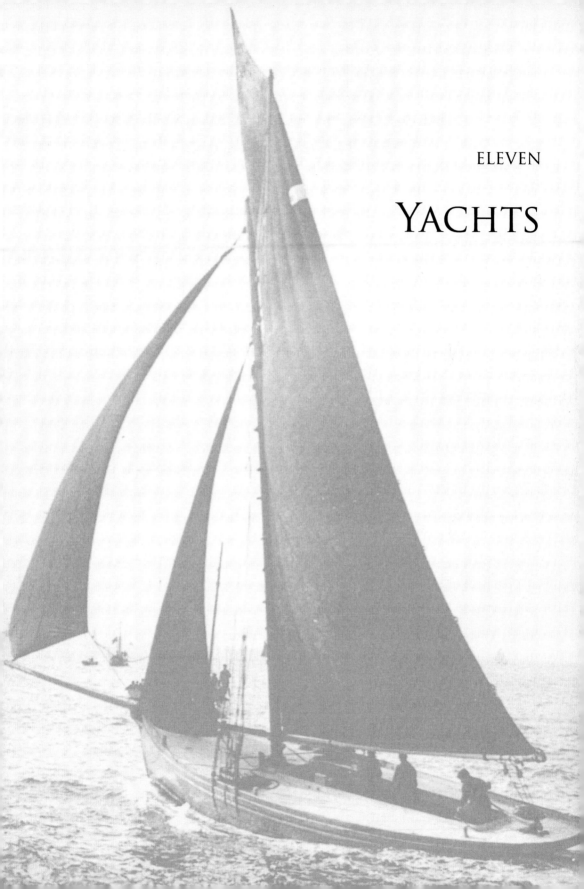

ELEVEN

YACHTS

The oldest yachts were small scouting and dispatch vessels for a sailing navy. By tradition the first English yacht was *Mary* which was given to Charles II in 1660. She was used for the Government mail and passengers service from Parkgate on the Dee to Dublin, until her destruction in 1675. The finds from her wreck are in the collections of Merseyside Maritime Museum.

Leisure yachting on the Mersey seems to have started in the early 1800s and regattas were popular spectacles. The first yacht club – the Royal Mersey – was founded in 1844. This was an elite organisation and many of its members were wealthy shipowners and merchants. They could afford to pay for a professional crew and their large yachts toured many of the other summer regattas. Their own annual regatta was attended by large visiting yachts including the Royal Yacht *Britannia* until the disastrous re competed until they stopped arriving in 1893. At the same time, their regatta also included classes for pilot boats, small open boats and shrimpers as well as various rowing races.

Towards the end of the nineteenth century (and especially from the 1890s) a whole range of sailing clubs were established for the smaller sailing boat owner. These included a club for sailing canoe owners and clubs based in outlying resorts such as Southport, Hoylake and West Kirby. These in turn developed One Design classes of yachts. These were all built as closely as possible to a definite specification which would place a premium on the skill of the crews and not on the design of the boat. Some of these early One Designs continue to be raced locally including the Stars at West Kirby, the Operas at Hoylake and the Half-raters (or Seabirds) at Wallasey.

Dinghy racing in standard designs was also a new development. It was underway in the early twentieth century, and there were some local designs such as the Clipper class at West Cheshire or the Tyrers at Blundellsands Sailing Clubs. But it really took off as a sport with the introduction of nationally popular designs in the 1950s. Some of them like the Mirror could be built from kits at home which reduced the cost of acquiring a boat. The amount of suitable sailing water also increased with the building of marine lakes at Southport, where sailing at sea had been finished off by silting, at West Kirby and later at Crosby. Local regattas still attract large entries, and events such as the twenty-four-hour race at Southport for Enterprise dinghies attract a national following.

Opposite above: The first English yachts were royal vessels. They were used not only by the king for pleasure but also for transporting dispatches and officials. They were highly decorated ships as can be seen in this model of the first one, the *Mary* of 1660. She sailed between Parkgate on the River Dee and Dublin. Parkgate was favoured for passenger traffic over Liverpool in the late seventeenth and early eighteenth centuries. The Royal Yacht *Navy* was stationed at Liverpool between 1689 and 1693.

Opposite below: Regattas or water frolics with rowing and sailing races were popular spectacles in the early nineteenth century. This one at New Brighton took place in the 1820s. There were some large cutter yachts together with rowing boats.

The Warrington Regatta of 1843 on the upper Mersey was another local example of a popular regatta, again with a combination of sailing and rowing races. Gambling on the outcome of the races was a common adjunct to Victorian regattas.

Early nineteenth-century yachts were generally large-decked cutters which needed a rich man's budget and a paid crew. By 1908, even the Royal Mersey Yacht Club had partly converted to racing in One Design boats.

Paid hands and skippers were often local fishermen and gig boat men who spent the summer yachting. A regular wage and a supply of good clothing were a great attraction. The lucky ones might be retained for maintaining the yacht when she was laid up in the winter.

The *Inyala* was typical of the yachts sailing around the Mersey and Liverpool Bay at the beginning of the twentieth century. She was a gaff-rigged 12-ton cutter built at Crossens near Southport in 1901 and could be used for racing or cruising.

The 350-ton auxiliary yacht *Sunbeam* was among the largest local yachts. She was built at Seacombe in 1874 for Lord Brassey, a rich railway contractor. She was rarely seen in the Mersey and her trips included a circumnavigation of the globe.

The Opera One Design was introduced at Hoylake Sailing Club in 1902. At just over 16ft long, they were more affordable racing boats. Their suitability for the local waters is proved by the fact that they continue to race at Hoylake.

The Rivers class was introduced to the Royal Mersey Yacht Club in 1911. It was based on the Jewel class raced by the Blackpool and Fleetwood Yacht Club. No.1, the *Styx* was photographed off Rock Ferry carrying a small shrimp trawl for some fishing instead of racing.
(Dr D. Chapman)

The Rivers yachts were 23ft long and were similar in shape and layout, if not length, to a fishing nobby. They were built by Crossfields of Arnside who also built many of the nobbies. (Dr D. Chapman)

The Mersey Mylne class was introduced in 1935. They were of similar size to their predecessors but had a modern hull shape and rig. Seventy-one years on they are still raced and No.1 *Mersey* is still winning. (RMYC)

The joy of messing about in boats! Three yachtsmen and a boatbuilder are preparing their boat at Rock Ferry, about 1910. (Dr D. Chapman)

The joy of messing about *with* boats! Some miniature yachtsmen display their home-made boats around 1900. (Williams Collection, the Trustees of National Museums Liverpool)

TWELVE

TRAINING
SHIPS

There were two types of training ship on the Mersey. The first were static retired wooden sailing warships. By the end of the nineteenth century there were five of these and four were moored off Rock and New Ferries on the south bank. The fifth was moored in Salthouse Dock. Those on the south bank were school ships for various types of boy and the *Eagle* in Salthouse dock was for training recruits to the Royal Naval Reserve. All had flotillas of naval gigs and whalers for rowing and sailing, and in the case of the school ships they were the only method of bringing in supplies and people from the shore.

There were no training ships in the modern way where young people were taken to sea for recreational or redemptive purposes. The school ships taught seamanship to equip their pupils for a career at sea. The same was true for the two deep-sea sail-training ships that were once based at Liverpool . The full-rigged ship *Mersey* was operated by the White Star Line between 1908 and 1914 and the brigantine the *James J. Bibby* was attached to the orphans' training ship *Indefatigable* between 1902 and 1914.

After that, sail training as such lapsed locally. There were some discussions by the directors of the Blue Funnel Line about building a three-masted barque in the 1930s and preliminary plans were drawn and not realised because of the dire financial situation, and then the outbreak of the Second World War. Other nations continued to value sail training. Most of the Swedish and Finnish grain ships arriving at Liverpool and Birkenhead up to 1939 were largely manned by apprentices. The 1950s saw the establishment of formal long-distance ocean races for sail training ships. These became known as the Tall Ships' Races and became immensely popular as a public spectacle at the departure and arrival ports. Liverpool hosted them in 1984 and 1992 and will do again in 2008. The participants range from four-masted barques to ketch-rigged yachts. But it is the bigger square riggers who draw the thousands of spectators down to the Mersey.

Sending young people to sea under sail has increasingly been seen to have a therapeutic value rather than training for a sea career. It calls for self-discipline and team work and there is a certain amount of hardship and excitement. Since the 1980s, several local schemes have got underway including the building of a replica pilot schooner for sail training, a north western branch of the Ocean Youth Club and the conversion of two Baltic sail traders into locally based training ships. In addition, there has been a regular stream of visiting sail training ships arriving at Liverpool both for special annual events such as the Mersey River Festival and also for crew changes.

HMS *Eagle* (later *Eaglet*) was based at Liverpool as a training base for naval reservists from 1862 to 1926. She had been built as a seventy-four gun third rate in 1804. In her second role she was given a Noah's Ark kind of floor over her upper deck. Her figurehead still survives at the present RNR headquarters. Notice the iron three-masted barque in the background. (The Trustees of National Museums Liverpool)

HMS *Conway*'s last figurehead was installed as part of her refit in the late 1930s. She had been built as HMS *Nile*. The vessel was the third HMS *Conway* which was a fee paying sea school for future officers.

HMS *Conway* (ex *Nile*) was moored off Rock Ferry on the south bank of the Mersey from 1876 until the Second World War. She was towed to the safer waters of the Menai Straits and was wrecked there in 1952 while under tow to Liverpool for repairs. (The Trustees of National Museums Liverpool)

The *Conway* was the last of four retired wooden warships that acted as boys' training schools moored near Rock Ferry. HMS *Akbar* was established a reformatory ship for Protestant boys in 1857. This vessel was the second to be borrowed from the Admiralty. The ship and its harsh regime lasted until 1907. HMS *Clarence*, a similar floating reformatory for Catholic boys was also moored at Rock Ferry. (The Trustees of National Museums Liverpool)

The final member of this quartet was HMS *Indefatigable* which was a school for sailors' orphans. This large single-deck fifty-gun frigate was served until 1914. The school then continued in a redundant cruiser before moving ashore to Anglesey in 1939. (The Trustees of National Museums Liverpool)

Sailing ships visiting Liverpool became increasingly rare events until the arrival of the Tall Ships' contestants in 1984. The brig *Maria Assumpta* and the barque *Marques* were conversions from Spanish coastal traders which were used for film contracts, carrying small numbers of passengers and trainees. The *Maria Assumpta* was photographed in Princes Dock in 1982.

Her companion had just left Waterloo lock and was about to set her sails. Her rig was based on that of HMS *Beagle* the naval research ship that had Charles Darwin among the scientists on her global expedition between 1831 and 1836.

Left: The American three-masted barque *Nantucket* was berthed in the Albert Dock in June 1934. She was among the first of the foreign sail training vessels that have called at Liverpool. (Keith Lewis)

Below: Sail training at the end of the twentieth century was carried on not only in traditionally rigged ships, but also in modern fibreglass yachts such as these ketches owned by the Ocean Youth Club in 1980 (The Trustees of National Museums Liverpool)

The German barque
Gorch Fock was among the
larger vessels that arrived
at Liverpool at the end of
the Tall Ships Race in July
1984. She was at anchor
at the Mersey Bar waiting
to receive her pilot like
hundreds of sailing ships
before her.

The barque *Kaskalot* was
converted from a Danish
wooden motor vessel. She
has been a regular visitor to
Liverpool over the last three
decades. She carries trainee
sailors among her crew but
her owners earn a living
from film contracts and
corporate hospitality.

The brigantine *Soren Larsen*
was another conversion
from a Danish coaster. She
was berthed at Canning
Half-tide Quay in August
1992 after completing a
voyage from Australia via
Cape Horn. She has since
returned to the South
Pacific to run trips from
New Zealand.

She was accompanied by another conversion, the *Eye of the Wind*. She was rigged with the eighteenth-century style of brigantine with a square topsail and topgallant on her mainmast. Today, she provides cruises around the Scottish Western Isles and visited Liverpool again in July 2006.

Many nations' navies have sailing ships to provide sailing experience for their recruits. It is believed to offer a valuable experience in seamanship but also fosters team spirit and morale. Many hands make light work in setting sail on the barque *Gloria* outward bound from Liverpool in 1984.

The Columbian Navy's *Gloria* under full sail with a British schooner yacht of modern design under her stern. The *Gloria*'s profile, as with so many other modern sailing vessels, is marred by a large and ugly bridge and deckhouse.

Above: The quay outside Merseyside Maritime Museum is the most popular berth for most Liverpool's sailing ship visitors since its restoration in 1984. The Irish brigantine *Asgard II* is one of the regulars.

Right: Their presence adds to the experience of visiting the Museum whose galleries display paintings, scale models or fragments of ships such as this figurehead from the unfortunate barque *Lottie Sleigh* which blew up in the Mersey in 1863.

The brigantine *Zebu* (and the ketch *Glaciere*) are 'residents' and are important for their educational work, such as helping visitors to grasp how these docks of the sailing ship era used to be.

Modern sailing ships are used not only for youth training but for promoting campaigns for the environment. Their use of 'green energy' for propulsion makes them suitable vehicles for bodies such as Green Peace and the National Trust's Operation Neptune to preserve the unspoiled coastline of England. The latter body hired the replica eighteenth-century frigate *Grand Turk* for a tour of British ports in 2000. She was already famous as the star of the *Hornblower* television dramas.